Pan Breakthrough Books

Pan Breakthrough Books open the door to successful self-education. The series provides essential knowledge using the most modern self-study techniques.

Expert authors have produced clear explanatory texts on business subjects to meet the particular needs of people at work and of those studying for relevant examinations.

A highly effective learning pattern, enabling readers to measure progress step-by-step, has been devised for Breakthrough Books by the National Extension College, Britain's leading specialists in home study.

Jacquetta Megarry is a freelance journalist who specializes in computers and related subjects. She has extensive experience of installations of all sizes, from mainframe to micro. Her interest in computer education has embraced work for industry, colleges and universities and for the British Government's microelectronics education programmes. A frequent contributor to The Times, *and* The Times Educational Supplement, *she is the author of* Computer World, *published under the Piccolo imprint of Pan Books.*

Jacquetta Megarry lives in Glasgow.

Pan Breakthrough Books

Other books in the series

Background to Business
The Business of Communicating:
　Improving Communication Skills
The Business of Data Processing
The Economics of Business
Keep Account:
　A Guide to Profitable Book-keeping
Making Numbers Work:
　An Introduction to Business Numeracy
Management: A Fresh Approach
Marketing: A Fresh Approach
Practical Accounts 1
Practical Accounts 2
Practical Business Law
Practical Company Law
Practical Cost and Management Accounting
Supervision: A Fresh Approach
Understanding Company Accounts
Understanding Industrial Relations
Understanding Office Practice
Using Statistics in Business 1
Using Statistics in Business 2
What Do You Mean 'Communication'?
　An Introduction to Communication in Business

Pan Breakthrough Books

Computers Mean Business

An introduction to computers in business

Jacquetta Megarry

Pan Original
Pan Books   London and Sydney

First published 1984 by Pan Books Ltd,
Cavaye Place, London SW10 9PG
9 8 7 6 5 4 3 2
© Jacquetta Megarry 1984
ISBN 0 330 28448 7

Phototypeset by Input Typesetting Ltd, London
Printed and bound in Great Britain by
Cox & Wyman Ltd, Reading

This book is sold subject to the condition that it
shall not, by way of trade or otherwise, be lent, re-sold,
hired out, or otherwise circulated, without the publisher's prior
consent in any form of binding or cover other than that in which it is
published and without a similar condition including this
condition being imposed on the subsequent purchaser.

If you wish to study the subject-matter of this book in more depth, write
to the National Extension College, 18 Brooklands Avenue, Cambridge
CB2 2HN, for a free copy of the Breakthrough Business Courses leaflet.
This gives details of the extra exercises and professional postal
tuition which are available.

For Dave
who gave me so much encouragement
in the first place

Acknowledgements

Authors commonly acknowledge the accuracy and patience with which their wives or secretaries typed their manuscripts. It is a sign of the times that my first acknowledgement is to Computer Concepts Ltd, whose friendly and flexible word processing chip (Wordwise) not only helped me to turn my jumbled thoughts into this book, but also made the process of revising it as painless as possible. The many revisions resulted from comments made by long-suffering friends who acted as guinea pigs for the self-check questions and commented on the text: I am particularly grateful to Keir Bloomer, Susie Stewart, Denis Sullivan and David R. F. Walker. I am also indebted to Gemini Marketing Ltd and to Hilderbay Ltd for spreadsheet, accounting, data base and payroll software and to Pafek Ltd for permission to reproduce the graphic on page 41. I would like to thank Ken Smith for his work on the illustrations.

I am also indebted to the library staff at Jordanhill College of Education for unfailing helpfulness and for the toleration extended to my two-year-old son, who sometimes had to accompany me. Finally, I would like to thank June, who made it possible for me to write at all, and my husband, for unflagging moral and practical support.

Contents

	List of figures	8
	Introduction	11
	Part 1: What is a computer?	
1	What's inside the boxes?	21
2	How does it work?	43
3	Some systems and their users	70
	Part 2: How can computers help business?	
4	Keeping account	103
5	Data bases	120
6	Word processing	138
7	Software options	155
	Part 3: Computers in business practice	
8	Acquiring software	173
9	Acquiring hardware	186
10	A taste of programming	200
11	Serious software	218
	Part 4: Computing and the organization	
12	Managing the computer	237
13	The employee's viewpoint	253
14	Computers and training	264
15	Computers and business futures	279
	Appendix 1: Sources of advice and information	287
	Appendix 2: Further reading	293
	Glossary	301
	Index	329

List of figures

1. Cartoon *15*
2. Plan of this book *17*
3. Humans and computers deal with information in four basic stages *22*
4. This bar code gives the price and International Standard Book Number (ISBN) of a paperback book. Above it the same information is printed in an OCR typeface *28*
5. A computer has some internal memory (RAM and ROM) backed up by external memory *30*
6. A floppy disc being loaded into a disc drive *33*
7. Specimen output from a dot-matrix printer and from a daisy-wheel printer *36*
8. A typical small business microcomputer system *38*
9. From left to right: low, medium and high resolution graphics *40*
10. These images of a universal joint show the computer's power to display three-dimensional shapes *41*
11. Some ways of storing software *47*
12. Excerpts from the same program written at different levels of language *52*
13. Relationship between the level of language and time to write *54*
14. Relationship between level of language and time to run *54*
15. Different levels of programming languages *60*
16. Operating systems form a crucial link between hardware and applications software *64*
17. A low-priced personal computer system *71*
18. Inputs and outputs for the kennel accommodation system *72*
19. Inputs and outputs for the kennel accounts system *73*
20. An integrated system covering sales, payroll, stock control and purchases *77*
21. Flow of information involved in bureau processing of the DTU's membership information *80*

List of figures

22 Microcomputers at different locations can communicate by telephone *84*
23 A network allows a number of microcomputers to share access to expensive facilities like a Winchester and telex *89*
24 An example of a hand-held computer system which includes a full-size keyboard, small printer and screen and floppy tape as 'external' memory *92*
25 An acoustic coupler allows computers to communicate over long distances using ordinary telephones *93*
26 A videodisc player under computer control provides fast access to a huge range of still and moving colour pictures *97*
27 Inputs and possible outputs of a sales ledger system *104*
28 Inputs and possible outputs of a purchase ledger system *108*
29 Inputs and possible outputs of a nominal ledger system *109*
30 Jenny Bruno's summary of income and expenditure for her first year of operation (dogs) *113*
31 Alternative spreadsheet for first year based on hypothetical cats, created from Figure 30 by changing just two formulae *116*
32 Spreadsheet for possible second-year operation based on cats and dogs (compare Figures 30 and 31) *117*
33 The author catalogue file contains a record for each book; each record has several fields giving details of the book *121*
34 The complete author catalogue might be held on a single floppy disc; each book record might fill a screen, with each field occupying one or more lines *122*
35 Holes on an edge-punched card can be destroyed selectively to represent some of the information recorded in its middle *123*
36 Edge-punched cards can be sorted by putting a needle through the holes. Cards whose holes have been destroyed will drop off *124*
37 Prestel provides a vast data base and communications link which helps homes and offices to locate information and make purchases *135*
38 Microwriter: a hand-held word processing input device. Inset: two examples of letter codes *142*
39 First version of paragraph with simple format commands *151*
40 Second version of paragraph with more elaborate format commands *152*
41 The software spectrum *157*
42 Apple's LISA system with overlapping windows shown on the screen and 'mouse' input *165*

10 List of figures

43 If the user chooses 'shades', a menu offers 36 options for shading the 1980 bar   *167*
44 Some options for acquiring software   *181*
45 Sample of output from JARGON program   *215*
46 A cardboard disc jargon generator; each disc corresponds to an array in JARGON   *216*
47 Flow-chart showing processing of data in a payroll program   *224*
48 Excerpt from Gemini Payroll, an example of serious payroll software   *227*
49 Some standard shapes used in data and program flow-charts   *231*
50 Program flow-chart for JARGON   *232*
51 Structure chart for JARGON (compare Figure 50)   *233*
52 Some features of a well-designed vdu work-station   *261*
53 Some environmental threats to data on a floppy disc, showing relative sizes   *267*

Introduction

If the motor car industry had progressed at the same rate as computer technology since 1945, a Rolls Royce would now be as cheap as this book; more powerful than the world's fastest train; could go round the world 3000 times on a single tankful of petrol; and would be so small that you could park eight of them on this full stop.

Such profound and rapid change is not without its penalties. It has revolutionary implications for the nature and structure of industry and for our methods of conducting and organizing business – indeed, for the very fabric of our society – yet conventional methods of education and training cannot adapt fast enough to catch up with the computer revolution. For men and women who are actively involved in business, the need to get to grips with the world of computing is very urgent: the rewards of successful computerization can make the difference between a profitable future and extinction. For business students, an understanding of computer systems can make the difference between being able to choose a job and being unemployed.

The technology continues to improve, prices are still tumbling and the technological imperative seems ever stronger. The rapid convergence of previously distinct technologies keeps changing the rules of the game (some would say moving the goalposts) before some people have learned to kick the ball. The risks of being left behind seem considerable. Yet the hazards of rushing into the wrong choices are even worse: experience of the last quarter-century has demonstrated conclusively that computer systems *can* be expensive, time-consuming and inefficient. The number of expensive computer disasters is widely underestimated: the firms involved are understandably reticent about them – if they are still in business, that is.

Some of the blame should be laid at the door of the computer industry – for too long an inward-looking group of professionals with little contact with its clientele. Computer professionals describe their customers distantly as 'end-users' and resolutely refuse to consult them or even speak their language. Some fault undoubtedly attaches to poor managers, who have under-estimated the implications of computerization and entrusted far too much to an internal data processing department or to an external computer salesman – forgetting that responsibility for managing the business is *theirs* alone. If a computer is to be worth its keep, it must become intimately involved in the organization: a manager delegates responsibility for it at his peril.

Some of the problems are not really the fault of either side, but reflect the difficulty of establishing communication between two such disparate groups. In addition to the artificial problems created by technospeak, there are genuine problems in conveying technical information to lay people, and subtler difficulties created by the culture gap between groups who have different training, contrasting priorities and few common assumptions.

The business world and the ordinary citizen have to realize that the accelerating bandwagon that is the computer industry has no one steering it and no one at the brakes. Business people need to climb on board and shout out their wishes until they make their destinations heard. The computer industry has suffered from a critical shortage of articulate and computer-literate consumers.

The analogy with motor cars is instructive in a different way. In the early days of motor cars, drivers were an enthusiastic élite, often oblivious of the convenience of the general population. Cars were unreliable and accidents all too common. Drivers accepted the need to carry out frequent maintenance and minor repairs. Because little was standardized, drivers expected to have to learn a new set of controls when they moved from one car to the next and adjusted to a different number and arrangement of gears. Manufacturers and consumers alike assumed that the drivers would learn about and adapt to the machinery, not that the machinery should be designed to make life easy for the driver.

Just fifty years later, these assumptions had all been overturned. In developed countries, at least, it is taken for granted that any motivated citizen of normal abilities should be able to drive a car. The benefits of standardized controls and gear layouts no longer need to be stated. There is even a near-unanimous international convention about which side of the road to drive on! Many drivers have no idea how an internal combustion engine works. As long as the car goes, they are pleased to drive it, and if it goes wrong, they take it to a specialist (garage). If a vehicle based on some other principle (electricity, perhaps) were more reliable and economical, they would happily change their allegiance, regarding the internal combustion engine simply as a means to an end.

We are already in a society in which computers are widely available in chain stores for less than the minimum weekly wage. The capabilities of the very cheapest micros are limited, compared with the big giants, of course, and computer professionals are fond of deriding them. There is a good reason for this: high priests seldom welcome developments which threaten their monopoly on mystical powers, nor do they embrace offers to translate and disseminate their closely guarded secrets, hitherto only whispered in mumbo-jumbo.

It is the cheapness and availability of micros that is so splendidly subversive. It puts a 'Model T' computer within the financial reach of any but the poorest in our society. Some independent tests performed in San Diego in 1983 found that a $2,000,000 mainframe was only 16 times as fast as a microcomputer costing $28. What are the implications of putting into the hands of the ordinary citizen computer power of a kind which only ten years ago was restricted to research laboratories and large organizations? No one really knows. Somehow the purchaser has to try to compensate for the half-century immersion in computer culture which she or he has missed. In our motorized culture, when people buy a car they don't expect to be taught about speed limits, how and where to park, motorway signs or the need for petrol; they absorb this kind of information as they grow up. Yet people who lack a basic grasp of computer concepts buy, and are expected to deal with, computers at their places of work.

What this book tries to do

My aim is to explain from first principles what computers can and cannot *do* for their users; how software can help in business; and how to get the system to earn its keep. If you can grasp the underlying concepts, principles and vocabulary of computing, you will be able to evaluate the claims made by salesmen and computer professionals for yourself. If you have the confidence born of mastering this material, you will not be afraid to tell such people that you cannot follow their jargon and will insist that they explain themselves in terms you understand. If you are familiar with most of the words in the glossary (and know where to look up the rest), you will be able to read the manufacturers' literature and computing magazines for yourself. Naturally, one book cannot hope to include everything you need to know. In any case, computers change so continually that learning more about them may become a lifelong pastime for us all. The aim of this book is to get you started. This might sound simple, but most people find the first step the hardest.

It may save misunderstanding if I mention at the outset some of the things this book does *not* attempt to do:

- It does not teach you how to program. You need a quite different book for that, and preferably some access to a computer. However, it does try to help you decide if you want to learn to program (Chapters 10 and 14);
- It does not try to persuade you to buy a computer, or to expand an existing system, because computers may not be part of the solution to a business's problems at present. However, even businesses that would currently find them more trouble than they are worth cannot afford to ignore computers, as they may well become important to the business at some future date;
- It does not try to advise you which computer to buy. A book is no substitute for discussing your needs with someone personally (ideally with an independent consultant or colleague). In any case, you need up-to-date information and advice about local dealers which no conventionally published book

could provide. However, it does discuss the issues you should consider and explains how to prepare yourself to benefit from independent advice (Chapters 8 and 9);
- It does not try to avoid technical language, because computers are ingenious and complicated machines and some technical terms simply have to be learned if you are going to deal with them. However, it does explain each new term when it is first encountered and avoids unnecessary jargon.

An important feature of the book is its alphabetical glossary of *all* the terms that it introduces (plus a few extra, in case you meet them later in magazines and sales literature). This is to help people who read the book in a different order; who forget what a term means; or who want to refer back to the glossary when reading other material.

Figure 1.

How to read this book

The sequence in which the material is presented was carefully planned so that the student who begins at the beginning and reads straight through should find everything in a logical order. Each term that appears in the glossary is highlighted in **bold** the first time it is used. However, psychology, as well as logic, influences how you read a book. Some people won't have time to read the whole book when they first buy it, or will be looking for information on some specific point. Others like to work backwards or skim-read bits that don't interest them. Others again will already know quite a bit about some aspects and will be looking for something to fill in the gaps.

Recognizing all of this, I have tried to make it easy for you to choose your own sequence. Using the contents page and the index, you should find your way to any topic of interest. If you have dipped into the middle of the book, you'll have to decide for yourself whether it's worth checking the meaning of a word in the glossary. If you have to consult the glossary too often, that may be a sign that you ought to go back and read at least Chapters 1 and 2 straight through, but you'll find that out for yourself. Figure 2 shows how the book builds on understanding and applying the basic concepts towards acquiring, managing and planning.

Whatever strategy you use to read this book, you will need to combine reading it with other activities, to get the most out of it. Computing is not just a theoretical subject. If you have never used a computer, the sooner you get your 'hands-on' the better; it doesn't matter what computer, what language or what software – although it's ideal if it relates to some problem you are interested in anyway. If you don't know anyone with a home computer, a local club, college, ITeC or Microsystems Centre should be able to help (see Appendix 1 for contact addresses).

You may also want to pursue the subject by other methods. It is always helpful to visit an office, college, school or factory where computers and telecommunications are in use. There is also a wide range of television and radio broadcasts and a variety of other sources of advice and courses (see Appendix 1).

Introduction 17

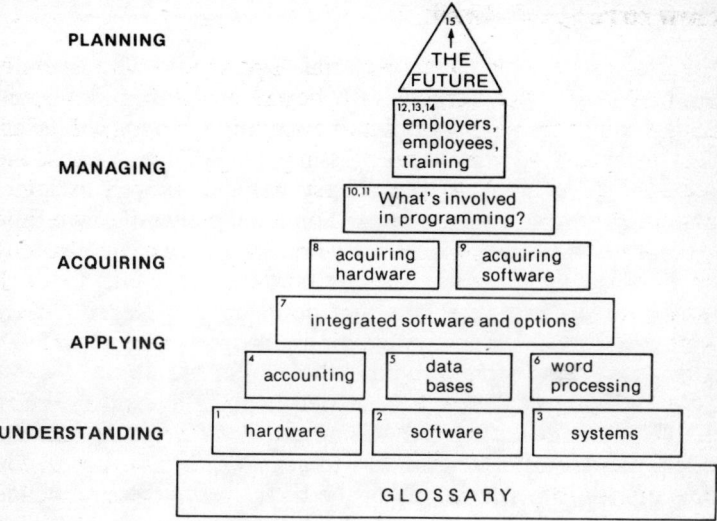

Figure 2. Plan of this book

Finally, each chapter contains a number of self-check questions. You will probably learn most thoroughly (and certainly feel more confident of progress) if you make a habit of writing down your answers before looking at mine, which are always given immediately afterwards. You may prefer to cover my answers with a card. Some of the self-checks are quite brief questions to check a small point before you proceed. Others – usually towards the end of the chapter – draw together several threads and help you to review what you have learned. Both kinds are the enemy of passive learning. Learning about computers means *active* learning. Good luck!

Part 1
What is a computer?

1 What's inside the boxes?

Computers come in all sorts of shapes and sizes. You may hear them referred to as **mainframe**, **mini** and **micro**. These impressive-sounding terms basically mean big, middling and small. Generally speaking, mainframe computers are expensive, powerful, have large memories and are split into many separate parts. Microcomputers, on the other hand, are cheaper and smaller and usually have some or all of their different bits packaged together. They also generally have smaller memories and may work more slowly. Minicomputers come in between micros and mainframes.

Mainframe computers are generally used by large organizations, which have different needs from small firms with minicomputers. Different again is the one-person business or home user, for whom a micro is often more than adequate. Some effects of these differences are explored later in the book. At present, the main point is that no matter what a computer looks like or costs, it works on the same lines. The fundamental principle to grasp is that of separating **hardware** from **software**.

Hardware and software

Hardware is the general name given to all the equipment which makes up the computer – the boxes and screens that you see in shops and magazines. Software consists of the **programs** and **data** which together make the hardware do useful work – or produce garbage, as the case may be.

Programs and data

A program is really just a list of instructions that the computer can obey, written in a special **programming language**. Data is

22 What is a computer?

the information which the program processes. For example, in Chapter 10 we will work out a simple program to calculate an employee's wage packet, written in a language called **BASIC**. But one program can be made to work for many employees and to suit different firms, if the data about employees and their rates of pay is stored separately from the instructions about how to process them. This is discussed further in Chapter 11.

Programs and data are usually prepared in advance and stored separately. So before a user can run any program, it has to be loaded into the computer. Once the output has been obtained, another program can be fed into the computer, or it might be switched off. The first program will then have been 'forgotten' by the computer and cannot be run again without being reloaded.

If you have a hi-fi system, you can think of all the equipment (record player, amplifier and loudspeakers) as the hardware. It cannot produce any sound by itself. In fact, its sound quality is only as good as the software (records and tapes) which you give it to play. This analogy should not be pushed too far, however, as a hi-fi system can only do one thing – namely, reproduce music. A computer, on the other hand, can do any job which can be spelled out in detail in a program. The secret of how a computer can be general-purpose lies in the way that one program can easily be replaced by another.

The four-stage model

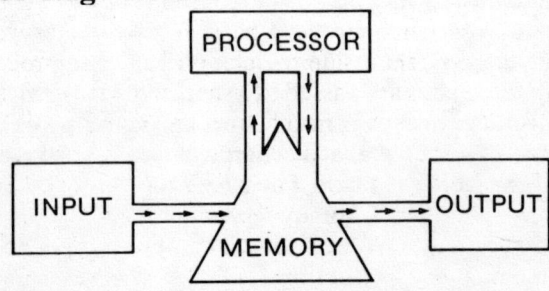

Figure 3. Humans and computers deal with information in four basic stages

What's inside the boxes?   23

Any system which processes information can be thought of as having four stages: **input**, **memory**, **processor** and **output**. Even humans, who have many unique qualities in addition to these, process information according to this model.

Imagine you are sitting at a desk, perhaps doing the accounts. 'Input' is any information about the outside world which reaches you through your senses. An invoice or letter in your in-tray, a telephone call or personal caller – all these are forms of input. This information is then stored in your memory and processed by your brain. The result is output, in the form of written or typed accounts. On occasion, output might be in the form of spoken or dictated instructions.

Sometimes you will have to retrieve information from other sources to complete the task. For example, you might have to look up last year's accounts, consult a book about income tax or work something out on a calculator. Other times, you may have all the information you need in your own head. In computer terms, this corresponds to the difference between **external memory** and **internal memory**.

Computers are much less flexible than humans about how they handle information. They need input devices to turn words and figures into a form which they can handle. We shall look at some of the various input devices shortly. Once the information has been transferred from the input device into the computer's internal memory, the processor acts on it according to the instructions contained in the program.

Programs usually have to be loaded from external memory for the purpose, though some very basic or frequently used programs may be **resident** inside the computer. Once processing is complete, the results are passed to a special output device, which turns the information back into figures and words again.

Many people imagine that all computers have huge memories, but this is far from the truth. Their *internal* memories are often surprisingly limited and usually **'ephemeral'** – i.e. everything is forgotten when you switch off. So all computers depend heavily on external memory – sometimes called **backing store** – to store almost unlimited amounts of software.

Computers vary very widely as to how much they can hold

What is a computer?

inside their 'boxes'. The smallest microcomputer memory could not store half the words on this page, though a more expensive micro could hold several chapters of the book and a mainframe could store the whole book ten or twenty times over. Even so, compared with many computers, humans tend to carry more of their 'software' around in their heads!

> ### Self-check
>
> Computers and humans may have some similarities when it comes to processing information, but there are also a lot of differences. Think of a specific routine task which you do regularly. For example, you could consider doing household accounts, sending out Christmas cards, or issuing invoices. Draw up two columns and note the good and bad points about using a computer, as opposed to doing it yourself.

ANSWER

Naturally your answer will depend on the task which you selected. If it was something fairly routine, the computer column might contain entries like 'accurate, fast, never bored or forgetful'. However, you may have noted that humans 'don't need to be programmed, can go to pillar boxes, will query unusual amounts, apply common sense'.

Analogue and digital

Deep down inside, a computer's operations are **digital**. Digital means something broken down into units which can be counted. However, many everyday things like time and temperature are 'analogue' – they vary continuously.

Conventional clocks and watches have hands which sweep continuously around the clock-face; their movement is an 'analogue' for the passage of time. Modern digital watches work on a different principle, counting the seconds and showing an exact figure, like 18.56 p.m.

Although some computers work on analogue principles,

nearly all modern computers are digital. No matter what form the input takes – letters, numbers, drawings or speech – it has to be coded into numbers by the input device before the processor can deal with it. Like Morse code or knitting patterns, this code looks strange unless you are used to it.

Self-check

What is the analogy for temperature in an ordinary thermometer?

ANSWER

The length of the column of mercury is proportional to the temperature being measured, rising and falling as it changes. Digital thermometers give a direct reading in degrees.

The binary system

The counting system that we are used to is based on the number ten and powers of ten, like a hundred, a thousand and a million. Computers do not count in this way. Instead, they use the **binary system**, which is based on the number two and powers of two, like four, eight, thirty-two and two hundred and fifty-six. This means that they can express any number, no matter how large, as a string of binary digits – 1s and 0s. For instance, fourteen would be written 14 in everyday (base-ten) numbers, but 1110 in binary (base-two) numbers.

Contrary to what many people believe or expect, you do not need to understand binary arithmetic to get the most out of a computer. The vast majority of computer users never see a binary number in the course of a day. Even among computer programmers, binary numbers are little used; very few people ever write programs in **machine language** – the computer's own language, consisting of 1s and 0s (see Chapter 2).

Some people believe that we developed our counting system based on tens because we have ten fingers. Whether that is true or not, base-10 numbers certainly have the advantage of being used by people all over the world. Because humans find base-ten numbers more manageable than long strings of 1s and 0s, programmers soon invented ways of getting the computer to translate our numbers into binary automatically.

The processor

It is in the nature of electronics that binary numbers are more suitable for computers than our own. Inside the processor, thousands of tiny electrical switches are either 'off' or 'on', and it is natural to make each 'off' or 'on' represent a binary '0' or '1'.

The processor doesn't deal with these binary digits, or **bits**, individually, any more than we read a book letter by letter. It groups them into 'words' consisting of 8 bits – e.g. 01000001. The early microcomputers dealt with **8-bit 'words'**, and you may have seen references to 8-bit micros. More recent and larger micros can process 16 bits at once and larger computers may have 32-bit or 64-bit 'words'. Although, *in theory*, the more bits a processor can deal with at once, the faster it will work, there are many other important limitations. For example, speed also depends on the speed of the system's internal **clock**, which keeps all the operations in step with each other. How quickly the processor can move information in and out of its memory is also very important. In practice, whether a 16-bit microcomputer will actually deliver results faster than an 8-bit micro also depends on the software which is controlling it.

For most purposes, bits are too small a unit. A **byte** is a group of 8 bits, and it can be made to store any **character** you are likely to want to feed in; characters include capital and small letters, numbers and symbols. So an 8-bit micro can process one byte at a time.

A **microprocessor** is simply a processor on a single **chip** of silicon. Modern microcomputers owe their performance, price and compactness to these remarkable chips. They tend to have rather obscure names, which give you little idea of whether they are 8-bit or 16-bit. For example, the **Z80**, **8080** and **6502** microprocessors are all 8-bit, whereas the 8086, 68000 and Z8000 are all 16-bit! You may meet these unhelpful names in advertising material or book titles, but you don't need to remember them.

The important point about binary numbers is not to be able to do arithmetic with them; the processor does that. What you should remember is that everything that goes in or out of a computer has to be turned into bits at some stage. The processor's apparent 'cleverness' all depends on doing basic operations like adding and comparing 1s and 0s according to detailed instructions – and doing them incredibly fast and accurately. It is impossible for 1s and 0s to exercise any common sense, unless humans find a way of analysing this uncommon quality in such detail that it can be programmed!

Most of the time, however, users are blissfully unaware of the binary goings-on inside the processor. They are fascinating if you are interested in that kind of thing, but largely irrelevant to this book. The other parts of the system – input devices, memory and output devices – have greater implications for the user.

Input

Input devices are used to turn programs and data into a form which the computer can deal with. In the early days, input usually depended on machines which punched holes in cards or paper tape. A hole meant a 1, and no-hole represented a 0. The cards or tape were then fed into a card-reading machine attached to the computer.

This two-stage process was rather clumsy and sometimes unreliable. When I learned to program in the early 1960s, the machines which did the punching sometimes failed to punch all the holes they should have. Days later, the program would refuse to run, and I had to 'read' along the tape until I found the mistake and punch an extra hole with a hand-held punch! Nowadays, such devices are literally museum pieces. Input is often made directly to the computer and can be in a wide variety of forms, each requiring an appropriate input device.

Keyboard

The commonest input device is a keyboard, with keys arranged like a typewriter; this is sometimes called a **QWERTY** keyboard,

28 What is a computer?

after the top row of letters. Many microcomputers are controlled from their keyboards all the time. However, even the fastest typist cannot hope to keep up with a computer. Some direct way of feeding in data is called for whenever computers are handling large volumes of data of the same kind. This is not only quicker than having everything 'retyped', it also avoids the main source of mistakes.

MCR and OCR

Banks have to process large numbers of cheques, and it is quicker and better for the information on them to be fed straight into the computer. This is made possible by special symbols printed in magnetic ink on the bottom of each cheque. This system is called **Magnetic Character Recognition (MCR)**. Figure 4 shows another system called **Optical Character Recognition (OCR)**, which depends on printing information in a special typeface so that it can be 'read' by a machine. The **bar codes** which nowadays appear on groceries and books are another way of coding information so that it can be fed in directly.

Figure 4. This bar code gives the price and International Standard Book Number (ISBN) of a paperback book. Above it the same information is printed in an OCR typeface

What's inside the boxes? 29

There are other systems which allow ordinary typewriting and even handwriting to be fed in, but these systems are still under development. Some can only deal with capital letters; others have to 'train' the writer to make letters a particular way. We are still some way from the input device which can decipher a doctor's handwriting!

Speech input

You may be wondering why we can't just tell the computer what to do. It would certainly be more convenient, but, unfortunately, turning spoken instructions into binary numbers is even harder than dealing with handwriting. People have widely different accents and dialects; their 'voice-prints' are as individual as fingerprints. Furthermore, we tend to leave many things unsaid, assuming that the listener will guess them from the context. To make a computer do this kind of 'filling in' needs a very sophisticated approach to programming. Such systems are – for now – confined to research laboratories. Voice recognition units can only respond to a limited number of words at present, but they may become much more important in the future.

Other forms of input

Most business uses of computers depend on processing letters and numbers. However, you should know that other input devices allow other kinds of information to be input directly. For example, **graphics tablets** allow shapes to be 'traced' with a 'pen' and loaded directly into the computer. The tablet turns the movement of the 'pen' into electrical impulses which the computer can process. Other devices (called **A-to-D Converters**) can convert analogue information into digital form, allowing computers to control **robots** and production processes. Others again, like **modems** and decoders, can handle information from telephone lines and television broadcasts. These are important when computers are being shared by many users or used over long distances.

Self-check

Going back to the hi-fi system analogy, can you think of more than one 'input device' for the music?

ANSWER

Music can be fed into most amplifiers by a record turntable, a cassette deck, a radio tuner or (live) through a microphone. In computer terms, these are all input devices.

Memory

We have already seen that computers have some internal memory, but most of them depend heavily on external memory to back it up. Naturally, information can be retrieved (fetched) much faster from internal memory, but it is more expensive to provide than external memory. Microcomputers usually have small internal memories, both to save money and to keep them small.

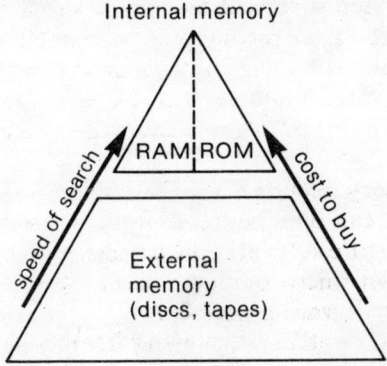

Figure 5. A computer has some internal memory (RAM and ROM) backed up by external memory

Internal memory

Random Access Memory (RAM) Internal memory is of two kinds, RAM and ROM. Random Access Memory (RAM) is the

What's inside the boxes?

computer's short-term working-space. During a few seconds or minutes of its working life, a computer's RAM may be 'overwritten' with new programs and data thousands of times. The size of a computer's RAM is measured in **Kilobytes**, or **K**, equal to about a thousand bytes. We saw on page 26 that a byte can store a single character.

> ### Self-check
>
> Work out how many Kilobytes would be needed to store a page of this book. Assume that there is an average of 7 characters per word (6 letters and a space) and 330 words on the page. (For simplicity, we'll assume that there are no diagrams.)

ANSWER

You need 1 byte per character, i.e. 330 times 7 bytes, altogether: 2310 bytes, i.e. just over 2 Kilobytes.

You may have been surprised by this answer if you have seen advertisements for a microcomputer with just 1 K of RAM: it couldn't even hold half a page of this book! Even 64 K of RAM (generally considered quite respectable for a business micro) would only hold about 30 pages of this book at any one time.

Read Only Memory (ROM) Read Only Memory (ROM) differs from RAM as it can only be 'read' from, it cannot be 'written on'. It is used to store software which will always be needed. For instance, my own microcomputer has a ROM chip installed which turns it into a **word processor**.

Comparing a computer system with a home hi-fi system again, ROM resembles a record disc that can only be played, not recorded. RAM is more like a blank cassette tape which can be recorded, wiped clean, and recorded again. However, the computer can get to, or access, any part of its internal memory (RAM and ROM) at random. In this way, RAM is quite unlike a cassette tape, which has to be searched by playing it through in order.

32 What is a computer?

External memory

Cassettes The same audio **cassette** you might play in a music centre can also serve as external memory for a computer. It isn't ideal for the purpose, because it is **serial-access**. This is the opposite of **random-access**; it means that if something is at the end of the tape, you have to play through all of it to reach the end. Since the tape travels at its usual speed of under two inches per second, this means that the computer is reduced to a snail's pace; even a simple program can take minutes to load. But cassette recorders are cheap and widespread, and many home computer users rely on them for external memory.

Floppy discs Businesses need something faster for serious use. **'Floppy' discs** (floppies) are like very flimsy 45 rpm records enclosed in a paper sleeve. You insert them into a special **disc drive**, shut the door and the computer, making them spin round at high speed, can locate information very fast. It can 'read' large amounts of information from the disc and 'write' (i.e. record) it on to the disc in seconds rather than minutes. Unfortunately, disc drives are expensive – they cost more than many microcomputers. Also, the discs are easily damaged by dust, magnetic fields or rough treatment, so it is essential to make copies of important information and programs as **back-up**. It is surprisingly easy to accidentally **overwrite** something you need, so discs can be **'write-protected'** (safeguarded). For 5¼-inch discs, this is done by sticking a bit of paper over the notch. (For 8-inch discs, you take the paper *off*; this is typical of standardization in the computer world!)

Most business systems include a twin disc drive, despite its high cost (almost double that of a single drive). This has several advantages: (a) it makes copying discs much faster; (b) it gives a back-up in case of drive failure; and (c) it means that software can be organized so that the program is on one disc and the data on the other. This last factor is decisive for businesses that need large, complicated programs or that handle large volumes of data.

What's inside the boxes? 33

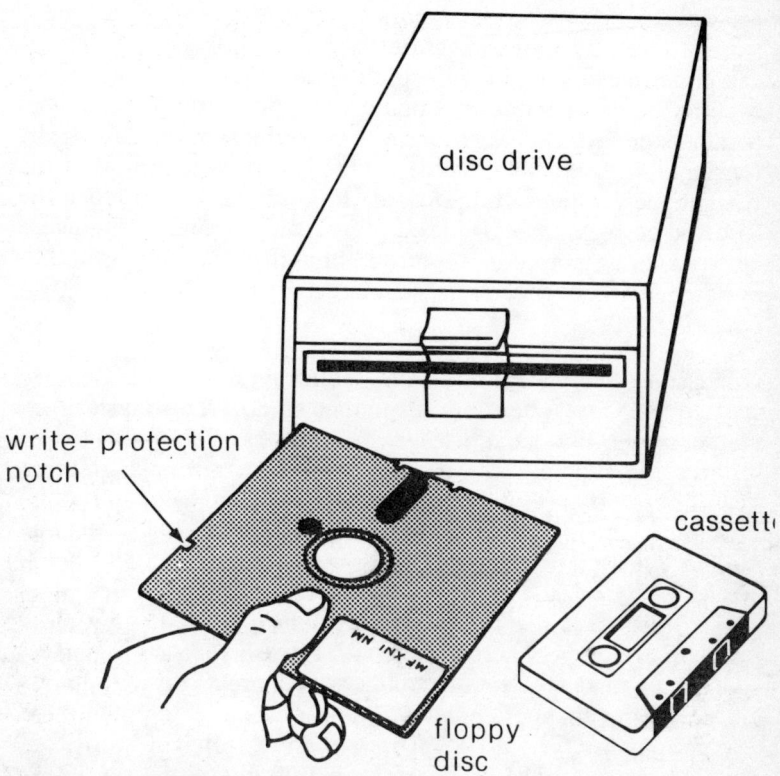

Figure 6. A floppy disc being loaded into a disc drive

Floppy discs have a wide range of different storage capacities, depending on whether they are 5¼- or 8-inch in diameter, single- or double-sided, single- or dual-density. A commonplace disc could be expected to store around 50 pages of this book, but some floppies could hold the complete book several times over.

'Floppy tape' It may seem surprising that recently some business software has begun to be distributed on **micro cassettes**: these are the miniature cassettes as used by dictating machines, which typically run for 15 or 20 minutes per side. In principle, they suffer from the disadvantages outlined above for standard audio cassettes. However, it is possible to control their motors more accurately, to pack information more tightly on the tape and to arrange for faster storage and retrieval of programs and data. Such systems are sometimes called **'floppy tape'**, to indicate that their capacity, speed and price are intermediate between floppy disc and cassette tape. Typically, 55 K can be packed onto each side (around a chapter of this book), and the compactness of the system is attractive for portable microcomputers.

Other storage Minicomputers and mainframes need far greater storage capacity. There are a number of different devices for mass storage, like **hard discs** and **disc-packs**. These also store information magnetically, but their capacity is so much greater than floppy discs that it is measured in a different unit – a **Megabyte**, or Mb. One Megabyte is about a thousand K (over a million bytes). For example, a disc-pack of 6 discs might hold 300 Mb.

Hard discs are fixed, sealed units which rotate many times faster than floppies, and storage and retrieval times are correspondingly faster. They also hold vastly more information and are becoming cheaper, smaller and more easily integrated into microcomputer systems. **Winchesters** are a series of hard disc units which were derived from the mainframe world but have become very popular on smaller machines. (They got their nickname from the first IBM small hard disc drive, whose model number was 3030, the calibre of the classic rifle.) The first Winchesters were 14-inch, but they have followed floppies in size reductions to 8-, 5¼- and, recently, 3.9-inch diameters. They are increasingly being used with microcomputers because of their tumbling prices and improving reliability. There is also a new series of removable **hard-disc cartridges** which may become cheaper and more powerful than floppy discs, without the disadvantages of Winchesters. Hard-disc technology is moving very rapidly and our present ideas of price and capacity may soon be out of date.

Videodiscs Videodiscs are already being used in conjunction with computers. They are much more robust than floppy discs and their capacity is immense. A single videodisc could store from 2000 to 20,000 complete books of this length! A videodisc-pack could hold around 300 times as much information in the same space as a magnetic disc-pack. At present, they can only read information pressed onto them at the factory, so their immediate applications are in computer-based training (see Chapter 14). However, **laser** videodiscs are being developed which will allow the user to 'burn' information on to unused sections of the disc. Because the capacity of a videodisc is so huge and its price so low, the fact that it cannot be erased hardly matters. Videodiscs may become an important form of computer storage in the near future.

Output

The ultimate value of any computer program depends on how easily humans can interpret its output. Most computers can send information to a number of output devices at once – usually a **printer** and a **screen**.

Anyone who is interacting with a computer needs a screen on which to see what is happening at any moment. Most personal computers can be connected to ordinary domestic televisions – colour or black-and-white. However, business people usually prefer special **'monitors'**, which take up less space and give better results. The best ones enable the user to adjust the viewing angle – very important in prolonged use. A monitor is also sometimes called a **visual display unit** (vdu). Health factors and vdu's are discussed in Chapter 13.

Screens are essential for immediate results, but in most cases you would still need to have a permanent record of the computer's work. After all, the screen goes blank when you switch off, and floppy discs aren't much use if the person you want to communicate with hasn't got a computer, or if their computer system needs a different type of disc. So most serious users still regard a printer as essential, for all the talk of the 'paperless office'.

36   What is a computer?

Computer printers

Printers vary enormously in cost, quality and speed. Small computers are usually used with **dot-matrix printers**, which form each letter or number from a pattern of dots. When these printers work at high speed, you can see the dots quite clearly. Some can produce better-looking results at lower speeds (some sales literature calls this '**correspondence-quality**'). Different letter sizes and **graphics** can also be printed by using special control codes (see Figure 7). Four-colour dot-matrix printers became available at low cost during 1983 and can produce striking results.

```
Normal typeface shows up the dots clearly.

Bold looks a bit blacker,

and double-strike better still.

You can also choose a condensed typeface

or  an  enlarged  one

or even enlarged-condensed.
```

```
Daisy-wheel printers produce better
quality than the dot-matrix type, but
changing the typeface or printing
special characters usually means
stopping the printer to change the
daisy-wheel.

Most can do shadow printing like this,
but they are not nearly as versatile as
dot-matrix printers.
```

Figure 7. Specimen output from a dot-matrix printer and from a daisy-wheel printer

To get the kind of quality produced by a good electric typewriter, a different method is needed (see Figure 7). Letters are arranged like petals on a rotating **'daisy-wheel'**, a bit like a typewriter 'golf-ball'. It can be exchanged for a different daisy-wheel when a change of typeface is needed. Daisy-wheel printers tend to be slower than dot-matrix printers and may cost two or three times as much. A printer **buffer** is a useful device which stores output until the printer is ready for it, thus releasing the processor to do other work. Paper **feeders** are almost essential if you want to use cut sheets of paper (see section on paper-handling in Chapter 6).

There are much faster printers called **line printers** and (recently) **laser printers**. They are not used widely, partly because of their high cost, but also because there is little point in producing huge quantities of print-out at high speed unless somebody wants to read it and will act on it. A slower printer often makes people think more carefully about what really needs to be said.

Computer sound

Many computers can also produce some kind of sound output. Beeps and hoots can be useful to attract the user's attention to an error, or to signal the need to load some data. Some computers can also manufacture music and speech, using special **synthesizers**. Their quality varies enormously and some synthesized speech sounds very peculiar – the kind of speech you might expect from a robot. But speech output is already very useful for the partially sighted, and for people who have to watch other instruments, or drive a lorry, at the same time as attending to the computer.

Self-check

You can see what a typical small business microcomputer system looks like in Figure 8. See if you can identify the major parts, which have been labelled **a** to **e**.

38 *What is a computer?*

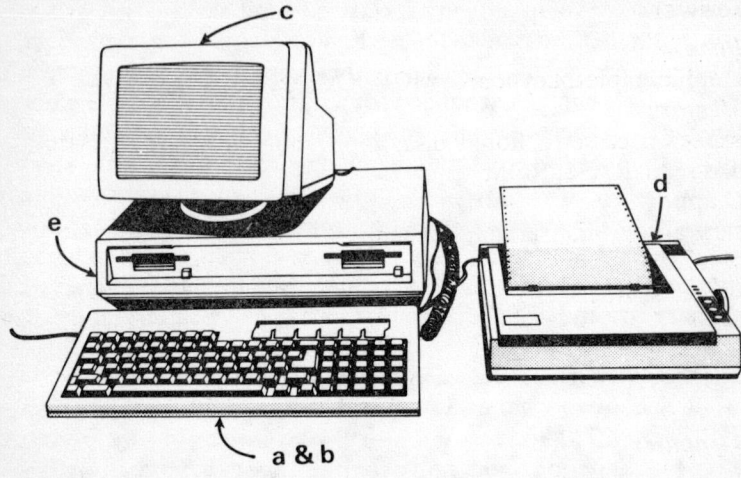

Figure 8. A typical small business microcomputer system

ANSWERS

a and **b** combined keyboard and processor
c monitor (or vdu)
d printer
e twin disc drive

Self-check

Now that you have met all the major forms of input, memory and output, it's a good moment to take stock of all the technical terms. Here is a jumbled-up list for you to rearrange logically under appropriate headings and sub-headings. For example, RAM should appear under 'Memory', which could have a sub-heading, 'internal memory'.

Cassette, daisy-wheel printer, dot-matrix printer, floppy disc, floppy tape, graphics tablet, hard disc, keyboard, MCR, monitor, OCR, RAM, ROM, speech synthesizer, television, videodisc, visual display unit, voice recognition unit.

What's inside the boxes? 39

ANSWERS
Input
graphics tablet, keyboard, MCR, OCR, voice recognition
Memory
EXTERNAL cassette, floppy disc, floppy tape, hard disc, videodisc;
INTERNAL RAM, ROM
Output
PRINTERS dot-matrix, daisy-wheel;
SCREENS monitor/visual display unit (vdu), television;
speech synthesizer

Graphics

Graphic output is not only important in design and engineering. It allows the computer to display information so that it is clear and easy to digest. This helps busy managers to grasp trends quickly, and can contribute to good communications generally. It can also be exploited in computer-assisted training.

Colour Many modern computers can produce a colour display, for example on an ordinary colour television screen. Used with discretion, colour can be a helpful addition to any display, text or graphics. Most people also prefer coloured displays if given a choice. However, the potential of colour is only beginning to be exploited in business software, and the majority of displays are on monochrome monitors. Green or amber screens are generally considered more restful than black-and-white.

Resolution Resolution is a measure of the fineness of the lines that can be drawn on the screen (see Figure 9). **Low resolution graphics** divide the screen into about 40 squares across by about 20 down. The 'squares' are called **pixels** (picture cells). You may see a computer's power to produce graphics advertised by its pixels e.g. '**high resolution graphics** (720 × 300)' meaning 720 pixels across by 300 down.

40   What is a computer?

Low resolution is good enough for bar charts and simple diagrams, but curves need **medium resolution** (about 300 times 200). Accurate maps and drawings need high resolution, which means at least 500 by 500 pixels have to be controlled separately. This uses a lot of processing power and memory – more than most microcomputers can manage. To take full advantage of high resolution graphics, a good quality monitor (as opposed to a television) is essential.

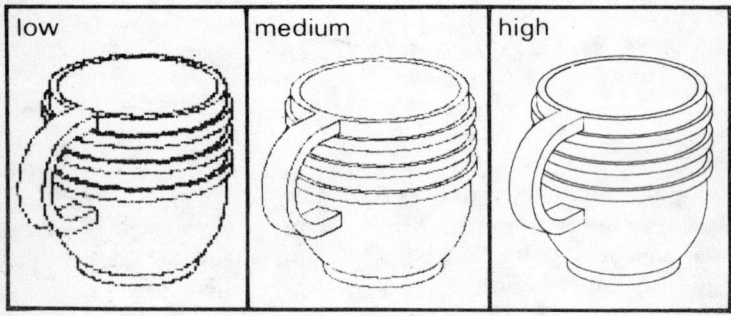

Figure 9. From left to right: low, medium and high resolution graphics (graphics by courtesy of D. R. F. Walker, L. Jenkinson and D. Bennett of Loughborough University)

Animation Animated graphics are moving images. Animation can be produced quite easily on many computers. It works very well in educational programs and games, but is of limited use in business applications.

Three dimensions The images shown on page 41 were produced using special graphics software. The computer needs a large memory to control the screen display, and a lot of processing power to work out what the object would look like from different angles. Programs can also show cut-away views of objects and fill in the hidden parts. These possibilities are very useful to people like architects, engineers and designers.

What's inside the boxes? 41

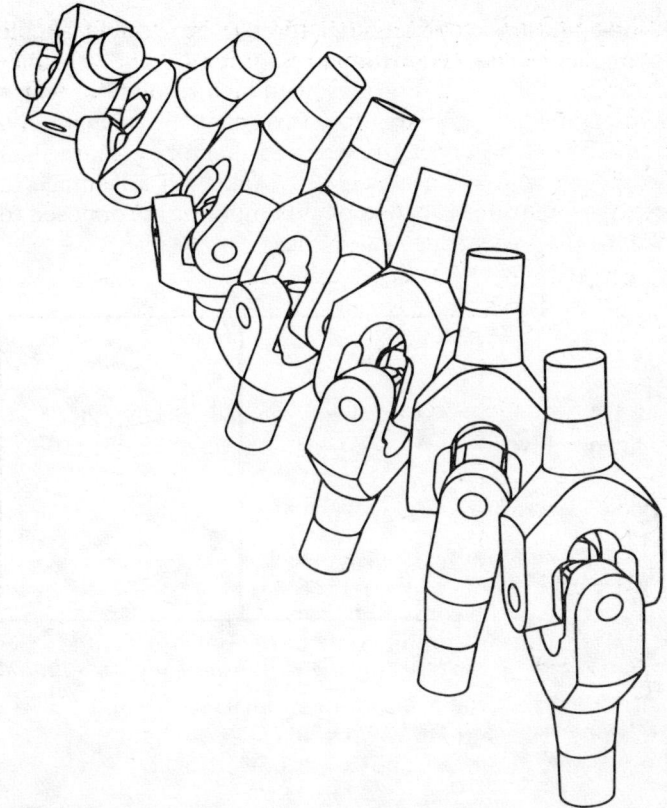

Figure 10. These images of a universal joint show the computer's power to display three-dimensional shapes (graphics by courtesy of Pafek Ltd of Nottingham

Self-check

HIDDEN WORDS

You have met a lot of computer words in this chapter, many of them unfamiliar. See if you can find them by joining up letters in the square overleaf to match the clues given below. For example, if the clue was 'Feeds information into the computer (5)', the five-letter word INPUT

42 What is a computer?

could be found. The lines need not be straight and the same letter can be used twice

```
L  S  P  A  M
E  X  I  R  C
T  M  A  T  O
O  D  U  T  W
U  T  P  N  I
N  E  M  O  R
```

If you find this too difficult, consult the Further Clues given below.

Clues

Cheaper and more flexible than a daisy-wheel (3,6)
Magnetic Character Recognition (3)
Typeface which computers can read (3)
Low resolution graphics only have about 40 by 20 of these (6)
Better than serial-access for memory (3)
Can be read, but not written on (3)
Everyday numbers count on its powers (3)
The base of the binary system (3)

Further clues

- Look back at the words listed in the Self-check on page 38. Some of them crop up here, too.
- The clues above are in alphabetical order of their solutions.

ANSWERS

Dot-matrix, MCR, OCR, Output, Pixels, RAM, ROM, Ten, Two.

2 | How does it work?

Why software comes before hardware

It is all too easy to be distracted by computer hardware. You can see it, touch it, even – if you feel inclined – kick it! Software is less tangible but much more important. The strengths and weaknesses of nearly all computer systems depend on the quality and appropriateness of their software. There are currently probably a hundred different kinds of microcomputer whose hardware is adequate to the needs of any small business. Whether *any* of them will be useful in practice depends on whether appropriate software can be obtained cost-effectively.

Systems software and applications software

Most people don't realize that if all you had was hardware – no matter how expensive or sophisticated – you would see nothing but a blank screen when you switched on your computer. You wouldn't be able to make the system obey you by typing instructions at the keyboard, nor would you be able to load or run any programs you might buy. What you would be missing is called **systems software**. This chapter is devoted to explaining what that is, and why it is even more vital than its better-known counterpart, **applications software**. This is the software that most people have heard of; it is designed for applications like accounting, word processing and financial forecasting. We will be looking closely at some such software in Chapters 3 to 7.

However, it is the systems software that determines which **packages** you can run and what sort of programs you can write. You can think of it as the behind-the-scenes software; sometimes it is supplied by the manufacturers on ROM chips, which are fitted into the computer. Additional or alternative systems software can sometimes be loaded into the computer from disc. For various reasons, many micros cannot do this, and this is a very important limitation. It restricts their owners' choice of applications software and it makes it much harder for them to keep up with improvements.

Most newcomers to computing underestimate the problems of software **compatibility**, especially among microcomputers. Those who expect to be able to take a disc working on one micro and load it into a micro of a different kind are in for a rude awakening. Appearances are misleading. One disc may look much like another, yet they can differ fundamentally in their invisible structure and be incapable of being run on the same kind of computer.

The only safe assumption about computer software is that, if a program runs on one computer, it won't run on any other without modification. If you start from this generalization you will sometimes get a pleasant surprise, especially if dealing with mainframes; but most of the time, depressingly, you will be correct. However, the degree of modification needed will vary from minor changes in odd words or punctuation to a total rewrite; the skill and experience needed by the person who modifies the program will range from negligible to immense. Chapter 8 discusses how far it is advisable for the business user to become involved in programming and Chapter 10 should give you an idea of the sort of skills involved.

For most people, the practical implication is simple but surprising: decide what software you are likely to use first, and only then start to look at hardware. Some computer dealers are beginning to see the other side of this coin: software sells hardware. If a local dealer stocks appropriate software as well as hardware, an early visit may be rewarding in giving you ideas about what can and cannot be done; if not, you will make more progress at a desk with a notepad. Assuming that you are not going to spend hours and weeks programming, you need a very clear idea of exactly what you want the computer to do, so that you can decide whether the programs available will suit the way you operate. Only afterwards does it make sense to consider hardware and compare performance and specifications. This is covered in more detail in Chapter 9.

Why isn't software transferable?

The main reasons why software tends not to transfer readily from one machine to another are historical. There is no good reason *in principle* why programs should not be easy to transfer between different computers unless they make use of facilities which might not be available on another machine.

> *Self-check*
>
> Can you give two examples of such facilities? (It may help to look back to Chapter 1.)

ANSWERS

- Internal memory: if a program occupies, say, 34 K of RAM, it cannot be run on a computer with only 16 or 32 K of RAM.
- Graphics: if a program produces high resolution colour graphics, it will not work properly on a computer with low resolution or which cannot handle colour. (However, the program can be *used* – though not enjoyed to the full – if the computer has the right capabilities, even if the display screen is monochrome and of limited resolution, like a black-and-white television.)
- Special inputs: if a program depends on graphics tablets, OCR input or other special devices, it will have to be modified before it can run on a computer which lacks these. (Similarly for output effects, like **3-voice music**, etc.)

Although there is a huge body of business software which easily *could* have been made compatible, unfortunately it wasn't worth anyone's while to ensure that it was. It would have taken a major cooperative effort among hundreds of different manufacturers at a time when the computer industry lacked any centralized direction, either from within or by governments. In the early days, there was little attempt at standardization and negligible consumer protection and things are little better today. Explosive technological progress and plunging raw material costs have combined to allow private enterprise to run riot in a seller's market. Consumers have been too bemused to complain about the chaotic results and too ill-organized to take effective action.

The result is that some business users buy expensive systems only to discover almost immediately that the system either cannot do what they want or expect or, in some cases, does not work at all. Others again find that, as their business grows, or as major improvements come on the market, they are unable to **upgrade** their system because their original purchase has locked them into a particular straightjacket. When the system's limitations become insupportable, there is a painful choice to be made between admitting the mistake and starting again from scratch or leaving the thing alone to gather dust with other expensive but useless executive toys. It is often debatable which is the more costly option in real terms.

Such mistakes are easily avoided if you look before you leap and understand the underlying principles. This will take us into some mildly technical aspects which you may prefer to skim over at a first reading, especially if you are not likely to be involved in any immediate decisions about purchasing hardware and software. However, you will need to re-read this section at some later stage.

First, it is essential to grasp the different *levels* of incompatibility which thwart the user's understandable ambition to transfer a useful program from one machine to another. They can be grouped under three headings, which we will examine in turn:

- physical form
- programming language
- **operating system**.

What does software look like?

In a sense, software is invisible and intangible. A program consists of instructions which never *need* to be written down (though in practice they usually are). Although software can be

How does it work? 47

stored in a variety of ways (see Figure 11), to the naked eye a blank disc looks the same as one containing a program. Inside the processor, the instructions are represented by microscopic changes in the electrical states of the processor, which profoundly change its capabilities.

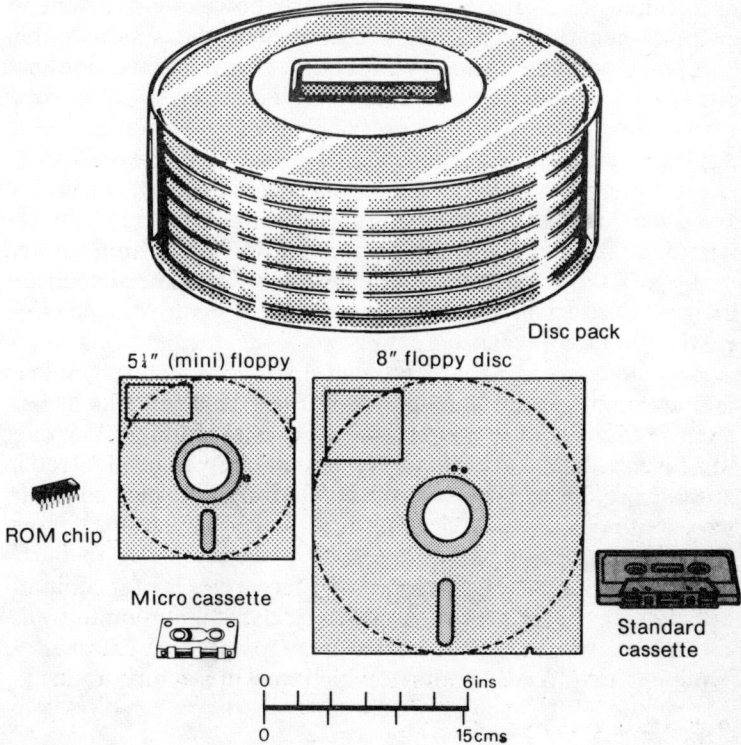

Figure 11. Some ways of storing software

Programs are generally sold, loaned or exchanged in one of the forms shown in Figure 11. The commonest are floppy discs and, mainly for personal and schools computers, standard cassettes. Floppy discs dominate the business software market. Unfortunately, they are one of the least standardized aspects of computing today. The two prevailing sizes of floppy discs at present are the 8-inch and 5¼-inch sizes mentioned on page 32; these are sometimes called floppies and **minifloppies** respectively.

However, continuing progress in packing more and more Kilobytes of information onto a minifloppy disc has had an unfortunate side-effect. Nowadays it is becoming common to find high-density discs storing 400 K, 800 K or even up to 2000 K (2 Megabytes); as these are far larger than most programs require to store them, various manufacturers have devised smaller discs called **microfloppies**. Alas for the consumer, floppy discs are now being produced in diameters of 3 inches, 3.25 inches, at least 3 incompatible formats of 3.5-inches, 3.8 inches and even 3.9 inches! Although their storage capacities are remarkable for their size (ranging from 200 to 2000 K in 1983) this proliferation of incompatible sizes is not in the consumer's interest. Disc drives are expensive and tailor-made for a particular size of disc, so early agreement on a standard for microfloppies would be highly desirable.

Even if software is available on a 5¼-inch disc, there is still plenty of scope for incompatibility. Discs vary in the way they store information: in technical language, they may be **40-track** or **80-track**, for instance, and **'hard-sectored'** or **'soft-sectored'** (consult the glossary if you want explanations at present). They also vary as to how closely information is packed on them; in place of single-density you may see advertisements for 'double-density' or even 'quad-density' discs. The result of all this is that before you can be confident that a disc drive attached to one computer can 'read' a disc from a different one, you have to know quite a lot about it in addition to whether it will physically fit the slot!

By contrast, the same cassette recorder can play any standard cassette, whether it is a C12 or a C90, whether the coating is ferric oxide or chromium dioxide, etc. Because of the limitations of cassette systems (see page 32), they are seldom used in business, except for very small businesses with modest data-handling needs. Dictation-style micro-cassettes, of course, need different equipment again.

The most compact form of software is that supplied on ROM

chips. These are designed uniquely for a particular system and are plugged into the inside of the computer. As they can only be installed by taking the cover off the computer, and cannot be modified by the user, ROMs are sometimes described as **firmware**, on the basis that they are intermediate between software and hardware. The commonest uses of ROM software is for word processing (see Chapter 6) and for programming languages (see below).

> *Self-check*
>
> It has been said that the parts of a computer system can be divided into those which cannot be changed, those which are often changed, and those which are seldom if ever changed. Can you think of a single word for each of these parts?

ANSWER

Hardware, software and firmware.

Software can also be provided in the form of plug-in cartridges (commonly used in home computers or arcade games), as a print-out of the listing (an impossibly slow and unreliable method, except for very short programs) or transmitted from a distance directly into the computer's memory, a process known as **telesoftware**). However, at present mini-floppy discs are the commonest vehicle for business software.

Consider the following extracts from a current business software price list. The first shows the main headings:

1 Accounting
2 Financial planning
3 Word processing
4 Data base management systems
5 Programming languages
6 Operating systems
7 Utilities

Numbers **1** to **4** are kinds of applications software which we shall be discussing later. The last three headings are all different kinds of systems software. If you looked up the entries under 'programming languages', the first few might read something like this:

- ADA, requires OS CP/M-80, 48 K RAM, £250
- BASIC-80 Interpreter, requires OS CP/M-80, 32 K RAM, £225
- BASIC-80 Compiler, requires OS CP/M-80, 48 K RAM minimum (54 K recommended), £280
- COBOL-80, requires OS CP/M-80, 48 K RAM, £550

If all that looks like gobbledygook, don't worry; after studying the rest of this chapter, its significance should be clear! Actually, if you stay calm and read it twice, it soon emerges that all the entries are in the same form: the first name is presumably that of the language and the last item is clearly the price! In between are the requirements for something called **OS** (they all seem to need **CP/M-80**, whatever that is) and RAM, which is presumably the amount of internal memory they take up. That still leaves some unsolved mysteries:

- Why would anyone want to buy a language other than the one that came with the original computer? Why do they have to take up RAM space which the user wants for programs? Which language is best, anyway?
- What is the difference between a **compiler** and an **interpreter**, and which one is best? (Since the compiler costs more and seems to take up more space, you might wonder why anyone would want one.)
- What is an OS and why is it important? What does **CP/M** stand for and why does it keep cropping up?
- What are **utilities** and why do you need them?

The rest of this chapter will enable you to answer questions like these.

Programming languages

High-level languages, assembly language and machine language

You may already have heard of the programming languages called **BASIC** or **COBOL**. There are many other such languages, the most important of which are introduced in the next section. They were designed for the programmer, rather than for the machine, and are sometimes called **high-level languages**, because they use words and symbols which are miles 'above' the primitive 1s and 0s in which the computer operates deep-down. Remember (see page 27) that all instructions have to be turned into this binary form – known as machine language – at some stage. You can see a sample of it in Figure 12.

If the only instructions that a processor can understand and act on are in the form of long strings, like 11101101 11011010, you may be wondering how anyone ever learns to program a computer. Humans don't take kindly to this sort of language! Although it is possible (for some) to learn to program in machine language, it is difficult and time-consuming; tracking and correcting mistakes (**bugs**) is even worse, and it is not recommended for people without the patience of a saint.

Fortunately, it is very seldom necessary to write programs this way nowadays. Early on, computer scientists invented superprograms which could *automatically* translate instructions in higher-level languages (e.g. 'LET C=A+B') into machine language. These super-programs are called compilers or interpreters, and we will deal with them in the next section. By loading different translation programs, you can make a single computer seem to understand different languages.

High-level languages allow the programmer to think out and write her or his program in terms which resemble ordinary language. This is much easier for humans to handle, so programs are quicker to write and less prone to error than programs written in binary 1s and 0s. The only disadvantages are the extra time it takes for the translation to be done, and the fact that the compiler or interpreter program itself occupies some of the

52 What is a computer?

computer's memory. Whether this matters or not depends on the nature of the program and the way it is used. It also depends on the particular method used for translation: compilers and interpreters do it rather differently, as we shall see.

In practice, situations where the system is held back by waiting for the processor are rarer than you might expect. Rotating 3-dimensional graphics, word processing and repetitive sorting of large volumes of data are examples where programs written wholly in high-level languages would be unacceptably slow. Even so, it is not often necessary to resort to machine language as there is a halfway house called **assembly language**, which can be used on its own or mixed with a high-level language.

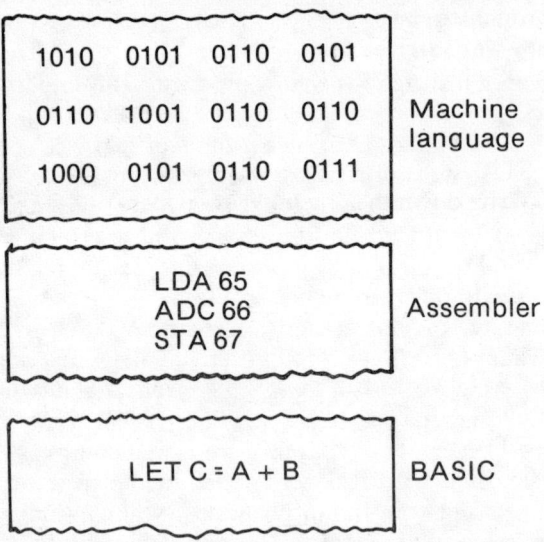

Figure 12. Excerpts from the same program written at different levels of language

Assembly language makes use of **mnemonics**, which are shorthand versions of English words (see Figure 12). For example, LDA 65 stands for 'Load the accumulator with the contents of box number 65', ADC 66 means 'Add the contents of box number 66' and STA 67 means 'Store the answer' in box number 67'. If you happened to know the standard code for storing letters in computers (see **ASCII** entry in glossary), you would know that 65 stood for A, 66 for B, 67 for C and so on. The relationship between the assembly language version in the middle of Figure 12 and the line of BASIC below it should now be clearer.

> *Self-check*
>
> (If this one doesn't appeal to you, don't worry too much about writing down the answers for yourself; just read through the answers and check that you understand how they were arrived at.)
> 1 What is the BASIC equivalent of:
>   LDA 78
>   ADC 77
>   STA 76
> 2 Write down the assembly equivalent of LET D=E+F

ANSWERS

1 If 65 is code for A, 78 is code for the 13th letter in the alphabet after A, i.e. N (78 − 65 = 13). Similarly, 77 stands for M and 76 for L. So this bit of assembly code means
   'LET L=N+M'
2 LDA 69
   ADC 70
   STA 68

The advantage of mnemonics like these is that the processor just refers to a master table with the machine language equivalent of each assembly instruction. This allows it to translate assembly programs into machine language quickly. Although not exactly friendly-looking, mnemonics are certainly easier for humans to handle and check than binary numbers. The graphs in Figures 13 and 14 indicate the relative merits of the three 'levels' of programming languages.

54 What is a computer?

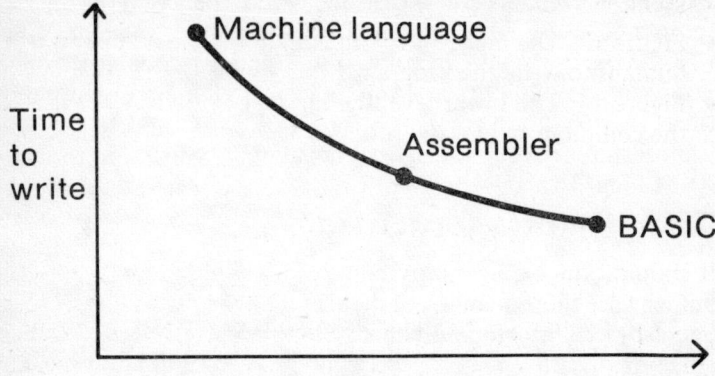

Figure 13. *Relationship between the level of language and time to write*

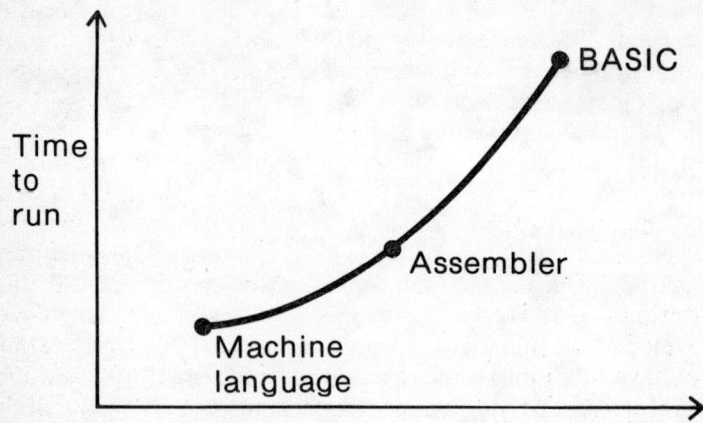

Figure 14. *Relationship between level of language and time to run*

Self-check

Re-state the information in Figures 13 and 14 in ordinary English. You may find it easier to use a separate sentence for each graph.

ANSWER

- Figure 13: The higher level the language, the quicker it is for humans to write the program.
- Figure 14: The lower level the language, the quicker it is for the computer to execute (obey).

Which high-level language is best?

It should now be clear why high-level languages are so useful, but why are there so many of them and how do you choose which one is best? Unfortunately there are no simple answers to these questions. With some microcomputers, the second one is meaningless as you may not have a choice at all: BASIC is sometimes built into the machine on a ROM chip. This is convenient, because you don't have to load it every time you want to use it and it doesn't occupy precious RAM space that you need for programs. But there may come a time when you want to use a different language, so it is important to keep your options open – or at least to be aware that you may be closing certain doors when you buy a particular machine.

Unlike micros, most mainframe computers can be made to obey almost any high-level language, though buying the necessary compiler (translation super-program) can be a significant expense. This variation between the different sizes of computers is partly historical accident and partly a matter of marketing decisions. Until recently, many of the traditional languages, developed on mainframes with huge memories, simply would not have fitted into a micro's much smaller memory. Now that RAM and ROM are getting cheaper and more compact all the time, and larger and more powerful micros are spreading into an ever-increasing number of business settings, making an appropriate choice of language(s) is becoming ever more important.

Like human languages, programming languages have grown up to meet different needs and to suit different groups of people. A universal programming language – a sort of computer Esperanto – might be the ideal, but it just hasn't happened yet and there are various practical and commercial obstacles in the way.

The nearest approach to it (and it is miles from the standardization of Esperanto) is BASIC.

The ubiquitous BASIC

BASIC stands for Beginners' All-purpose Symbolic Instruction Code. It was developed at an American college in the 1960s to help beginners learn to program computers. It is an easy first language for newcomers to learn, as you will find out if you work through Chapter 10. Some form of BASIC is widely available on computers of all sizes. Its compactness makes it especially suitable for microcomputers, and its flexibility means that it can be used for a wide range of applications. Unfortunately, it has serious limitations as a programming language, especially for complex programs.

Perhaps the most annoying feature of BASIC from the user's viewpoint is the number of different versions, or **dialects**, which have grown up. Unlike human dialects, where the listener might understand nine words out of ten and still get the gist of what was being said, BASIC dialects are generally incompatible. Even the most trivial difference between the dialects used by different machines can prevent a program written on one machine from being run on another. Sometimes the modifications needed are quite small, but if you are unfamiliar with the two dialects, the barrier can still seem insuperable. Some of the variations arise because different manufacturers were too lazy or too perverse to use the same conventions. Others represent truly worthwhile improvements over the original language. With a bit more effort, most could have been made '**downwards-compatible**', i.e. able to run all programs written in the original BASIC and some more besides. Having to modify programs written in one dialect of BASIC to work in another is the source of a lot of frustration and wasted effort.

However, BASIC has the great advantage that most people who can program at all know *some* sort of BASIC. This means that there are lots of good introductory books to help beginner-programmers learn the language, and there is masses of reasonably-priced BASIC software. Some of it might have been more compact, more professional or faster-running had it been written in a different language – but much of it might never have been written at all.

Although BASIC has enjoyed huge popularity as a language which makes it easy for novices to get into programming, it is not necessarily unsuitable for serious business software. Professional programming techniques, careful documentation and the use of an extended dialect can overcome many of BASIC's inherent disadvantages.

COBOL

COBOL stands for Common Business Oriented Language. It was introduced in 1960 especially for commercial data processing, and it specializes in the handling of alphabetic, as opposed to numerical, information. It can also handle basic mathematical operations (rather inefficiently). COBOL was developed in the belief that a commercial programmer will prefer to use words rather than mathematical symbols, e.g. ADD in place of +. COBOL programs tend to be rather verbose and COBOL compilers (the super-programs which translate it into machine language) tend to be greedy for memory space.

Transferring COBOL programs from one computer to another is much easier than for BASIC programs but still not trouble-free. Despite early efforts to standardize it (mainly thanks to Univac and the US Navy), various 'improved' versions of COBOL have been developed, some of which need less internal memory space. This development reduces the value of the original standard. Unless the new version is available to a different range of computers, or has some really worthwhile additional facilities, it may not be much of a benefit. For example, in the late 1960s IBM decided to replace one version (COBOL F) by another (ANSI COBOL). American users alone spent between 2,000 and 3,000 *million* dollars on converting their programs! Recently, COBOL has become available on small computers in trimmed-down versions. COBOL is of great importance to business users, if only because it is the most commonly used language for business applications on mainframe computers.

Other high-level languages

There are many other specialized business languages to choose from. RPG (Report Program Generator) is a stripped-down business language used by many smaller IBM installations. Many traditional mainframe languages are fairly general-purpose. For example, FORTRAN (FORmula TRANslator) and ALGOL (ALGOrithmic Language), although more commonly used for scientific and mathematical applications, *can* cope with most business needs; they are simply less convenient for the programmer.

Many other more recent languages have taken features from the traditional languages and improved on them. PASCAL dates from the mid-1970s. Unlike BASIC, it *obliges* programmers to display clear structure in their programs. It is rapidly becoming available on various microcomputers. PL/1 was developed by IBM with the aim of meeting the needs of both commerce and science. It derives features from ALGOL, COBOL and FORTRAN, but is in some ways easier to learn, as simple programs can easily be written without a full knowledge of the language. PL/M is the scaled-down version for microcomputers.

There are literally hundreds of other programming languages, with names like PROLOG, APL, LISP, COMAL, LOGO and ADA. In 1983, ADA joined the ranks of FORTRAN and COBOL in being adopted by **ANSI**, the American National Standards Institute. It was developed by the US Defence Department and has been billed as the likely universal programming language of the next decade. However, a new language has to be fully standardized, learned by a new generation of programmers and have its software widely distributed. This is a long process, and their huge libraries of proven software give the established languages considerable momentum. This creates a climate in which guinea pigs usually suffer: it may actually pay to be *behind* the times if you don't want to have to write all your own software.

How does it work? 59

Anyone who is familiar with any programming language is likely to disagree with some of the above. It is a controversial field, and every language has its loyal adherents and its virulent critics. It is difficult for most people to be objective about the merits of programming languages; it takes quite an effort to learn a language and many people get all too comfortable with the one they learn first. They prefer to think up reasons why *their* language is objectively the best, rather than face learning another.

With a bit of ingenuity, most computers can be made to do most things with *any* language. Unless you are going to write programs yourself (see cautions in Chapter 11), the important questions are (a) will you be buying software, and if so what language is it written in? and (b) who will the programmers be, and what languages do they already know or can they easily learn?

Self-check

List four or more features of an ideal programming language. Note any which are likely to be in conflict with each other.

ANSWERS

1 Exists in a single agreed version which is interchangeable between computers.
2 Quick, natural and easy to learn for humans.
3 Fast for the computer to execute.
4 Universally available on all sizes and makes of computer.
5 Capable of handling all applications (business, scientific, educational).
6 Produces programs which are easy to understand and amend, and whose structure is clearly visible.
7 Makes modest demands on the internal memory of the computer.

Numbers **2** and **3** tend to be in conflict, and number **2** is also hard to combine with number **7**. This in turn means that number **4** is problematic; if a language requires a lot of internal memory,

60 What is a computer?

it won't be possible to run its full form on microcomputers. This in turn jeopardizes number **1**, as scaled-down versions will be needed. These trade-offs partly explain why we are so far from the goal of a universal programming language.

Author languages

Author languages get their name because they are designed for the author of the program, rather than for the machine or for a professional programmer. The author might be a trainer, a manager or even a pupil. Author languages are even further removed from machine language than programming languages (Figure 15). They allow the author to write instructions in near-normal English, according to certain conventions.

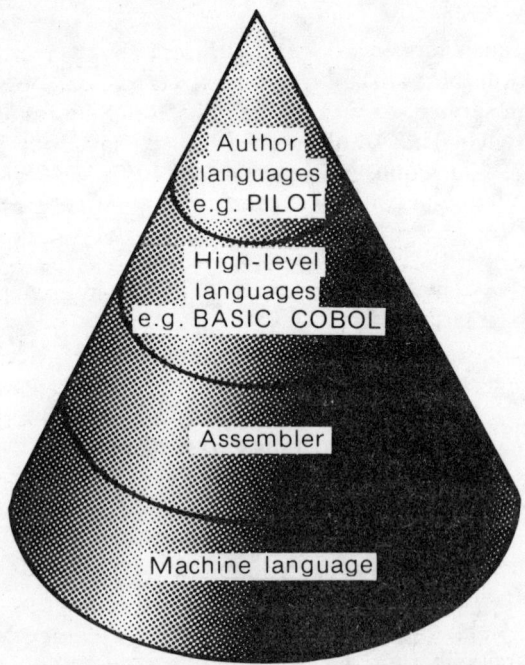

Figure 15. Different levels of programming languages

How does it work? 61

Author languages are of especial importance to businesses interested in computer-based training (see Chapter 14). Although general-purpose languages like BASIC *can* be used to produce programs for education and training, special-purpose languages can help people involved in training with no experience of computers to produce working course material more quickly. One example is PILOT, which is available on some minicomputers and a variety of microcomputers. Another is MICROTEXT, which was developed at the National Physical Laboratory and is widely available on micros. Others include IIS (available on IBM medium and large mainframes) and TUTOR (available as part of Control Data's PLATO system).

Compilers and interpreters

We have seen that the facility of programming in any language other than machine's own depends entirely on super-programs, which perform the translation automatically. A compiler is like a translation service, to whom you might send a book of short stories in French. They translate the ones you have specified into the language you requested – German, say. Only after you get the German text will you know if they have done the right ones. An interpreter is more like a simultaneous translator at the United Nations. Each sentence (line of program) is translated (interpreted) as it is heard (read in), so that errors are easier to identify as you go along.

Let us now forget this analogy, which will mislead us if we try to push it too far. Once the machine-language program has been compiled, it can run without interruption, very rapidly. And since you need no longer store either the original program or the compiler, large amounts of RAM are available for data. Although the BASIC compiler program on page 50 *looks* as if it takes up a lot of RAM, actually the interpreter will leave *less* space for the user's program and data to run. The reason for this paradox is that the interpreter and the program being interpreted have to be held in memory all the time while the machine language version is translated and executed line-by-line.

Not only do interpreters limit the RAM space available, they also make the program run more slowly. Most programs contain instructions to the processor to jump back to some previous line and 'loop the loop'. The interpreter has to re-translate all these lines over again. If the **loop** is to be repeated 100 or 1000 times, the re-translation must be done 100 or 1000 times. The whole process is very inefficient compared with running a once-and-for-all compiled version of the program. Interpreted programs tend to take around three to five times as long to run as compiled programs and they leave less usable space inside the computer.

You may now be wondering why anyone ever has programs interpreted if they could have them compiled. The answer is two-fold. First, programmers spend far more time getting mistakes out of programs than they do writing them. This process (called **debugging**) is much quicker and easier with an interpreter because errors are identified as each line is read, and helpful messages can be displayed telling the programmer what kind of bug and which line it occurs in. Second, although the fully debugged program would run faster and occupy less space if it were compiled, in practice that may not be worth doing, because unless the system is fully stretched, the program may be quite fast enough already and there may be RAM space to spare in any case – especially if the interpreter itself is supplied on a ROM.

Self-check

You see a description of two programs for microcomputers, both written in BASIC. One is a simple set of mathematical tests, designed for use and modification by school pupils and their teachers. The other is a commercial program for sorting and rearranging large mailing lists. Which would you expect to be intended for computers with interpreters and which for those with compilers? Explain why.

ANSWER

The mathematical program would be meant for use with an interpreter. This would help any teacher or pupil making modifications (e.g. making the sums harder) to get their amendments right. In any case, when the program is running, the computer will probably spend over 99 per cent of its time waiting for the pupil to make a response, so the program execution speed is hardly critical. The space taken up by the interpreter is irrelevant since the program will be quite small and there will be very little data.

The business program, on the other hand, would benefit from being compiled. It should already be fully debugged and its users are much less likely to be able to modify it anyway. Mailing lists require lots of RAM to store them, and sorting of large amounts of alphabetic data is a slow job in computer terms. So compactness and efficiency may both be quite important.

Operating systems

The computer's operating system is the resident control program which is running all the time when nothing else is (apparently) happening. It supervises all the activities, like input and output, decides what jobs the processor should give priority to and deals with the computer's external memory, saving and retrieving programs. You will see operating systems referred to as OS for short; in systems which can handle discs, the bit of OS that deals with disc operations is called the DOS (**Disc Operating System**).

The OS is also the computer's personality. It determines whether the user finds the computer cryptic and unfriendly or whether the system seems avuncular and helpful, giving explanations of what is happening and what input is required. (The latter style tends to need a larger OS than the former, though not all large OSs are friendly!) Operating systems vary enormously in size and capabilities. Systems which have to deal with several users at once (**multi-user** systems) or several programs at once (**multi-tasking**) need more complicated operating systems than single-user, single-task micros. For example, the OS will have to sort out the priorities when there are conflicting demands.

Operating systems are closely related to computer hardware (Figure 16) so different OSs are needed for different types of processor: 16-bit processors need different systems from 8-bit

64   What is a computer?

ones. 8-bit micros usually have relatively simple operating systems. Had the 'Big Three' first micro companies (Apple, Commodore and Tandy) agreed on a chip, they could have cooperated to produce a common OS. Unfortunately, all three went their own way to produce three incompatible machine-specific OSs, even though two of them were using the same basic processor anyway. This lost opportunity is responsible for many of the early problems of transferring programs between micros.

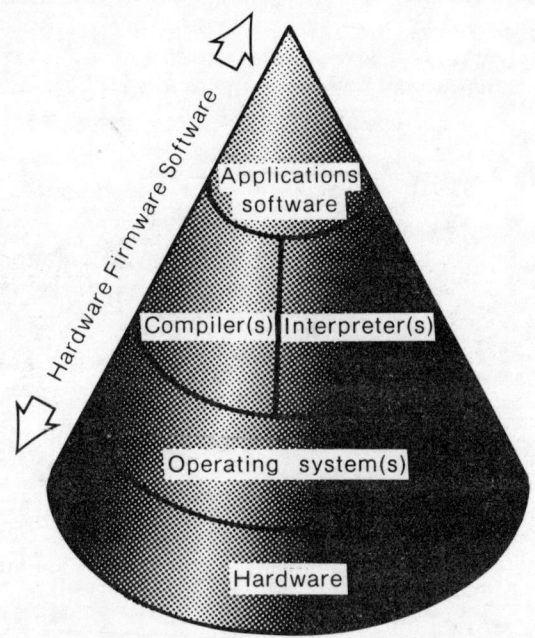

Figure 16. Operating systems form a crucial link between hardware and applications software

Mainframe OS facilities are more standardized and the problems of software transference are correspondingly simpler. Mainframe computers have to have much more sophisticated operating systems to deal with lots of different users, often running different programs simultaneously. The smaller micros

How does it work? 65

don't have enough processor power and memory space to make it worth sharing out in this way. However, the new generation of 16-bit microcomputers tend to have more flexible OSs, and they sometimes offer two resident operating systems as a way round the incompatibility problem.

When things are going well, the user should hardly notice the OS. So why is it important for the business user to bother about the operating system? First, the character of the OS will affect the demands made of those who use the system and will inevitably influence their attitudes to working with it. For example, it is easy for a beginner to forget to close the door of the disc drive, or perhaps to try by mistake to 'read' a write-protected disc (page 32). The current prevailing business OS will respond to these easily-made mistakes with an error message like

BDOS ERR ON B: BAD SECTOR

at which, understandably many beginners will panic! It would be no more difficult for it to say 'Please close the disc drive door,' or, 'Sorry, can't read write-protected disc.'

For small-computer owners, the OS is especially important, because non-professionals are more likely to be dealing with the system. Even more important, the OS is more likely to determine what applications software can be run than is the programming language originally provided. Many micros can run additional languages just by plugging in another ROM or by loading them from disc. Unless the original OS provides for it, however, there is no escaping the computer's operating system! In particular, the features of the disc operating system (DOS) determine what discs can be read, and this is of great practical importance to all business users who want to run disc software.

As with programming languages, the general lack of standardization is lamentable. The nearest approach to an industry standard for single-user 8-bit microcomputers is called **CP/M** (Control Program for Microprocessors). You will also see it written as CP/M-80 (to emphasise that it is for the Z80, 8080 and 8085 processors). It was devised in the late 1970s to help programmers to develop software. It was taken up by the micro market with enthusiasm as the first OS to allow a program to be transferred from one microcomputer to another. It managed this by separating the basic input/output section (BIOS), which is specific to the processor, from the section which deals with discs (the DOS). This is a bit like providing different shapes and sizes of plugs on a travelling iron so that it will be compatible with sockets in any country. The processor has to be told to pull in CP/M off the disc, so part of the program includes a routine to load CP/M automatically. This technique is known as **bootstrapping**, as the system 'pulls itself up by its own bootstraps'.

Because it was the first OS to make software transference easy, more software by far runs under CP/M than any other OS. Thus it has become a *de facto* standard and even though it was based on technology which is now out of date, the mass of proven software which runs under CP/M guarantees its immediate future. This inertia is not entirely a good thing, since CP/M does not use the full power of the processor for which it was designed, nor does it take full advantage of vdu technology. The result is that it uses more memory than it should, is slower in retrieving from disc and not as **crash-proof** as it should be. Nor is CP/M as friendly as it might be, as the error message above shows. (The printed manual is if anything less approachable!) Nevertheless, in operating systems, as in programming languages, it may be more in users' interests that a standard exists than that it be the best standard. Any business user who plans to buy in software should certainly think twice before cutting himself off from the vast CP/M libraries of tried and tested software.

CP/M can run on any 8-bit micro which uses the processor mentioned, providing it has at least 16 K of RAM (24 K is preferable), at least one disc drive and an OS designed to bootstrap CP/M. Individual software packages may need minor modifications to work on particular machines, so it is always worth checking this point. There have been several updates of CP/M; in 1983, version 2.2 was the current one for micros with up to 64 K of RAM. CP/M Plus (or CP/M 3.1) is an extension designed to address more memory than this; it is also more compatible with the other enhancements of CP/M mentioned below.

How does it work? 67

A modified system called **CP/M-86** was devised for 16-bit microcomputers, but it has not achieved the same monopoly as the original 8-bit CP/M. The main rival at present is **MS-DOS**, the system commissioned by IBM for its Personal Computer (where it is called PC-DOS). Because IBM is the world's largest manufacturer, other 16-bit micro producers soon decided to follow its footsteps. Some manufacturers are hedging their bets (and hence keeping the user's options open) by offering both these systems – a wise precaution.

Derived from CP/M is MP/M II, the 1982 release of a multi-user operating system for micros. This has not achieved the same popularity as CP/M, and a system called **Unix** has been widely adopted for 16-bit micros doing 'multi-user multi-tasking'. One of the business examples of multi-tasking most commonly cited is that of printing out a long report in the '**background**' while using the micro to run a program in the 'foreground'. A similar effect can be achieved with a printer buffer, however. Since processors are (relatively) cheap, many businesses find it more cost-effective to network several micros and share expensive peripherals.

Self-check

A business colleague is interested in buying a microcomputer. He is hesitating between various 8-bit micros at attractive prices and a newer but more expensive 16-bit machine. All have twin disc drives. After a visit to his dealer, he has been completely baffled by technical talk. He appeals for your help. What help can you give him on the strength of this chapter? Assume that he will be buying all his software, and that the system will only have one user. Suggest what questions he should ask about programming languages and operating systems.

ANSWER

There is no short answer to this, as it raises major issues stretching over several chapters. Apart from offering to lend him this book, you could offer:

- *Languages*: does it support BASIC, and if so what **dialect**? What other languages are available?
- *Operating system* 8-bit: can it run CP/M-80? 16-bit: can it run *both* CP/M-86 and MS-DOS?
- *Software* Has he seen programs which will fit the needs of his business? If so, on which of the machines he is contemplating will they run? If not, who is going to write his software and has he costed this operation . . . etc?

Utilities

Utilities are mundane but vital programs which do jobs like copying discs, telling you how much space remains and preparing output for printing. Some may be supplied with the original computer or disc drive, but there are many useful ones which are marketed independently. For example, you can get utilities to recover the contents of deleted discs and to copy programs from one format or density to another.

> *Self-check*
>
> Look back at the questions on page 50 and try to answer them now.

ANSWER

You will find all the answers on pages 51–68. Re-read this material now, or else return to it later, if you are not sure of the answers.

> *Self-check*
>
> You are advising a self-employed friend who has rashly bought a computer for book-keeping, but cannot find a program suitable to the way she records and receives her fees and expenses. Having noticed a magazine advertisement for a software package aimed at freelances, you ring her up to tell her about it. She becomes very excited and is about to jump into her car and drive sixty miles to the dealer to collect one. You advise her to telephone first. What should she ask about it?

ANSWER

Apart from the obvious questions like whether it is in stock, she should try to find out (a) whether it will run on her computer and (b) form an impression of whether it is likely to be worth buying. If the dealer is knowledgeable, telling him what machine she has *might* be enough, but it is safer to check the three things mentioned in the chapter: format, language and operating system. Even if all seems to be in order, she should still double-check whether any special facilities are needed (individual computers often come with different options for RAM size, or optional colour capability). She should ask if the dealer has ever successfully run the package on her particular machine, and whatever the answer, she should take her computer along with her unless it would be impracticable.

How far it is worth discussing the package is more debatable. If your friend is desperate and the package moderately-priced, her journey will probably be worthwhile as long as the program runs. However, if her time is precious and if alternatives are offered by reps willing to visit her, she should try to satisfy herself of its appropriateness or else ask for printed details to be posted.

3 | Some systems and their users

This chapter introduces seven computer systems in use in different sorts of businesses. At present, we are not going into the details of how each system works, as these examples are only intended to be suggestive; their purpose is to give you ideas about how computers could be useful in businesses with which you are familiar or even directly involved. We shall be looking at four specific types of software package in more detail in Chapters 4, 5, 6 and 11.

The self-checks in this chapter all have a common purpose: to get you to think of other businesses that might find a similar computer system useful. This can be both challenging and entertaining if you avoid the obvious. Try to devise plausible examples as *far* removed as possible from the one described.

Jenny Bruno

Jenny Bruno was brought up on a farm and had always kept her interest in animals. At school, she was good at maths and business studies and she went on to study for a degree in business administration, including computing. However, she never really felt at ease in the big city and was bored by her image of a future of office routine and big corporation bureaucracy. In her second year at college, her steady boyfriend left her, and just afterwards her favourite uncle (a wealthy bachelor) died, leaving her £8000. At the age of nineteen, Jenny decided that the time had come for a change of direction and, after heated arguments with her parents, she dropped out of college to buy a boarding kennels.

Her college studies stood her in good stead in her subsequent dealings with bank managers and building societies. She found a run-down cottage with an acre of ground in beautiful, hilly

Some systems and their users

country just ten miles from a major conurbation in the Midlands. A large mortgage enabled her to buy it and finance the necessary alterations to house sixteen dogs. When she was ready to open, in April, she had no trouble filling the places. Lots of pet-owners seemed to be going on holiday and liked the idea of giving their dogs a stay in the country with someone whose fondness for them was so obvious. Her former college was a good source of recommendations, too, and Jenny was soon thinking about expanding.

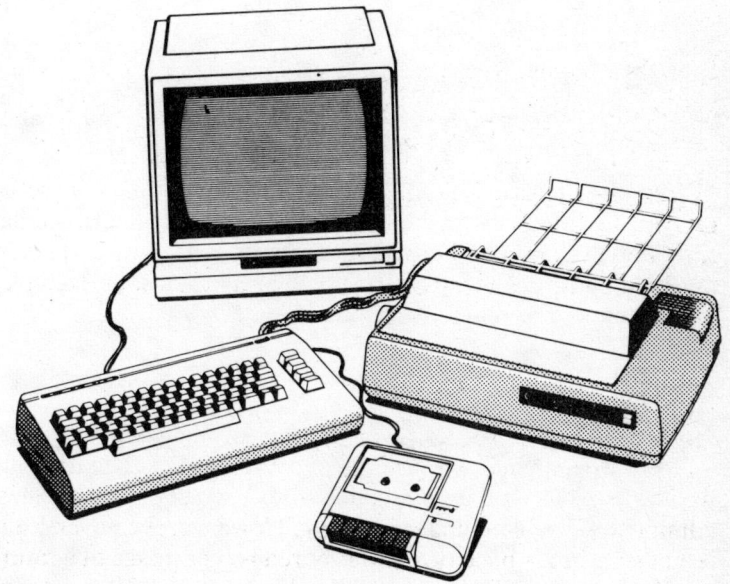

Figure 17. A low-priced personal computer system

However, Jenny was beginning to wonder if she could cope with exercising all the dogs herself on top of the paperwork involved in bookings, correspondence and doing the books. She was also secretly beginning to wonder if her brains might atrophy without a challenge! So she bought a medium-priced personal microcomputer and a dot-matrix printer, hoping that she would

72 What is a computer?

remember enough programming to write software to help run the kennels. Her system is shown in Figure 17. She already had a black-and-white television and a mono cassette recorder, and she bought the micro and the printer new for £450. With cables and supplies, the whole system cost just under £500. The micro had 48 K of RAM, a proper full-size keyboard and a built-in BASIC interpreter. It would not run CP/M (it was based on the 6502 chip) but this didn't worry her, as she didn't expect to be able to afford to buy software or a disc drive.

In the first two months, she found that writing programs 'for real' took her a lot longer than those college exercises, where mistakes didn't really matter. She also discovered that cassette loading and saving was driving her mad, so she bought a disc drive after all. This speeded things up dramatically and encouraged her to finish debugging two programs: one covers accommodation (Figure 18) and the other accounts (Figure 19).

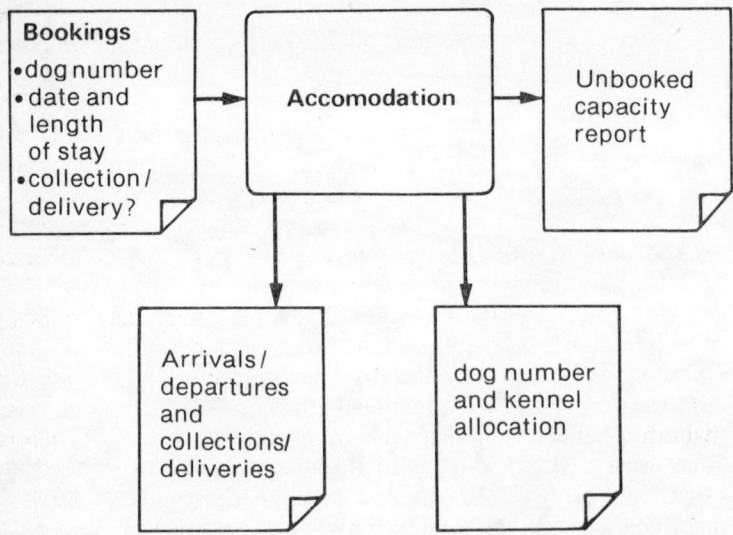

Figure 18. Inputs and outputs for the kennel accommodation system

Some systems and their users   73

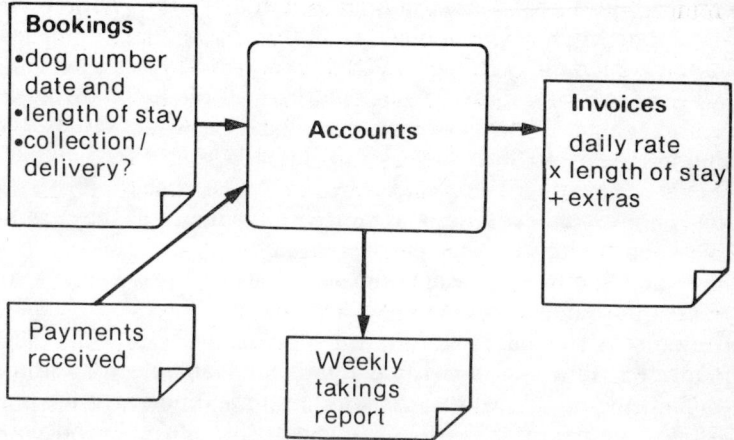

Figure 19. Inputs and outputs for the kennel accounts system

Twice a week Jenny enters booking details (dog number, date, length of stay, whether collection/delivery is needed) into the accommodation system. The dog number is a code which not only identifies the dog but also shows its size; the daily rate charged depends on size, and she has three different sizes of kennel. (All phone bookings have to be confirmed by letter, so she does this job in one sitting at her leisure.) The accommodation system produces a list of dogs and kennel allocations for the forthcoming two weeks and also confirms which kennels are vacant. (In practice, Jenny keeps this on a wall-chart opposite the telephone, anyway, so that she always can tell at a glance whether to accept a booking.) The program also lists all dogs arriving or departing, together with their kennel numbers and whether collection/delivery is required. Dogs whose departures are imminent are asterisked to remind Jenny to prepare the invoice. (Jenny's terms are cash on collection.)

Once a week, she enters the same details into the accounts system, and also enters payments received. The program stores the three daily rates, and the dog code indicates which one to apply. It prints an invoice showing the daily rate and length of stay and adds any extras, like collection/delivery. The system also reports the weekly takings and shows up any discrepancies between payments received and invoices issued.

These two programs do not take care of all Jenny Bruno's book-keeping. They ignore her outgoings, for which she uses a simple notebook. She buys dogfood in bulk, runs a secondhand car (used mainly for dog collection/delivery and shopping) and notes household expenses and mortgage payments as they arise. She keeps details of dogs (names, ages, food preferences, owners' names and addresses) on a simple card index, which also has her dog codes written on it.

Her next purchase was a word processing ROM chip. She plugged it into her micro and found it invaluable for letters (confirming bookings, dealing with enquiries) and also for the articles she now writes for magazines for dog-lovers (and personal computer users!). She is also working on a simple program to help her to do financial forecasting. We will meet this again in Chapter 4.

Self-check

1 What other businesses might need the kind of software which Jenny has been writing?
2 Suppose you were such a business and were thinking of adopting her system. What change(s) would you want made to it?

ANSWERS

1 Anyone involved in advance booking and invoicing – for example, a guest-house/hotel, a car-hire firm, a canal-boat owner.
2 Apart from the general need to tailor the programs to suit the business concerned, there are two major limitations of her system: its incompleteness and the separation between programs which means that the same details have to be entered twice over.

Beau Brummel

Beau Brummel is a small-town retailer of carefully selected men's clothing, from suits and shirts to small items like handkerchiefs and cuff-links. The owner, Julian Dapper, is a self-made businessman who made a great success of his first shop by concentrating on a small number of colour coordinated lines. Dapper built up a reputation for quality and found that his small items attracted gift-shoppers. A year after opening his second shop in a nearby town, he was thinking of buying a third.

However, expansion was making it increasingly difficult for Dapper to retain close personal control of the shops. Apart from the amount of his time that went on routine paperwork, two management problems were worrying him. He had no clear picture of the relative profitability of the different garments, lines and suppliers, and his sales assistants conveyed vague and sometimes conflicting impressions. He also had mounting doubts about the honesty of two of them, but couldn't spare the time either to prevent pilferage or to prove that he was right and dismiss them.

Dapper thought that a micro could help him solve these problems but whenever he asked suppliers about software, he found that it was geared to a multiple chain of retailers, couldn't handle his system of four discount levels or wouldn't operate the commission basis he used to pay his assistants. Being resolute that he wanted the micro to do *all* his paperwork in an integrated way, he decided that since the necessary software wasn't available 'off the peg', he would just have to have it made to measure. Realizing that it would be prohibitively expensive to 'go it alone', he used a network of independent retailers to identify seven others who were in a similar position. They agreed jointly to commission a software house to produce programs to their specification, and to split the cost eight ways.

The programs were written to operate under CP/M, and the software house agreed to instal and maintain it on each of the five different makes of microcomputer that the retailers wanted to buy. Dapper bought two systems like the one shown in Figure 8 (see page 38), except that the one in his original shop has a medium-speed daisy-wheel printer (total hardware cost £2500), whereas the other shop has a dot-matrix (£500 cheaper). (Since the micros and disc drives are interchangeable, he can always take a disc with him to the other shop if he needs a high-quality print-out for some reason.) Dapper's share of the software cost was £1500 and his total initial outlay £6000.

Figure 20 shows the four main sections of Dapper's software: sales, payroll, stock control and purchases. Each of these automatically produces various documents (bits of paper) and will also generate reports (management information) whenever Dapper asks for them. Let's start with the documents by seeing what happens when a suit is sold. Details of the garment (product code), the price (with discount code if appropriate), type of sale (cash, credit card or account) and the employee code (to identify who made the sale) are entered into the system. In the case of credit sales, it will produce invoices, statements of account and a monthly analysis of outstanding payments by period overdue (aged debtors list).

Details of the sale are also sent to the payroll section. This holds details on all employees, including their commission rates, so as to calculate their wages according to the sales they have achieved. Weekly payslips are printed automatically at the original shop, but at present Dapper prefers to write cheques longhand.

Simultaneously, details of the sale are used by the stock control section to update the stock levels. If these fall low enough, repeat orders are generated automatically, though Dapper checks these personally before mailing them. When goods arrive, the delivery note is fed into this section, which updates the stock level and checks it against the invoice, which sometimes arrives later.

The suppliers' invoices are simultaneously analysed by the purchases section of the system. This holds details of all the different suppliers' credit arrangements and settlement periods. This allows Dapper to time payment to achieve maximum settlement discount without paying unnecessarily early. Remittance advice notes are printed automatically, but, as for wages, Dapper chooses to use his own pen and chequebook.

Some systems and their users 77

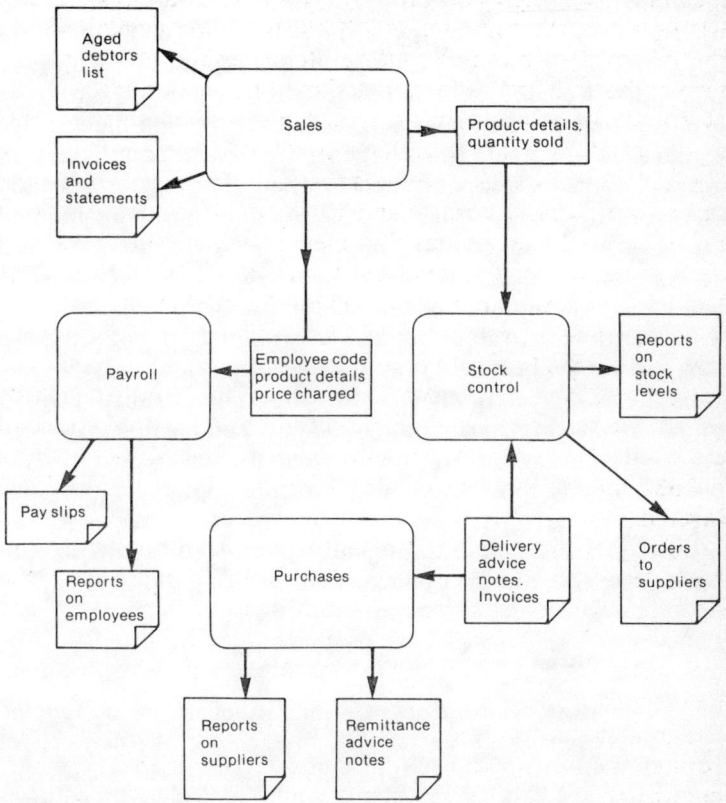

Figure 20. An integrated system covering sales, payroll, stock control and purchases

Reports from the different parts of the system help Dapper to exercise tight management control. The sales system naturally produces all the information and totals which Dapper used to have to work out for his sales ledger (accounts receivable). In addition, it gives him a detailed breakdown of the pattern of cash and credit sales and automatically highlights any sales assistants who are giving too many discounts or producing low sales generally. Payroll reports give him individual and cumulative information on each employee, including year-end summaries required for tax purposes. Stock control reports show him the times turnover for each supplier (the number of times the average stock holding has been sold in a year) and the average lead time for ordering (time between date of order and delivery note). This helps Dapper to decide whether or not to adjust the threshold level for re-order and whether to reconsider continued use of slow-moving goods or poor suppliers. He can also check on the individual profitability of each item if he wishes. The purchases system not only does all the routine purchases ledger work (accounts payable) but also helps him to manage his cash flow and get the best deal from his suppliers.

In the first year of the system's operation, Julian Dapper found that his profits increased by 13 per cent. He bought a word processing package and did extensive mail shots to advertise the opening of his third shop, which is proving to be the most profitable so far. The two employees of whom he harboured suspicions both left voluntarily, muttering about Big Brother, as the computer had come to be known.

Self-check

1 List three businesses who might benefit from Dapper's approach.

2 Jenny Bruno and Julian Dapper both run small businesses. Draw up two columns listing at least four differences between their approaches to computerization.

ANSWERS

1 You may have thought of almost any retail business: for example, an electrical discount store, a sweet or toy shop or a plumber's merchant.

2

Bruno	Dapper
used two separate programs	adopted integrated approach
has to enter same data twice	single-entry serves multiple purposes

Bruno	Dapper
wrote own software	commissioned software specially
built up gradually	went for complete system
worked in isolation	collaborated with other retailers
small, cheap system	ambitious system geared to future

The Democratic Trade Union (DTU)

The DTU is a small white-collar trade union with 50,000 members who work at 1500 different locations and mostly pay their subscriptions monthly through employers' deductions. Its headquarters are in London, where it employs a staff of thirty, two-thirds of whom do secretarial and clerical work. It publishes a monthly newsletter distributed by post to shop stewards at members' places of work. The DTU is proud of being run on democratic lines: once a year, it runs postal ballots of the whole membership to elect its national executive, using a system of proportional representation. Its local branches also run annual postal ballots and some have branch newsletters, which are distributed through the workplace.

Five years ago, DTU's office manager became concerned at the resources going into purely clerical jobs like addressing envelopes, counting and redistributing votes and posting out the results. It seemed an obvious case for computerization, but buying or leasing their own computer was out of the question: no one had the skills to operate or program it, the hardware costs at that time were astronomical, and the organization's need was sporadic, not daily. The solution was to use **batch processing** by a computer **bureau** which offered a complete service (consultancy on which applications were suitable for bureau service, design/adaptation of suitable software, use of machine time, etc.).

The result was the system shown in Figure 21. The DTU's membership list is held on the bureau's mainframe and updated quarterly by their headquarters, who receive information about

80 What is a computer?

new and lapsed members, changes of workplace, etc., from the local branches and collate it with their own information about those members who pay their subscriptions direct. Once a month, the bureau produces sticky labels with workplace addresses showing the number of newsletters to be sent. These are posted to HQ, where staff stuff envelopes with the newsletters and post them.

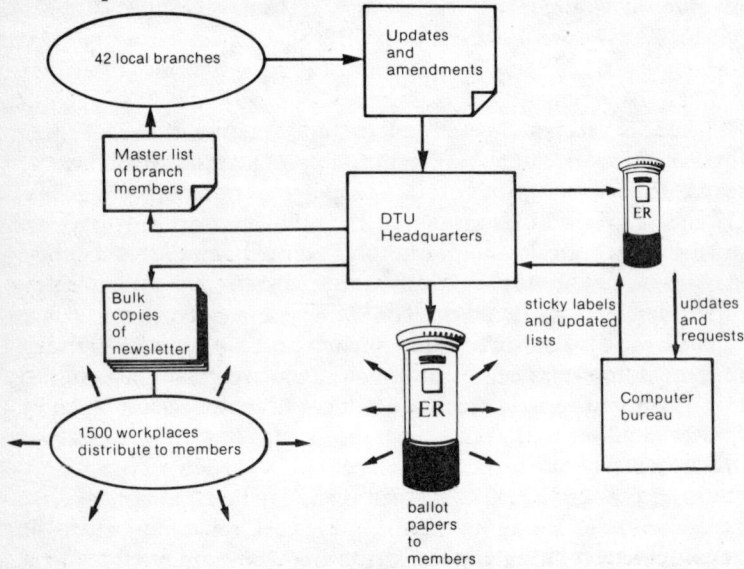

Figure 21. *Flow of information involved in bureau processing of the DTU's membership information*

Once a year, individual sticky labels are produced for direct mailing of the membership for the secret ballots and sent to HQ. (Some local branches also arrange to buy in sticky labels for their own local ballots.) HQ staff then stuff envelopes with ballot papers and stick stamps on them, but the pre-printed return address is the computer bureau's. On the cut-off date for return of papers, bureau staff open the envelopes, key in the numbers showing the members' preferences among the candidates, and the mainframe performs the complex arithmetic involved in

Some systems and their users 81

redistributing the votes until the correct number have been elected. (This used to take three HQ staff two full weeks to complete and check; the mainframe does the processing in a couple of minutes.) Nowadays the results are telephoned to HQ the day after voting closes.

The system has worked reasonably well, but the office manager is now worried about it. Some DTU members are becoming involved with computer technology at their workplaces and a new field officer with a degree in computer studies was appointed to the HQ staff. She is asking awkward questions about the cost-effectiveness of the system, which now costs £6000 per annum. She argues that they could buy their own system for less than the annual bureau payments *and* have greater control over turnaround time. Meanwhile, the bureau are suggesting that DTU should instal a **terminal** at HQ and transmit data to their mainframe down the telephone; this would cut out postal delays and allow DTU to use its own staff for the labour-intensive process of opening envelopes and keying in preferences.

To make things worse, the General Secretary is complaining that the computer does nothing but print sticky labels – and the HQ photocopier does that better! What the organization really needs, he says, is to be able to get quick answers to questions like how many members they have working on temporary contracts with degree-level qualifications at each location. Ideally, he'd like to be able to do sticky label runs selectively, so that if management took a decision which affected a sub-group within the membership, they could be contacted promptly. Surely that should be an easy job for the computer?

Self-check

1 What other organizations might have a similar use for batch processing by a bureau?
2 What strategic questions should the office manager clarify with the DTU management in order to decide whether to continue bureau batch-processing or invest in an in-house computer?

82 What is a computer?

ANSWERS

1 Any similarly-run trade union, political party, professional association or direct-mail organization might consider this approach. Apart from checking that the bureau charges are low enough to make it cost-effective, the key pointers are:

- large volumes of data processed on foreseeable dates;
- postal turnaround time acceptable;
- computer use confined to limited tasks with these characteristics.

2 This is an open-ended task. DTU would almost certainly benefit by hiring a computer consultant to explore the issues with HQ and report. Here are some of the issues he should consider:

- How often does DTU need the kind of information the General Secretary mentioned? How important would it be to have it within hours rather than days?
- How much would an in-house computer system with sufficient external memory to hold their membership records *as at present* cost to buy (complete with software)? What would be the likely manpower and other cost implications of housing, running and maintaining the system? (The field officer could be asked to do a feasibility study on this; given the way that hardware costs have tumbled while bureau charges have crept up, there is at least a case for looking carefully at this option.)
- Leaving aside the overt and hidden costs associated with the previous questions, are there policy reasons why DTU might want to buy a computer, e.g. to build up its own computer expertise and enhance its credibility in dealing with members' reactions to the introduction of computers in their workplaces? What priority should be given to these?

Good Wheel

Good Wheel is an Edinburgh bicycle shop and showroom with a large range, from children's bikes to small mopeds, and a wide selection of accessories, like child seats, dynamos and handpumps. They also custom-build racing bicycles of a famous Scottish marque in their workshop. These retail at anywhere from £350 upward, depending on the customer's choice of gear set, brakes, saddle, pedals and the rest. They supply these to special order through a chain of retail outlets in Europe and North America, and have won an award for their export performance.

Good Wheel also hold a huge range of spares for all lines, some of which are imported from the continent, and supply spares to smaller shops all over Scotland. Their workshop and stores are in an industrial estate three miles from the city-centre showroom. They build the racing cycles there and also carry out repairs and maintenance on *any* bicycle. Good Wheel has an enviable reputation for quality and reliability. Since introducing a computer system, they have put up a sign in the window offering a free bicycle to any customer who is let down on any firm delivery date given for any job. So far, none has been claimed. How is it done?

Figure 22 shows the computer system which they adopted a year ago. Both micros are of the same make and have a built-in modem, which means that they can be plugged directly into the public telephone network and communicate with each other very fast. The showroom micro has an 8-bit processor with 64 K of RAM and twin disc drives (holding 400 K each); it is linked to a good daisy-wheel printer (not shown). The warehouse machine has performance comparable to many minicomputers, with a 16-bit processor in addition to the 8-bit, 256 K of RAM and both a 21 Megabyte hard disc and a 400 K floppy disc; its printer (not shown) is a fast dot-matrix. The total cost of both machines was £8500, while printers and commercial software added another £3000. Both machines normally operate under CP/M, though the larger machine can also run three 16-bit operating systems.

Good Wheel uses the system to manage its accounts, using an integrated accounting package that they bought for £700; it operates similarly to Julian Dapper's system (see Figure 20). The major difference is an extension to the package which they commissioned to link the stock control system to bicycle production planning. Custom-built racing bicycles are built to order,

84 *What is a computer?*

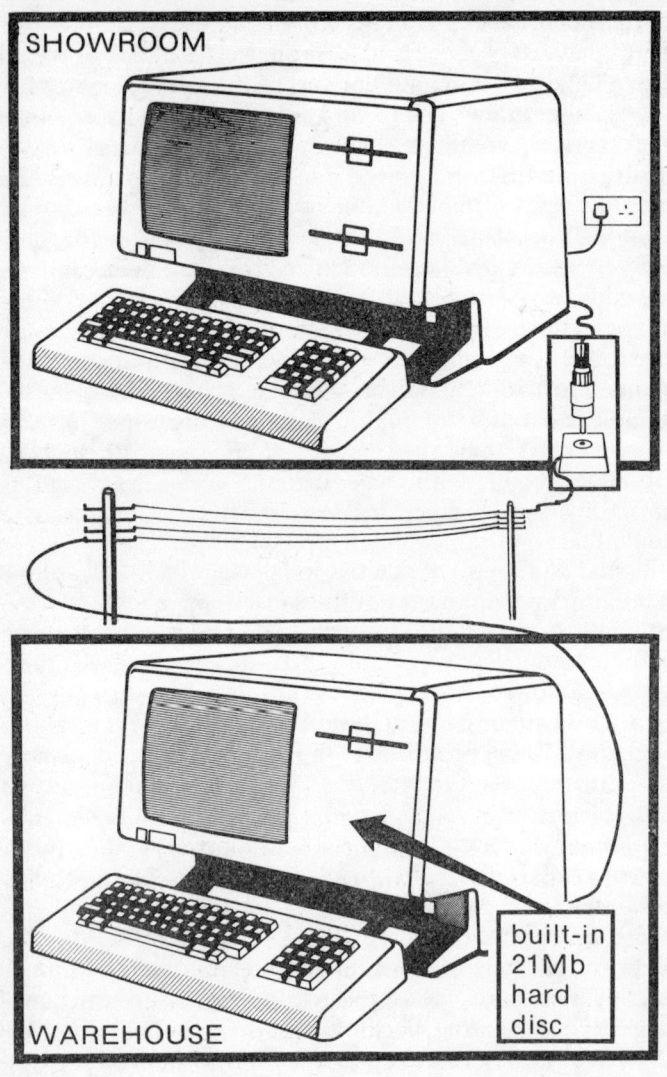

Figure 22. Microcomputers at different locations can communicate by telephone

using expensive components from a variety of sources, most of which have to be ordered several weeks ahead. It would be impossible for Good Wheel to stock *all* the parts which customers might specify, and even to keep most of them would tie up too much capital. However, freight charges make it attractive to order multiples of some of the faster-moving lines. Before the computerized system was introduced, stock control and parts ordering was a constant headache.

Even worse was the problem of giving the customer an accurate delivery date for his cherished machine. The showroom seldom knew what parts were in stock in the warehouse, let alone the current delivery times for the components which had to be ordered. The warehouse manager was much too fully occupied to notice if ordered parts were overdue. Usually the problem came to light when an irate customer was in the showroom asking why his bicycle wasn't ready; a phone call to the warehouse would establish that his gear set had been ordered six weeks ago and was presumed to be on its way from Italy!

Under the computerized system, things are very different. When the order is first placed, the showroom micro 'interrogates' the warehouse micro to find out the availability of the bicycle as specified. The instantaneous response shows not only a price breakdown and an expected delivery time-bracket but also highlights those components with the longest lead-time. If the customer finds the delay unacceptable, the program suggests an alternative gear set which is in stock. It even lists the specification and price of the ready-assembled bicycle closest to the one requested, which the customer could ride away that day.

After experimenting with various combinations, the customer may stick to his original order, but even then the system speeds things up considerably. This is because it stores average lead times for all the thousands of components which Good Wheel have ever ordered. It uses these to chase up orders by automatically initiating a progress enquiry letter to the supplier two-thirds of the way through the lead time. Apart from the salutary effect that this system had on suppliers' actual delivery times, it has the great benefit that by the time the enquiry arrives, suppliers usually know whether delivery is likely to be delayed, and by how long; they then usually phone Good Wheel to notify. This allows Good Wheel to adjust their production planning accordingly and advise the customer of a definite delivery date and/or options to vary the specification if the delay is unacceptable. This automatic progressing of outstanding orders for components had a tremendous effect on throughput of bicycles and also on customer relations.

Armed with this system, Good Wheel are expanding their export activities again. A small extra purchase will allow them to run telex and they expect this to pay for itself in boosting orders from abroad and speeding up deliveries still further.

> *Self-check*
>
> What other businesses might find this type of system useful?

ANSWER

There are really two aspects of the system. The use of communicating microcomputers might be attractive to any organization with split or multiple locations and large telephone, **telex** or **fax** bills. The stock control/production planning/order progressing system could be helpful to any manufacturer dependent on a number of suppliers with varying lead times and significant component costs.

Outer Temple

Outer Temple is a set of barristers' chambers in central London. Barristers are self-employed and the seventeen members pay the chambers' running costs out of a common fund, to which they contribute in proportion to the fees that they earn. The clerk of chambers and secretary are both paid salaries as a straight percentage of all fees earned, whereas the two typists are paid a weekly wage. Typing is charged to individual barristers at a fixed rate per page.

There is a heavy volume of repetitive typing associated with drafts of contracts and wills and some formal 'opinions' have to be retyped if extensive changes are made to the draft, which is usually dictated. High standards of accuracy are expected and typists' wages form a considerable proportion of the chambers' running expenses. Barristers' court appearances are irregular and of unpredictable duration and the typists find it difficult to plan the workflow so that urgent typing is ready when it is needed. When the typing backlog is too great, or if someone is off sick, barristers sometimes type their own work.

After finishing each job, the typist has to record it in her book, showing the number of pages typed and who originated the job. The clerk of chambers does all the book-keeping necessary to apportion internal expenditure, and also all the negotiation and collection of the barristers' fees. These are always paid in arrears, usually months or even years later, and chasing up slow payers had become increasingly important in view of high inflation.

It has become clear that the chambers will have to review its office equipment. Its telex equipment has become antiquated and unreliable and the most junior typist is keen to have an electric typewriter with a correction key in place of her manual machine. At a chambers meeting, replacement of the telex, another electric typewriter and the hiring of an additional part-time typist are all on the agenda. The combined cost would be at least £8000 per annum and the barristers failed to reach agreement on what the priorities should be. That night, one barrister discussed the problem with her husband, who works for British Telecom. He said, 'Look, I haven't kept up with the Computing Section, but I bet you could buy a **network** of word-processing microcomputers *and* have a telex facility for less than £8000. Why don't you get a consultant to look into it?'

With some difficulty, she managed to persuade her colleagues of the wisdom of this course. The consultant spent four days at the chambers, analysing the flow of information, sampling the usage of telex and dictation and analysing the amount and nature of typing. He also discussed the idea of introducing computers individually with the clerk and the three typists, and also with the four barristers who regularly typed for themselves. He demonstrated his own portable word processor and encouraged those who were willing to try it. He found that all the support staff and two of the barristers seemed willing and able to use word processing if appropriate, and that eight more of the barristers were willing to use it to correct and polish text as long as a typist did the basic keying in.

This reaction was promising enough for him to present provisional recommendations for adopting a computer network solution to the next chambers meeting for discussion. There was considerable interest when he explained that the system could handle all their internal accounting automatically and that it would also give them access to **Prestel** (useful for share prices and up-to-date companies information). As an option, they could subscribe to a conveyancing search facility or even a European data base of legal precedents, giving instant answers to queries which would normally take weeks to answer.

Encouraged by their reactions, he went away to research sources and to write a detailed report, which he submitted two days later. (The barristers were pleased to find that for all this work he charged £450!)

The system which was adopted after this exercise is shown in Figure 23. The micro in the clerk's office controls the whole network and also drives the telex system. It has 128 K of RAM, backed up by a 400 K floppy disc drive and a 10 Mb Winchester. Both the disc drives and the daisy-wheel printer (which has a built-in buffer) are shared with the other five micros, though in practice the barristers and typists generally use the 'local' dot-matrix printer to produce a working draft immediately and without having to walk to the clerk's office. One barrister finds this output quite adequate for the text of a legal textbook that he is writing, and another prefers it for her lecture notes because it produces bold and double-size letters so quickly. The typists use their dot-matrix a lot, because most of the barristers prefer to mark changes on its output; they only use the daisy-wheel for final versions of letters and documents. Most of the time, the users feel as if they have the system to themselves. Only if two users want to save or retrieve text simultaneously, or to produce daisy-wheel print-out simultaneously (both are unusual), does the network software have to sort out priorities and sent a

Some systems and their users 89

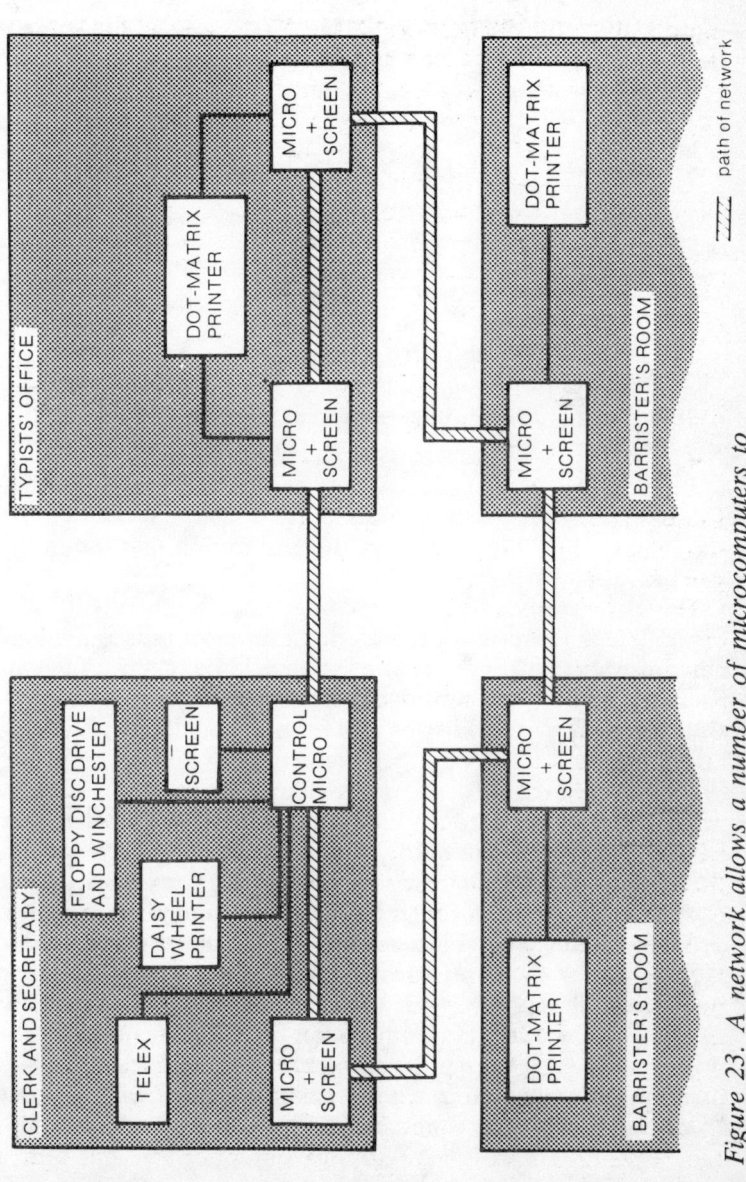

Figure 23. A network allows a number of microcomputers to share access to expensive facilities like a Winchester and telex

message like 'Printer busy, please wait'. The noise level is much lower than before, throughput is higher and running costs lower.

> *Self-check*
>
> What other organizations might benefit from a microcomputer network of this kind?

ANSWER

Any group practice – a doctor's surgery, architects' office, freelance consultants – *might* find such a system helpful; it depends on the availability of software suitable to their accounting practices, the extent of typing suitable for word processing and the attitudes of the people concerned to keyboard skills and operating computers.

Rothespierre Wines

Rothespierre Frères is a French wine growers whose headquarters are in a small town near their vineyards in the Côtes du Rhône. Their British subsidiary, Rothespierre Wines Ltd, imports and sells a small list of around thirty varieties of quality French wines, including their own Côtes du Rothespierre (VDQS).

The British company has its head office and warehouse near Dover. It sells wine through a network of ninety sales representatives (reps) who cover the mainland. The reps visit potential customers in their homes, clubs and offices and give them free tastings of a range of six to ten wines. Customers can then order these wines by the case; when taking the order (usually there and then), the rep writes out and calculates the invoice, usually on a cash-with-order (cwo) or cash-on-delivery (cod) basis.

Once a week, the rep posts his orders to head office in Dover, where a computer system keeps track of stocks of wine, checks orders against payments and calculates reps' monthly commission as a percentage of the value of orders processed. If the customer needs supplies urgently, the rep can telephone the order, but head office try to discourage this, as it leads to extra paperwork in subsequently linking the order, the despatch note and the payment. The rep keeps a handwritten note of all his customer contacts, tastings and orders. When head office receives an order, they enter the order and invoice total on to their computer, which checks that the sums agree and the wine is available. If everything checks out, it prints out the despatch note for the warehouse to make up the order, which is included in their next consignment for their carriers.

However, a high proportion of orders are rejected by the computer system and have to be processed manually. Problems arise with telephoned orders (which are becoming commoner), if one of the wines ordered is out of stock, if the vintage available is different from that specified, or if the invoice total is incorrect; since reps sometimes have to write orders out under considerable pressure at a tasting, such errors are not unknown. Head Office then has to contact the rep (not always easy since they spend most of their time on the road), who agrees any substitute wines and cash adjustments with the customer. These then have to be notified back to head office.

The sales manager was not convinced that Rothespierre's computer installation was justifying its cost. Although it functioned efficiently enough with the orders it processed, they were the straightforward ones which had never taken much staff time, anyway. He went to a computer exhibition in London and attended an advice clinic. He explained his worries to one of the consultants, who asked a great many questions and then said: 'I'm not surprised you're having problems. You've only done half the job of computerizing your operation, and the easy half at that! You should equip *all* your reps with microcomputers, so they can key in the orders direct and send them down the telephone to your mainframe. That way, any problems will be picked up immediately and you'll cut out most of the time-wasting. You'll also cut ten to fourteen days off your delivery times, reduce your phone bills and improve customer relations.

92 What is a computer?

More important, your reps will spend less time on paperwork and be able to increase their appointments and sales.'

'But reps couldn't possibly cart microcomputers round with them, and the reps would still have to fill in the order forms, because the customer would need something in writing', said the bewildered sales manager. 'Anyway, how could the computers talk down the telephone, and what would it all cost?'

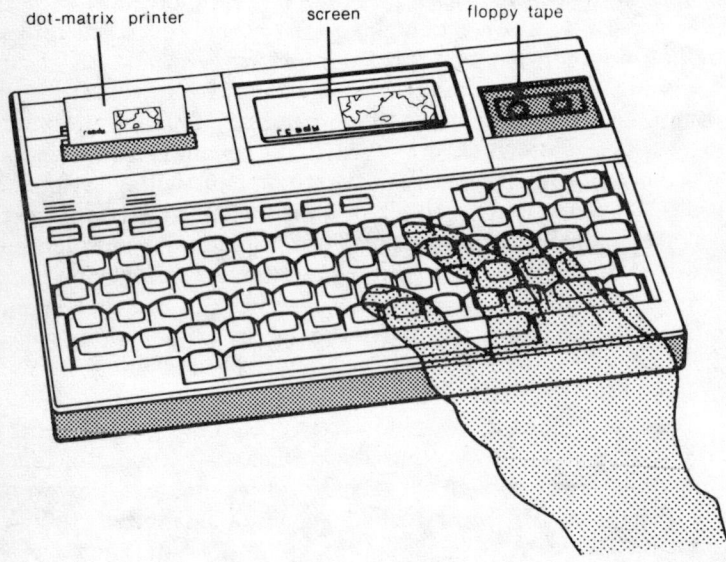

Figure 24. An example of a hand-held computer system which includes a full-size keyboard, small printer and screen and floppy tape as 'external' memory

But the consultant showed him a hand-held microcomputer system which was on display at the show, complete with newly-launched software packages (Figure 24). By pressing a single button, any one of five pre-stored programs could be run; they remained in its memory even after the micro was switched off.

Some systems and their users

Its battery life was 100 hours between re-charging, and a mains unit was supplied. The consultant wrote a demonstration program to work out wine order sub-totals, VAT and delivery charges and the grand total, printing out each item. (This took him about ten minutes.) The sales manager was impressed by how small and self-contained the system was (it was comparable with a large book) and by the quality and speed of the tiny printer – more than adequate for the customer's need for an order confirmation/receipt.

Transmitting the order to head office would require another gadget called an **acoustic coupler** to accept the hand-set of any standard telephone (Figure 25). This would enable the rep to 'phone in' the order direct to the head office mainframe from anywhere (even using the customer's own telephone if immediate confirmation was required) at any time. The total retail cost of the micro plus acoustic coupler was £500, so the cost of equipping the whole sales force would be £45,000 (in practice a large discount could be negotiated on an order of ninety).

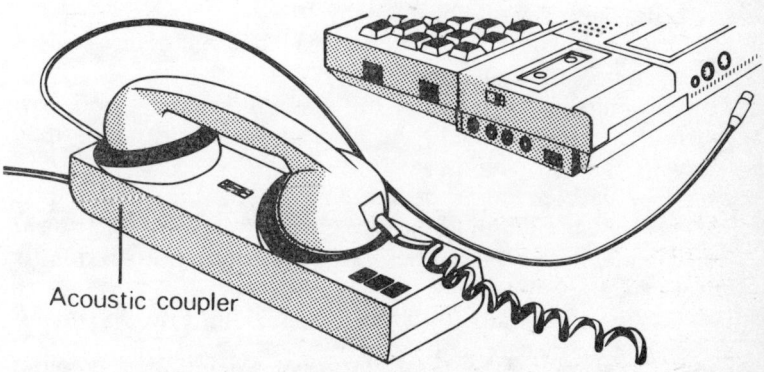

Figure 25. An acoustic coupler allows computers to communicate over long distances using ordinary telephones

94 What is a computer?

Self-check

1 What other businesses might benefit from a number of self-contained, hand-held microcomputers able to communicate by telephone with a larger computer?
2 Suggest other questions (at least four) that the sales manager should ask before adopting the idea?

ANSWERS

1 Any firm with a travelling sales force selling direct to the public – e.g. insurance, home improvements, office supplies.
2 A great many! In practice it is unlikely that an exhibition clinic is a good place to go into the details, but here are some examples of the *kind* of issues that should be explored by Rothespierre with a competent adviser, preferably together with head office staff and some reps:

- What would be the cost of adapting the mainframe software to receive orders in this form? How long would it take to commission?
- How much change would be needed in their office systems and stationery to cope with the changeover, and how much staff training would be needed?
- What happens if the phone is engaged or out of order when a rep tries to send an order in?
- How much lower would the running costs be, and how much staff time could the firm expect to save once they were familiar with the system?
- How widespread is dealer back-up on the micro? Has anyone adopted this system before? If so, what snags were encountered? Can Rothespierre contact them? and, if he is a cynic:
- Has the consultant any connection with the firm who manufacture or distribute the micro?

Sandycare Ltd

Sandycare is a chain store supplying baby equipment, toys and clothing for children up to 12 years of age. The big city branches stock a wide range of bulky equipment, like cots, climbing frames and bicycles. Small-town branches mainly supply clothing and smaller toys, though all branches have a 500-page catalogue with colour illustrations (published annually). This is sold to the public at £1 per copy, but sales are modest and do not approach its production costs of £5000.

Sandycare is reconsidering the future of the catalogue, because prices often rise within the lifetime of a single edition, and lines can become discontinued. Sales of goods on the basis of the catalogue alone have never been as great as anticipated. Customers don't seem to feel confident about ordering expensive items on the basis of a single photograph, and sales assistants cannot effectively reassure them about the robustness or safety features of equipment that they have sometimes never seen. Sandycare's delivery times (up to three weeks on large items) also seem to be off-putting to potential customers.

The firm is also worried by reports from sales supervisors. Many of the sales assistants are young, unmarried girls, some of whom have had little experience of babies. They have difficulty in answering customers' questions and are often too diffident to offer advice. The shops get a number of visits from people without children who come in wanting to buy a gift for first-time parents, but they quickly become bewildered by the variety available and leave empty-handed. Perhaps staff training could help with these problems, but bringing together all the assistants who need training for a residential course would be prohibitively expensive.

Another problem relates to customers' convenience rather than lack of staff training. Some mothers are so handicapped by push-chairs, babies and toddlers that they give up the attempt to shop halfway, or after the first bout of wailing; fathers seem reluctant to accompany young families on these visits! Some sort of attraction in a corner would make the store more attractive to harassed parents and would provide temporary 'child-minding'.

Although the head office operation is fully computerized in respect of accounts and stock control, the branches operate manually, communicating purely by post and telephone. Branches collect their own information about which lines are fast-moving and profitable, depending on the branch manager's skills and inclinations. Branches seldom manage to re-order soon enough to prevent blank shelves, because delivery times fluctuate according to what is in stock at the warehouse. Better communications between head office and the branches would help.

Sandycare's Training Manager has recently had these diverse problems drawn to her attention. She is a computer enthusiast who has also just found out how videodiscs can be computer-controlled and is very excited about their possibilities. She believes that videodiscs could solve the catalogue problem, and in addition could provide 'entertainment' in the stores which would combine health and parentcraft education with 'child-minding'. Outside shop opening hours, videodiscs could also provide an invaluable resource for staff training. She explains to her boss that a £10 videodisc can store an immense quantity of high-quality pictures and computer software (see page 35). The computer program can select which 'frames' should be viewed and can arrange for moving sequences to be alternated with still pictures, interspersed with text and questions produced by a normal computer program.

She suggests that each store should have a videodisc player controlled by microcomputer, with telephone link-up between the micros and the head office mainframe for instant feedback of stock information, staff information and an electronic newsletter. Figure 26 shows the basic equipment for the 'Video Corner' in each store. The trolley has adjustable shelves and can be wheeled to the office where an acoustic coupler and printer are kept for instant communication with head office.

A single videodisc could easily store the complete Sandycare catalogue. Unlike the static printed version, however, the videodisc would include action sequences. For example, after asking for information on children's slides a customer could not only see a short clip of children clambering on one but could also view

Some systems and their users 97

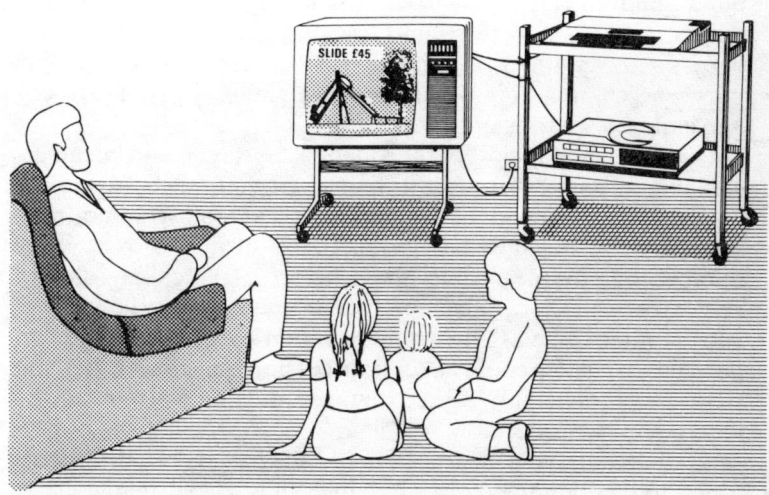

Figure 26. A videodisc player under computer control provides fast access to a huge range of still and moving colour pictures

the apparatus being assembled from the flat-pack in which it is supplied, or another action sequence which would show the safety test being applied to the joints. Any single item or sequence of shots can be located within a few seconds. Although it is expensive to produce a master videodisc, updates to the computer program are very cheap and almost instantaneous, so the problems of price changes or discontinued lines can be solved quickly and cheaply by showing appropriate messages on the screen.

There are many other uses for the videodisc under computer control. When customers were not using it as a 'live' catalogue, they could be encouraged to look at another disc which carries a number of short baby- and infant-care sequences. Some of these would be aimed at first-time fathers (e.g. a humorous sketch shows how *not* to change a nappy); others could be designed for older children (e.g. what to do if a stranger talks to you) and others again to show first-aid procedures (e.g. what to do if a baby swallows a marble). Other videodiscs could be available purely as 'child-minding', each one containing hours of cartoons and children's television.

Once the shop is closed, the videodisc system could become a valuable resource for staff training. Each branch supervisor would have a training pack comprising a videodisc and printed suggestions about how best to make use of it. For example, a number of episodes could show actors playing the roles of customers and shop assistants. One incident might show a nervous mother-to-be asking for information about brands of powdered milk. Notes could suggest discussion questions which the supervisor might put, e.g.: 'How well did the assistant in the video deal with the mother's actual question? Did she understand the underlying anxiety? Should she have taken the opportunity to mention the danger to babies of lead in drinking-water and explained how to avoid it?' Depending on how the group reacts, the computer program could be arranged to move on to a sequence showing how to prepare powdered milk or how to deal with anxious customers.

An alternative computer program could make the same video sequences work for individual training. The episodes would be chosen for replay on the basis of the trainee's answers to questions. Other sections would deal with basic induction training, covering topics like the operation of the firm and the control of cheques and credit card sales. These would be especially useful for newly appointed staff; if the videodisc system were in heavy use by customers, they could be given a crash course on a Sunday and time off in lieu during the week.

When the microcomputer was not needed for customer or staff training, it could be available for connection to the head office mainframe for instantaneous transfer of information and updated videodisc software.

> ### Self-check
>
> What other businesses might find videodisc/computer systems useful for staff training and/or point-of-sale consumer education?

ANSWER

Any organization with a large training budget might want to consider this possibility. Likely indicators are:

- there is a strong visual element to the training;
- it is difficult or expensive to get the trainers and trainees together;
- there is an adequate number of trainees to justify mastering a videodisc;
- the subject matter does not change rapidly, or the changing elements are easily separated out and confined to the software element.

Large chain stores, multi-location businesses, oil rigs, the armed forces, banks, travel agents and the hotel trade are all possible areas of application.

Part 2
How can computers help business?

4 | Keeping account

In Part 2, we look at the kinds of software which enable computers to help business efficiency, cash-flow and profitability. The practicalities of how to go about choosing and using software are dealt with in Chapter 8. What concerns us first is identifying just how and when computers can help.

This chapter deals with the traditional area of accounting packages (sales ledger, purchase ledger, nominal ledger and beyond). **Data base management systems** and word processing are covered in Chapters 5 and 6, and payroll is the subject of Chapter 11. Chapter 7 discusses the limitations of the package approach and considers some recent trends in business software.

If you are not already familiar with book-keeping practice, you may need to refer to another Pan *Breakthrough* book, *Keep Account*, by John Etor and Mike Muspratt, which is devoted entirely to book-keeping and includes helpful material on computer-based methods. This chapter can do no more than summarize the kinds of packages available and suggest some of the main issues to weigh before opting for computer-based accounting.

Sales ledger

Book-keeping has its own special language which can be just as off-putting as computer jargon if you're not used to it. The sales ledger is just an organized collection of details on all a firm's customers. You may have heard of it as a *debtors' ledger* or *accounts receivable*. Ledgers are not necessarily huge cloth-bound books; they can also be ring-bound or lever-arch files or (increasingly common) piles of computer print-out. The process of writing something in a ledger (or entering it through a computer keyboard) is called *posting* the ledger.

104 How can computers help business?

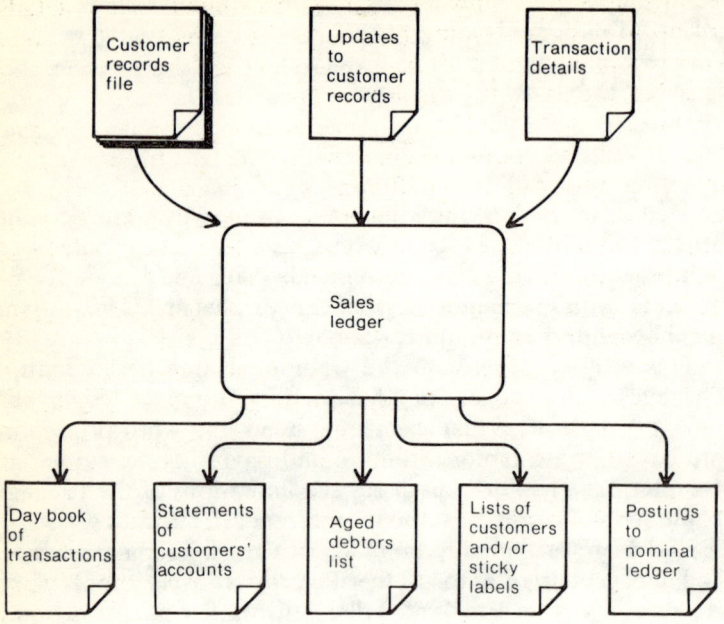

Figure 27. Inputs and possible outputs of a sales ledger system

Figure 27 shows typical inputs to a sales ledger package and the kind of outputs (sometimes called **reports**) it may produce. The customer file is the master list of details on all the customers to whom the business sells, and setting it up is a major task. It may include any or all of the following:

- name
- address
- account number
- credit limit
- balance brought forward
- previous transactions

Any business (other than a small retailer selling entirely for cash) will keep most of this information in some form or other – perhaps in a card index or notebook. Creating the customer records file is not simply a matter of checking that these details are up to date and typing them into the computer, however. Very careful thought must be given to how the information is to be **coded**, especially the account number.

Ideally, codes should be short, easy to interpret and to remember, difficult to make mistakes with and an efficient aid to analysing information in different ways. Since these requirements tend to conflict with each other, designing good codes is a difficult but important part of any accounting system. The limitations imposed by small computer memories tend to put a premium on compactness at the expense of the other criteria. There is helpful material on the design of codes in two other *Breakthroughs*: Chapter 11 of Etor and Muspratt and Chapter 3 of Carter's *The Business of Data Processing*. These should be studied carefully by anyone who is designing a coding system or contemplating changing an existing one to suit the requirements of accounting software.

The customer file is sure to need regular updating of its standing information – e.g. addition of new customers, amendments to addresses and credit limits, deletion of customers who cease trading.

The main activity on a sales ledger is posting transactions: for example, invoices and credit notes will be issued, cash received, balances updated. It is essential for the system to be able to relate cash received to invoices issued. Where the amounts agree, there are not many invoices per month on each account and payment is prompt, this may be a simple matter. The system need only carry forward any balance each month and set cash received against it. Book-keepers call this the *balance forward* method. When conditions are not so favourable, each posting must keep its invoice numbers attached to it so that the 'loose ends' (*open items*) can be traced back to individual invoices. This is known as the open item method, because instead of bringing forward a balance at each month end, the system brings forward open items. This obviously requires more capacity on the disc than the balance forward method but is more helpful in sorting out discrepancies and queries. Any business which already uses the open item method should think seriously before sacrificing this detail to suit the limitations of a small microcomputer or a cheap software package.

There are five main sorts of output from sales ledger packages. The day book (or *journal*) forms a kind of diary of all transactions; in some small manual book-keeping systems, it is literally a book written up every day. Day books are useful for *audit trail*, i.e. when auditors or others want to trace the various events between the placing of an order and its final settlement.

Statements may be sent to customers showing invoices issued, payments received and balances brought forward. These sometimes include detachable remittance slips for customers to return with cheques, to help the system link payments with invoices.

A debtors' list is often produced, showing all those whose credit limits have been exceeded and those with balances outstanding analysed by age of balance (*aged debtors*). If the sales ledger package is linked to a word processing package, it can automatically print out reminder letters to debtors.

In addition, the system may print out customer lists, either on plain paper or perhaps on to sticky labels for mailing. Some packages allow selective customer listing according to various criteria. These are useful for selective mail shots, e.g. to all customers who have not ordered for three months, who live in a specific area or whose accounts show excessive or aged balances. The usefulness of selective customer listing underlines the importance of designing account codes carefully so that such selections can be made efficiently.

Finally, if when they are posted transactions are coded according to their nature (as well as by customer), the system can print out all transactions analysed into different categories ready for posting in the *nominal* (or *general*) *ledger*. This is the ledger which provides an accounting summary of all a business's activities, assets and liabilities (see below). It would summarize counter sales separately from mail order trading, and in a large organization would show trading activity separately for the different departments. If the sales ledger output shows the nominal ledger codes, it can be used to post the nominal ledger by hand. In an integrated accounting system, sales ledger outputs automatically update the nominal ledger.

Self-check

What advantages would you anticipate from the introduction of a computerized sales ledger?

ANSWER

The most likely benefit is improved cash-flow because of aged debt analysis and the semi-automatic issue of reminders. The system should also help earlier identification of defaulters and thus help to reduce losses from bad debts. There may also be improved marketing from mail shots and possibly reduced clerical work, especially if the system is integrated with other ledgers.

Purchase ledger

The *purchase ledger* contains details on all the firm's suppliers; it is also known as the *accounts payable*, *creditors' ledger* or *bought ledger*.

The purchase ledger is the counterpart of the sales ledger, and Figure 28 shows how the inputs and outputs are comparable. Like the sales ledger, it contains a master file with standing information, e.g. suppliers' names and addresses and settlement terms, which has to be amended periodically. The transactions are posted to the purchase ledger in batches, after being checked and classified, e.g. with a code for the nominal ledger and perhaps showing what cost centre they belong to. Appropriate choices for such codes are just as vital for the sales ledger. Equally, different packages offer open item or balance forward methods for dealing with unpaid invoices which the firm has not settled.

The outputs are also comparable to those from the sales ledger. The day book lists the invoices posted, together with totals, VAT and control codes. The remittance advice accompanies outgoing payments and cheque or credit transfer may be produced automatically or optionally, depending on how much manual control the user wants or needs. The software can either decide on payment dates and calculate amounts automatically according to standing rules, or else it can produce lists for

108 How can computers help business?

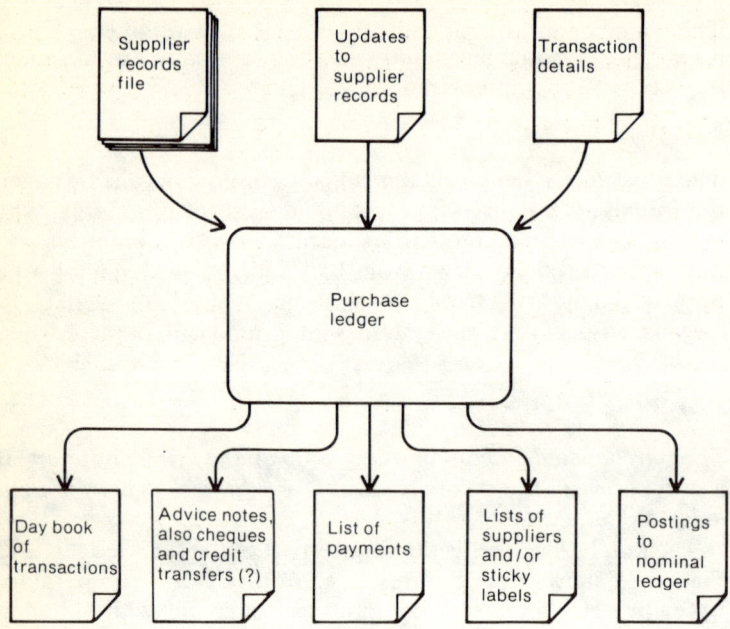

Figure 28. Inputs and possible outputs of a purchase ledger system

inspection, followed by manual processing. Lists of payments actually made correspond to the *cash books* kept by firms who process accounts manually. A list of suppliers' addresses and/or sticky labels may also be useful, for example if a firm changes its address or wants to forewarn suppliers of cash-flow difficulties. Finally, the system may list all invoices by nominal account, with totals ready for posting to the nominal ledger. As before, an integrated system will post the amounts automatically.

Self-check

What benefits would you expect from the introduction of a computer-based purchase ledger?

ANSWER

The main benefit is tight control over payments, allowing better cash management, cf. Julian Dapper's system (page 76).

Nominal ledger

The nominal ledger analyses income by source (e.g. sales, commission, rent, fees, royalties) and may be subdivided by department, section or location. Expenditure is analyzed by type (e.g. purchases, wages and salaries, rent, transport) and may be further analyzed by department or cost centre. An account is opened for each analysis head and transactions posted to it

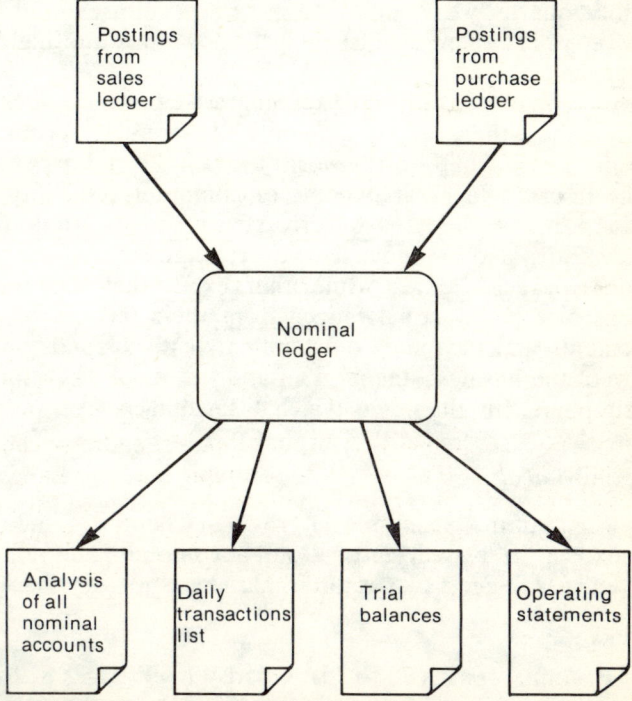

Figure 29. Inputs and possible outputs of a nominal ledger system

periodically. The nominal ledger thus summarizes all the activities covered by the sales and purchase ledger. It is the major source of information for financial planning and budgeting.

Figure 29 shows the inputs and outputs to a nominal ledger package. In a fully integrated system, the inputs would be made without manual intervention. The output should certainly include an analysis of all the nominal accounts in a suitable form for the auditors. It is backed up by the transactions list, which gives detailed records of all the daily transactions as recorded by the system. Trial balances can be produced at any time to provide verification that debits and credits are in balance and to give an overall picture of the state of affairs across all the different accounts. Operating statements may be produced monthly, quarterly or annually to show expenditure of different types, compare them against budget allocations and highlight discrepancies.

Any computer-based book-keeping system which does *not* integrate these three ledgers automatically should be scrutinized carefully to see whether it is worth the trouble and expense of setting it up. The great benefits of computer reliability and accuracy can be defeated by errors in manually transcribing invoice codes and amounts. However, some small firms work without a purchase ledger, while others expect their accountants to construct the nominal ledger from their records of cash movements and payments outstanding. It all depends on the nature of the business, the number and variety of its customers and suppliers, and the way in which it is managed.

Self-check

Which of the businesses described in Chapter 3 would you expect to benefit most from a computerized nominal ledger? Suggest two or three characteristics they share.

ANSWER

Beau Brummel (pages 75 to 79), Good Wheel (pages 82 to 86) and Sandycare (pages 95 to 99) might all find this facility valuable for various reasons. You could make a case for any of the others, but those were my first choices, as it seemed most likely that their managements might actually *use* the information. Nominal ledger analysis should benefit any reasonably complex or evolving business with a fair number of accounts, plenty of transactions, a number of different centres of activity and a management who will request and digest frequent reports on turnover and profit in different areas.

Beyond the ledgers

Some books give the impression that integrated ledger packages are the be-all and end-all of accounting by computer. But bookkeeping is actually the *end*, not the beginning, of a business transaction. Only *after* an order is given, a sale made or some stock moved is there any ledger activity. The principle of integrating different paperwork systems and using the output of one as input to another can be extended much further. The next self-check invites you to work out how. If you haven't just done so for the last self-check, it may help to skim-read Chapter 3 again, especially the sections on Beau Brummel, Good Wheel and Rothespierre.

Self-check

Apart from ledger activity, with what other paperwork could a computer assist a business?

ANSWER

This is a challenging question, with a great many valid answers. For a start, Jenny Bruno, Beau Brummel, Good Wheel and Rothespierre all used their computer systems to produce a *sales invoice*, sometimes on-the-spot. Furthermore, the Beau Brummel example showed how after each sale, information could be sent to update *stock control* and, if appropriate, to trigger a *purchase order*. In several cases in Chapter 3, other accounting information was needed by the *payroll* system: Beau Brummel, Rothespierre and Outer Temple all used some form of commission as a salary element. In the case of Good Wheel, sales order information was used not only by stock control but also in *production planning*. In addition, even after book-keeping is formally complete, there are many ways in which computer processing can assist in *budgetary control* and *financial planning*. The final section of this chapter looks at one popular tool for this: the spreadsheet.

The more integrated the system, the more likely it is to give a good return on the inevitable extra work invested in getting information *into* the computer in the first place. If a computer is useful for the accounting done at the *end* of each business transaction, why should it not be of assistance at earlier stages? After all, the objective of most businesses is to make a profit, and the computer must help toward that goal in order to pay its way. Equally, non-profit organizations must weigh the contribution the computer makes to the services that they offer against its cost.

Many people are misled by the fact that computerizing the ledgers is traditionally the first place to start in business computing. Certainly such software packages are very common, but that does not in itself make them cost-effective or even necessarily the best place to start. An aged debtors list may improve your cash-flow but it won't increase your productivity or generate new business. The reason that accounting packages established themselves so quickly may be historical accident, or a product of the background and training of accountants, rather than a considered decision by the business community.

Electronic spreadsheets

Financial planning packages can encourage managers to think critically about their business's past performance and to try to anticipate its future. Spreadsheets are a popular and simple type of package, of which VisiCalc was the first and is still the most famous example. Their name reflects the way they allow the user to *spread* out the firm's accounts on a *sheet* of paper. The user defines what headings he wants to use in the spreadsheet and what the relationships are between the entries. In effect, he 'programs' the spreadsheet to fit the way he does his books.

The value of a spreadsheet is not just that it then does all the arithmetic (totals and carrying forward) automatically. The point is that it encourages 'What if?' thinking. For example, by changing just one or two entries the user can discover the effect upon cash-flow and profitability of a major decision.

To see how, let's go back to the smallest of the businesses in Chapter 3: Jenny Bruno's kennels. She could use her own spreadsheet program to summarize her first year's trading, as in Figure 30. In what follows, we will refer to each entry in the spreadsheet by a code giving its column letter and row number, so the word 'Income' is entry A3, the income for the first quarter (£1456) is entry B3 and the Year total for income is F3. (Row 2 has been left blank for clarity.)

	A	B	C	D	E	F
1		1st qr	2nd qr	3rd qr	4th qr	Year total
2						
3	Income	1456	2184	2184	1456	7280
4	Wages	1092	1092	1092	1092	4368
5	Food	910	0	910	0	1820
6	Overheads	150	150	150	150	600
7	Total exp.	2152	1242	2152	1242	6788
8	Infl /outflow	-696	942	32	214	492
9	Balance b/f	500	-196	746	778	500
10	Balance c/f	-196	746	778	992	992

Figure 30. Jenny Bruno's summary of income and expenditure for her first year of operation (dogs)

114 *How can computers help business?*

> *Self-check*
>
> What are the codes for
>
> a total expenditure in the first quarter
> b wages in the second quarter
> c balance brought forward in the third quarter
> d income in the fourth quarter
> e total overheads for the year?

ANSWERS

a B7 **b** C4 **c** D9 **d** E3 **e** F6

To calculate entries B3 to F3, Jenny worked from average dog boarding figures as follows: in the first and fourth quarters, she had an average of 8 dogs at any one time, in the second and third an average of 12. Her average charge is £2 per dog per day, so with 91 days per quarter, entry B3 is 91 × 2 × 8. The program uses * as the symbol for multiplication, so what she actually typed was 'B3 = 91*2*8'. To complete the income section, she also typed 'C3 = 91*2*12', 'D3 = C3', 'E3 = B3' and 'F3 = SUM(B3,E3)'.

> *Self-check*
>
> Can you guess what SUM(B3,E3), is likely to mean?

ANSWER

It is shorthand for B3+C3+D3+E3. If you can follow how these equations are used to build up the spreadsheet, you are actually understanding a simple form of computer programming. But you don't need to follow every detail of all this to get the hang of why spreadsheets are useful.

In case you want to check the rest of Figure 30 for yourself, here are the figures it is based on: Row 4: Jenny pays herself wages of £84 per week (times 13 weeks per quarter), Row 5: she buys a six-month supply of dog-food twice a year and dogs cost on average £0.50 per day to feed. Row 6: her business overheads (accommodation, telephone, car) average out at £150 per quarter. To calculate row 7, she typed 'B7=SUM(B4,B6)' and 'REPLICATE' was the simple command which told the program to work out similar formulae for C7, D7, E7 and F7.

Row 8 shows her income minus expenditure (i.e. cash inflow or outflow for the period). Entry B9 is her opening balance for the first quarter, which is added to B8 to give the balance carried forward into the second quarter. Column F summarizes the year's activity: F8 shows that the excess of income over expenditure for the year was £492, which added to the opening balance (F9) gives a balance of £992 to carry into the next year.

Self-check

a Write down an equation showing the relationship between B8, B3 and B7.
b Repeat for F10, F8 and F9.

ANSWERS
a B8 = B3 − B7
b F10 = F8 + F9

Similar relationships hold good for all the other columns, and Jenny would again use the REPLICATE command instead of typing them out individually.

Figure 30 can show Jenny a number of interesting things about her business over the past year. But let's see how she might change things to explore possible futures. She has a nagging feeling that she might make more money if she took in cats instead of dogs. Although she would charge less (the going rate is £1.50 a day), she could handle more of them because they take less space and don't need to be exercised like the big dogs. If her top limit were 24 cats in the second and third quarters, she expects she would have 16 in the first and last. Cat food costs an average of £0.25 per cat per day. So she now changes a couple of entries to turn out a 'cats' spreadsheet for comparison. Figure 31 shows the result, except that one entry has been left out in each column.

116 *How can computers help business?*

	A	B	C	D	E	F
1		1st qr	2nd qr	3rd qr	4th qr	Year total
2						
3	Income	2184	3276	3276		10920
4	Wages	1092		1092	1092	4368
5	Food	910	0	910	0	1820
6	Overheads	150	150	150	150	
7	Total exp.		1242	2152	1242	6788
8	Infl/outflow	32	2034	1124	942	4132
9	Balance b/f	500	532		3690	500
10	Balance c/f	532	2566	3690	4632	4632

Figure 31. Alternative spreadsheet for first year based on hypothetical cats, created from Figure 30 by changing just two formulae

Self-check

Fill in the blank entries B7, C4, D9, E3 and F6. If you look carefully at the pattern, you won't have to do any adding or subtracting.

ANSWERS

B7 = 2152, C4 = 1092, D9 = 2566, E3 = 2184 and F6 = 600.

It only took Jenny a couple of minutes to change the formulae for income and food, and the program recalculated the whole spreadsheet in a couple of seconds. (Although the food figures look the same, this is coincidence: on average there are twice as many cats at any time, but costing half as much per day to feed, so this multiplies out to the same figure.) The change in the F8 entry is quite striking. Her profit for the year would have been £4132 instead of £492: over eight times as much!

Keeping account 117

	A	B	C	D	E	F
1		1st qr	2nd qr	3rd qr	4th qr	Year total
2						
3	Income	3640	5460	5460	3640	18200
4	Wages	2184	2184	2184	2184	8736
5	Food	910	910	910	910	3640
6	Overheads	150	150	150	150	600
7	Total exp.	3244	3244	3244	3244	12976
8	Infl/outflow	396	2216	2216	396	5224
9	Balance b/f	992	1388	3604	5820	992
10	Balance c/f	1388	3604	5820	6216	6216

Figure 32. Spreadsheet for possible second-year operation based on cats and dogs (compare Figures 30 and 31)

The only problem is that Jenny loves dogs and doesn't *want* to spend her time with cats! So she tries another experiment with the spreadsheet. Suppose that next year she employed an assistant and took in both cats and dogs? Figure 32 shows the new calculation, with changes made to rows 3, 4 and 5; the program calculates the rest automatically. It makes the same assumptions about numbers, income and costs as Figures 30 and 31 made individually, and also assumes that Jenny pays the assistant the same wages as she draws herself. Pet food is now shown as bought each quarter, to ease the load on her car springs and even out the cash-flow, and overheads are assumed to be unchanged. With her balance of £992 brought forward from the current year, she could expect to finish next year with £6216 *and* keep her beloved dogs!

In practice, of course, the decision to hire an assistant would not be made on financial grounds alone. We have also made a number of oversimplifications, e.g. she would probably incur some capital expenditure in converting more animal accommodation. Also, we have ignored the different rates for different sizes of dog and the collection/delivery service, etc. But this example may serve to illustrate what a simple and powerful tool a spreadsheet can be.

Note that each time users define their own headings (by putting text into row 1 and column A) and then 'program' their own figures and relationships into the spreadsheet, the results fit the way the business handles its accounts like a glove. Furthermore, the uses of spreadsheets are by no means confined to annual income and expenditure statements. *Any* information which can be expressed in the form of a table with relationships between its entries can be handled this way.

Self-check

Can you think of at least three other examples of ways of using a spreadsheet?

ANSWER

Forecasting of likely return on investments, comparison of the costs of buying versus leasing, processing the results of scientific or engineering calculations, tables for conversions between different units, costing exercises and presentation of tenders, break-even analysis.

The possible applications are almost limitless, but what about the overall *size*? It all depends on the amount of RAM available and the capabilities of the particular spreadsheet package used. Spreadsheets on large computers accommodate more information and process it faster than microcomputers. However, even the one I used to produce the examples above on my personal microcomputer (which has only 32 K of RAM) can take up to 26 columns by 50 rows before it runs out of space. The package cost only £20 and allowed me to vary the width allocated to each column individually to suit what was going into it. I could also select information from it to feed directly into a related program for display in graphical form, as a pie chart, graph or histogram (see Chapter 6 of Clark's *Using Statistics in Business 2*, in the Pan Breakthrough series).

5 Data bases

Data bases and data base management systems (DBMS) are simply forbidding-sounding names for information and ways of managing it. Data bases – whether they are stored on paper, card or in a computer – are just collections of facts organized in some way so that they can be retrieved. Every business has data bases, although they may or may not be efficiently organized or gathered in a single place. You can think of them as a giant filing cabinet containing the business's files on customers, accounts, contacts, suppliers or whatever.

If you go into a public library looking for a particular book, you will need to consult its data base – the catalogue. This is usually held on cards, one for each book, in banks of wooden drawers. If you don't know how the cards are arranged, or if you don't know the exact title of the book or how to spell the author's name, you will probably ask an assistant for help. The library staff are the intermediaries who help you to extract the data you need from the system.

In many cases, it may be helpful if a data base is computerized – for example, if the same information needs to be sorted in different ways, or if a number of people need simultaneous access to the same data. The DBMS is like the library staff: it forms the vital link between the user and the data he needs. Unless a DBMS is flexible and easy to use, it can be worse than an unhelpful library assistant; in effect it can be more like a padlock on the library door!

It is difficult to generalize about data bases, because they vary in so many ways. Some are small and localized, covering only a small part of the company's operation, and allowing any user unrestricted access to the information they contain. Others are immense collections of public and private records, capable of being accessed over thousands of miles by satellite and with elaborate systems of passwords and account numbers to control who gets access to what. As you would expect, the DBMS software needed to manage the second kind is more complex than that demanded by the first.

Files, records and fields

Standard terms are used to describe the different levels in a data base. A file is the top level in the hierarchy: it is a complete collection of information of a particular kind. In the library example, the list of books in alphabetical order by author (the author catalogue) is a single file although it might consist of thousands of cards in many separate drawers. The next level is called a record: each card in the author catalogue is a separate record. If the library holds many books by the same author, there will be a record card for each one. The bottom level in the hierarchy is the field, which is a single item of information, like a name, title or number.

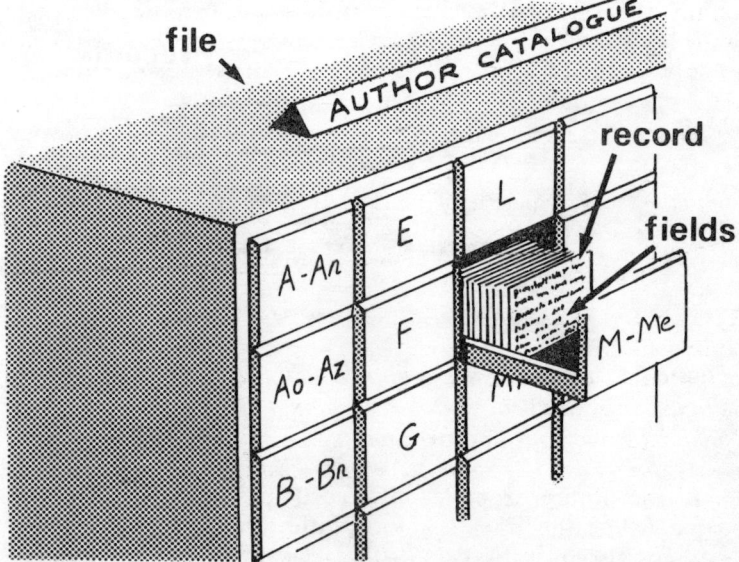

Figure 33. The author catalogue file contains a record for each book; each record has several fields giving details of the book

122 How can computers help business?

Thus the file contains many records, each of which consists of a number of fields. Although files, records and fields might look different in a computer system (see Figure 34), the hierarchy is the same. A file need not necessarily fit on a single floppy disc, and a record might be smaller or larger than a convenient 'screenful', but Figure 34 gives a rough idea of typical comparative sizes.

Figure 34. The complete author catalogue might be held on a single floppy disc; each book record might fill a screen, with each field occupying one or more lines

In the library example, all records probably contained the same fields: the book's author, title and classification code, perhaps also its publisher, ISBN, accession number and details of its format or contents. Different fields may be of different lengths: for example, an author's full name might consist of anything up to thirty characters, whereas the accession numbers might run from 1 to 99,999 (5 characters).

A data base on cards

For a small or specialized collection of books (or any other items), special edge-punched cards can be used to set up a data base with many of the features of a computerized system but at a fraction of the cost. Understanding how will help to prepare you to evaluate computer packages.

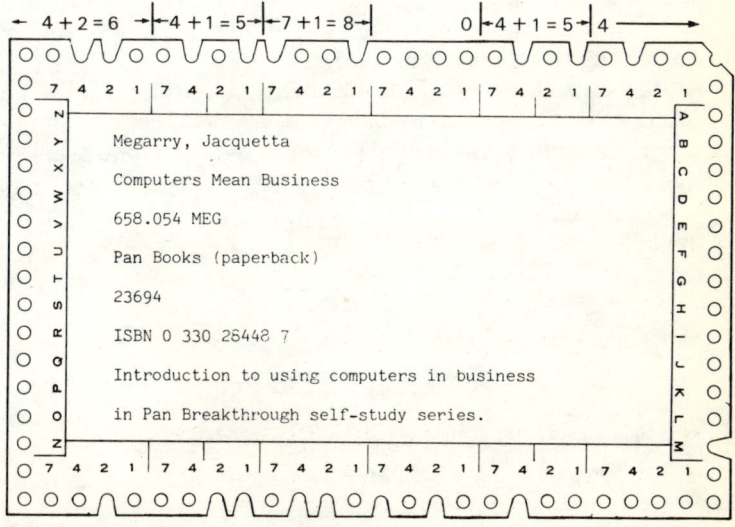

Figure 35. Holes on an edge-punched card can be destroyed selectively to represent some of the information recorded in its middle

Figure 35 shows a sample card from an imaginary library catalogue. Around its edge are the holes punched by the manufacturer, and next to them are pre-printed numbers in groups (7, 4, 2 and 1) and also letters (A to Z). The holes and pre-printing are standard; but users decide for themselves how to interpret each position and whether to interpret them individually or as a group. Having decided what information to code, the user would also select where on the card to destroy the holes in order to represent it.

For example, in Figure 35 the top row of holes represents the Dewey classification number (658.054); each group of four holes stores a number between 1 and 9. The bottom row shows the accession number (23694) coded the same way, with the last few holes reserved for showing whether the book is a reference copy (not for lending) and whether it is oversize (in which case it would be shelved separately). The holes at each side of the card show the first letter of the author's surname; there simply are not enough holes to code a whole name.

If the whole catalogue is on such cards, a knitting needle can be used to sort them by any field that has been coded (Figure 36). For example, if you wanted to check the stock in the oversize

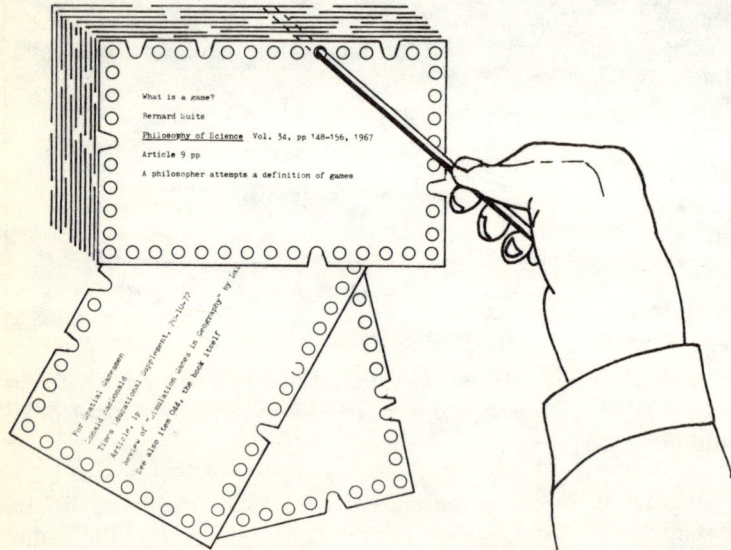

Figure 36. Edge-punched cards can be sorted by putting a needle through the holes. Cards whose holes have been destroyed will drop off

section, putting the needle through that hole would make all the cards for normal-sized books (whose holes are intact) stay on the needle while all the oversize ones (whose holes are destroyed) drop off. Searching for a book by its Dewey number or accession number is a bit more cumbersome because you have to use the needle repeatedly in each group of holes, though with experience this can be done faster than you might think. And searching for a particular author would involve 'needling' for the first letter and then scanning through all the cards which dropped off to find the right author 'manually'.

Generally speaking, edge-punched cards are not suitable for a library catalogue. If there are more than a few hundred books, the physical handling of the cards becomes difficult, and sorting can be unreliable because some cards stick with the pack when they should drop. Even with a larger size of card, it is hard to get enough holes to code alphabetic information like names. It is true that if you coded the letters of the alphabet as numbers (1 for A, 2 for B and so on), you would need only 6 holes (instead of 26) for each letter. But then the user would have to decipher the code, work out which holes corresponded to '13' and needle repeatedly just to isolate all the books written by authors whose names began with an 'M'; locating a particular book could be very slow and awkward.

All in all, you might think this is a suitable case for computer treatment. Before we look into this, let's summarize some points which emerge from the edge-punched card approach:

- Before you can design a suitable filing system, you need to anticipate how many records there will be (to see whether edge-punched cards are feasible) and how many fields of what size you need (to decide how many holes are needed i.e. what size of card).
- You have to work out what sort of questions the users will want to ask so as to make sure that the file can be sorted on those fields. (Edge-punched cards can carry information on their centres which is not also coded around their edges, but they cannot be searched for such information using the needle.)

- Before you begin, it is important to think carefully about how to code the information. In general, the more compact the code, the less obvious its meaning to the user.
- Once a coding system has been adopted, it is difficult and time-consuming to change. (Preparing, coding and punching cards takes a long time, so there would have to be overwhelming arguments for *changing* the system once holes had been destroyed. However, *adding* other items of information would be possible as long as vacant holes remain – in this case only one.)

> *Self-check*
>
> The edge-punched card system was introduced to introduce some features of data base design and retrieval. But can you think of an application where a simple, card-based system like this might be useful to a small business – possibly more useful than a computer package?

ANSWER

One possibility is employee records, as up to a few hundred cards can readily be sorted this way; additional information, like emergency phone numbers, can be written on the cards. Another possibility is the supplier or customer file; and you may have thought of others.

Whether or not these files would work better if computerized depends on the numbers involved, the nature of the business and the way in which other information is processed. What *is* certain is that a business whose records are held this way will be well-placed to assess whether a particular DBMS will suit its needs.

The main advantages of computerizing a data base are speed in retrieving the facts needed and flexibility in being able to sort them in a number of different ways. Computerized data bases can also be used conveniently by many people access to the same up-to-date information. A number of computer-based packages are available – variously called **file managers**, **information managers**, data bases and DBMS – which allow the user to search through a file, select records according to various criteria and display or print out the information held in each record either selectively or in full.

There are several possible problems with data base software as it has been designed traditionally; the recent trend is to make the software less rigid. Points to watch for are best expressed as a series of questions:

- Can it deal with incomplete information?
- Can it cope with varying sizes and formats for records and fields within a single file? Can these be changed after the data base is set up, or are they fixed for ever?
- Is it easy to add additional fields to some or all records?
- Can it search the file on the basis of *any* field (as opposed to insisting that the user commits himself at the outset)?
- Can it store free-text comments (like the bottom line on the card in Figure 35), and can it search through comments for the occurrence of specific words?
- Can it tolerate spelling mistakes and recognize synonyms (words with the same meaning)?
- Can you use it without having to learn a special language first?
- Can it produce reports in a form which you can use directly, or alternatively can it be connected with a word processing package?

Contrary to what some books and many salesman would have you believe, the answer to all these questions *can* be 'Yes', although some 'No's may not matter for some applications. In all computers, there is a trade-off between the space occupied by the program and the space available for data. For microcomputer users, the problem may be acute unless the software is available on a ROM chip. Faced with the alternative of having to buy a larger computer to accommodate all the records, users may be willing to accept some inflexibility in the software! As we shall see in Part 3, this is exactly the sort of dilemma which careful planning can avoid.

Single file applications

Many organizations make heavy use of a single file containing large amounts of information organized in a standard way, like a dentist's file of patients or an estate agent's file of vendors. A London theatrical agency keeps a file on all its artistes and uses a data base package to give immediate responses to requests like 'Availability dates of female tap dancers over 5 foot 8 inches and under 27 years who can also sing?'! The system can store up to sixty fields such as height, address, skills, etc., and it can search on up to eight criteria simultaneously. The results of the search can be sorted into order on any field selected (e.g. from youngest to oldest) and print out the results either as a simple list or – by linking with a word processing package – as part of a standard reply letter.

> *Self-check*
>
> Can you think of two other examples of organizations which might find a similar system useful? Identify what sort of information the main file would contain, and what sort of enquiries might be made of it. You could look back at the organizations described in Chapter 3, for a start.

ANSWER

The DTU sounds as if it needs to put its membership records on a data base (see page 81), so as to be able to search by members' qualifications, type of workplace, years of service, type of contract and perhaps also age and sex. Reports (showing how many members fall into a particular category and where they work) and sticky mailing labels (to send letters to them individually) would be useful for different purposes. Of course this all presupposes that such membership information is already available (or can be collected).

A political party or professional association might find this kind of facility equally useful, for mail-shots to market publications or conferences and for mobilizing interest groups within themselves (e.g. to locate by-election helpers, or when government action affects specific sub-groups).

A data base of jobs classified by their characteristics and qualifications required can be invaluable in careers guidance. The user feeds in his or her examination results, aptitudes and preferences and the program indicates possible 'matches' with jobs stored. The system has no preconceptions about the individual's talents or suitability: a computer is incapable of sex-stereotyping or race prejudice, unless it is explicitly programmed to discriminate.

There are many other possibilities: a data base of houses for sale can help an estate agent to deal with requests, e.g. for postwar semi-detached houses with three bedrooms, a small garden, central heating and within five miles radius of a given point. A computing dating or marriage bureau can help people to locate possible partners. A data base of package tours allows a travel agent to identify last-minute availability of 14-day Greek holidays with flights direct from Glasgow, a single room, sea view and daytime flights, and print them out in ascending order of price. If none were found, the customer could decide which criteria to relax until the search produced some results.

The police use computerized data bases for a number of purposes: for example, full details of the registered owner of any British vehicle can be radioed back to a patrol car which calls in with a registration number. Many Britons do not realize that the information they provide when they register a vehicle is automatically passed not only to the central police computer, but also to Customs and Excise, Inland Revenue and the Home Office. Computerized data bases are understandably controversial, especially where they contain facts and hearsay about people known for or suspected of criminal activity by the police.

Personnel records are a sensitive area generally, in government, health and education as well as in business, regardless of whether the information is held on a computer or not. All too often the 'subject' has no right to inspect and challenge the information recorded on him (which may be inaccurate and potentially damaging and is unlikely ever to be deleted). The power of large computers to link up information held in such data bases and compile detailed dossiers can undoubtedly be put to sinister purposes. Many people are already irritated by selective mail-shots sent by credit card and mail-order companies who buy and sell computerized mailing lists: the possibility that other, undisclosed organizations may also have bought such lists for more sinister purposes is ever-present. Many countries have legislation to protect citizens from such abuse; see page 226.

Using a DBMS

DBMSs vary enormously in how easy they are to use. Some are intended to be used in **command mode**, i.e. you have to know when and how to type in one of a restricted set of commands that the system understands; this can be a bit unnerving until you are familiar with the commands and how they work. **Menu-driven** software, on the other hand, offers a main menu listing the options from which you can choose. This is usually easier for a beginner, but going through successive menus can be tedious if there are a large number of possibilities.

To get the feel of the main stages, let's look at a simple menu-driven data base. Unlike too many commercial programs, this one presents the user with choices expressed in plain English:

> MENU
> 1 Create a file
> 2 Save a file
> 3 Load a file
> 4 Look at a file
> 5 Edit a file
> 6 Sort a file
> 7 Design a report
> 8 Delete a file

Suppose the DTU (see pages 79–82) were to use such a program. In the first instance, a master file of all the membership records would be set up under option 1. Creating this file would be a big undertaking, and careful thought should first have been given to what information needs to be entered and how it is to be coded. Using option 2, the file would then be saved on to disc (and back-up copies made and stored safely).

Next time the program was used, the first step would be to

load the file from disc (option 3). Option 4 allows the user to look at the file – for example, to discover how many members meet a given set of criteria (type of institution, length of service, qualifications held). **Editing** (option 5) allows the contents and format of the file to be changed; a much smaller file, consisting only of members meeting the criteria, could be set up (remember the master file would still be intact on the disc). Option 6 would allow this file to be sorted on any field, so that members could be arranged in order of length of service, for example. Designing the report (option 7) presents the print options: a report might be just a list of members on paper, or it could involve formatting their addresses suitably for sticky labels. Finally, option 2 might be used to save that sub-file in case it will ever be needed again. Periodically, option 8 would be needed to weed out superseded files. Separate menu pages would present choices for the entering, amending and updating of records, the design of fields and so on.

Not all data bases can be 'interrogated' in plain English like this. Some use a programming language such as BASIC, and others again have their own special languages, often referred to as **query**, or **enquiry**, **languages**. These are high-level programming languages supposed to help the inexperienced user to use the data base in command mode.

On-line data base searching

To see how searches are done using a query language, let's look at one of the most heavily used library data bases in the world – the ERIC system. This American data base contains over half a million summaries of educational books, articles, research reports and other documents. It is held on a large mainframe and can be searched **on-line** by institutions all over the world who link up with the computer by telephone and satellite.

ERIC's basic records typically consist of summaries of about a hundred words. Each summary is followed by a number of **keywords** which indicate the gist of what the document is about. For example, if this chapter were an ERIC document, 'data base' and 'on-line search' might be among the keywords listed.

How can computers help business?

> *Self-check*
>
> List at least five more possible keywords which convey the essential points in this chapter.

ANSWER

Data base management system, file, record, field, edge-punched card, on-line data base, keyword, query language.

There are other valid answers which you may have given, but this exercise should have helped you to see the difference between allocating keywords and indexing. For example, tap-dancers, libraries, satellites and Inland Revenue are all mentioned in the chapter, and such words may appear in the book's index. But they are not keywords because they are incidental to the main purpose of the chapter; if someone using ERIC was interested in one of these subjects, this would not be the place to direct them to.

Notice also that you may have given one of these words in a different form: 'DBMS' instead of 'data base management system', for example. Some authors write about 'databases' instead of 'data bases'. Remember how literally computers obey their programs? Depending on how the software is written, the data base may or may not be able to react sensibly to alternative or mistaken spellings by looking for 'near-matches' to terms that it *does* recognize. It is easy to get a program to disregard whether spaces are present in words like 'data base'. It is harder, but perhaps more important, to allow it to make responses like, 'Sorry, I do not understand "stock lever". Do you mean "stock level" or "stick lever"?' This is more constructive than a cryptic '?' or, even less helpful, 'syntax error'. In addition to dealing with spelling varieties, a dictionary of synonyms is useful – a bit like the section in Yellow Pages where you look up 'Doctor' and it says 'Doctors – see Physicians and Surgeons'. In a firm where the parts manager has always called something a part number, a dictionary is vital if the data base system calls it a product code.

But many data bases need more than just a list of synonyms. If you have ever been at a loss for the right word, you may have used an invaluable reference book called *Roget's Thesaurus of English Words and Phrases*. It gives lists of synonyms, antonyms (words of opposite meaning) and related words for thousands of crucial words in the English language. A large data base needs a **thesaurus**, too. Keywords may have different meanings in different contexts, so the user has to look at related terms to be able to decide whether the meaning is the one she or he wants. For example, someone who was looking for information about files, records and fields wouldn't want to be directed to articles about metalwork, music collections or agriculture! The thesaurus tells you about all the related keywords in the data base, and is an important guide to the relationships between different items.

The ERIC system allows the user not only to search by keywords, but also to *combine* keywords to define a field of interest. This is done in DIALOG, the system's special query language, using words like AND, OR and NOT. For example, if you were interested in all the books and articles relevant to business education and training using computers, you might define keyword combinations like this:

11 = computer-based OR computer-aided OR computer-assisted
12 = education OR training OR instruction OR learning
13 = business OR enterprise OR management OR administration
10 = 11 AND 12 AND 13

If you then search the data base on 10, it will list all the documents whose keywords include at least one of the 'synonyms' from *each* of the lists 11, 12 and 13.

Self-check

Suppose code 5 has already been defined as 'word processing'. Describe the subject matter of documents located by a new search defined by 6:
6 = 11 AND 12 AND 5

134 *How can computers help business?*

ANSWER

This might find articles on computer-based training courses in word processing systems, or on the use of computer-based word processing for education generally, or other combinations that you may have thought of. The user would then decide whether he wanted to see the full text by reading through the summary given.

ERIC is an example of a relational DBMS: that means that you make use of the relationships between records in searching the data base. Cross-references are suggested implicitly by the recurrence of the same keyword combinations in different summaries. This allows you to search the same records (the summaries of half a million documents) from a variety of viewpoints (defined by the unique combination of keywords you choose to reflect your particular interest). **Relational** DBMSs use a variety of ways of storing the relationships between different items; some have an explicit hierarchy, others define a formal network. There is no need to go into the details of these, but it *is* important to realize that when people talk about DBMSs, they may mean anything from a simple, single-file system to an elaborate structure which accurately reflects the complicated relationships between data in the real world, backed up by an extensive thesaurus of terms used.

Indeed, a largescale business DBMS may have sophisticated facilities which mean that it can carry out all the operations needed to process accounts, payroll and stock records – in effect, to conduct all routine aspects of the business's **data processing**. Such a system would contain *all* the business's standing records; after each transaction was entered, all the arithmetic, postings and updating would be done automatically. In effect, the DBMS would replace software packages for accounting (including costing and forecasting), payroll, employee records and much else besides. Clearly, the design and implementation of such grand systems is a specialist field in which professional advice is needed.

Prestel: a public data base

Prestel is the best-known example of a public data base and its implications for business are potentially immense (see Chapter 15). It is accessible to anyone with a telephone, a television and a keypad or keyboard linked to the system. Figure 37, in fact, shows Prestel in use with a microcomputer and an acoustic coupler, but there are other cheaper methods. Although launched in Britain, Prestel services are also being marketed in North America and Europe.

The Prestel computers contain a huge data base of hundreds of thousands of 'pages' (screenfuls) of information, provided by public and private bodies like government departments, private businesses, holiday firms, airlines, estate agents, financial and consumer information services and many others. Information

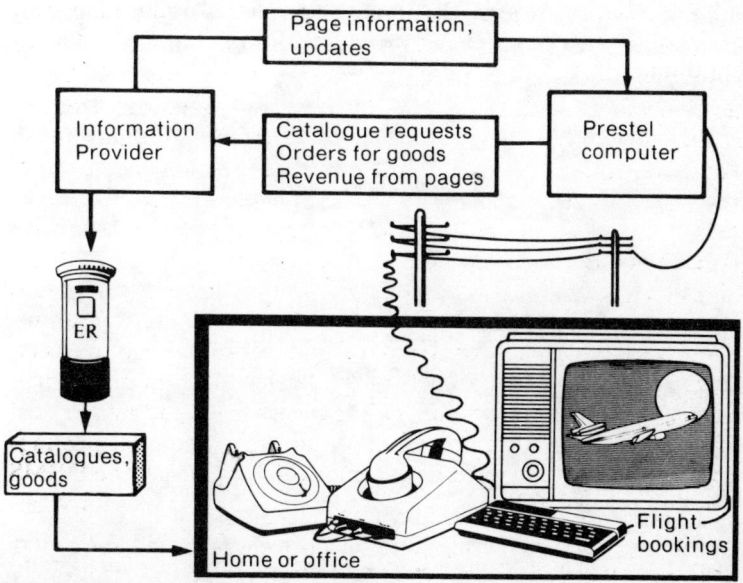

Figure 37. Prestel provides a vast data base and communications link which helps homes and offices to locate information and make purchases

136 *How can computers help business?*

Providers have the option of charging Prestel users for viewing their pages, although by 1983, over 80 per cent of the pages were still free. Users pay a small quarterly standing charge for Prestel services, and during office hours they also pay for connection time to the computer on top of standard telephone call charges. Since there is not just one Prestel computer but actually a network of 'local' Prestel computers, the phone calls are usually charged at local rates in Britain.

Prestel was the first example of a public **viewdata** system: viewdata refers to the tree-like structure which means that each page of information leads to a number of related pages which fan out to others again, like a tree trunk, branches and twigs. It is possible (although usually slow and often expensive) to find your way to the page you need by working through successive pages from the general index page. There are also directories of Information Providers (IPs), but their value is limited if you do not know who might have provided the information you are looking for.

Self-check

What aid could you suggest for searching through a data base like Prestel?

ANSWER

A good thesaurus would be invaluable to many users. (Work is in progress on a Prestel thesaurus at the time of writing.)

Public viewdata systems like Prestel are important to business for several reasons. First, they hold vast amounts of up-to-date information which can help in the running of a business – financial market reports, currency fluctuations, stock and share movements and the like. Second, they offer considerable marketing possibilities if your potential customers include current or likely Prestel users. Response frames allow the user to request further information or a catalogue at the touch of a button (no need for the customers to write out or dictate their names and addresses); details of these requests are passed from the Prestel computer back to the IP concerned, who can then post the material. Users can even use the system to order goods, with the charge being added to their Prestel bill. Clearly, this places special responsibilities on the security of the account number and password facilities.

The implications of Prestel stretch far beyond an information service and marketing medium, however. Businesses may also be interested in unlimited access to other data bases (including international ones), in **electronic mail**, telesoftware and **Closed User Groups** (CUG).

6 | Word processing

When word processors were introduced in the 1960s, they were large **dedicated** machines costing tens of thousands of pounds and operated by specially-trained staff. Big organizations needing large volumes of typing still use systems like that. However, much cheaper and easier word processing is beginning to spread to small businesses, voluntary organizations and the self-employed. This trend is mainly due to the rise of word processing systems based on ordinary microcomputers which can also be used for other purposes.

Why is word processing useful?

Word processing (wp) systems vary widely in the facilities provided by their software. The essential elements of any system should make it easy:

- to alter anything that you write, so that you can correct mistakes, substitute words, transpose sentences and paragraphs and try out alternative versions;
- to produce final documents, free of error and attractively laid out, showing no trace of alterations or previous versions, which can be printed rapidly and without human supervision;
- to compose text which fits precise limits on layout or word lengths without having to count words or print out unsatisfactory versions;
- to produce the same text in various formats – for example, single-spaced and double-spaced, or to suit different page sizes;
- to store standard documents, like letters, contracts, and minutes, and produce variations on them to suit individual cases

without having to retype or check the parts that are unchanged.

A wide choice of wp software already exists in various forms for computers of all sizes. Some microcomputer packages cost as little as £30–80 and do everything listed above and sometimes much more besides. (I am ignoring cassette-based wp software – which is even cheaper – because the slowness of cassette loading and saving rules it out for any serious wp system.) Additional facilities are available in more expensive software designed for minicomputers and mainframes: for example, the ability automatically to merge a customer file with a standard letter (variously known as **mail merge**, **batch infill** or **list processing**). Although microcomputer wp systems can produce 'personalized' mail, they tend to require human intervention.

To some extent, price tags of several hundred pounds tend to reflect the characteristics of a different market: mainframe and mini customers traditionally expect much more dealer support and may want to send their typists on wp training courses. Microcomputer customers are more likely to want to buy wp software which is sufficiently easy to use to make training courses unnecessary.

Some wp software has been designed to link with other programs, so that the output from a spreadsheet or data base search can be incorporated directly into a report. The more expensive systems often have facilities which go far beyond word processing as such: they may be able to check spelling or even query grammar and style (!), to carry out calculations, to conduct data base searches of their own, or even to connect directly with the telephone network, communicate with other word processors or with phototypesetting machinery.

How do you make it work?

You put words in (**enter** them) by pressing keys on a normal keyboard. As you key them in, the words appear on the screen, but nothing will be produced on paper yet. You then alter and rearrange the words as much as you like; this is known as editing.

On many systems, if you decide to delete something, the other words all squeeze up automatically. You can insert extra words freely, without having to worry about whether they will fit in the margin or between the lines.

Contrary to popular belief, you don't need to be a good typist to benefit from word processing. In fact, the more amateur the typist, the more he or she will appreciate how easy it is to remove errors without a trace. Once they are used to the system, most people type faster – often much faster – than on an ordinary typewriter.

Once you are completely satisfied with the wording on the screen, you **format** it – arrange the margins, spacing and page layout (see Figures 39 and 40, pages 151–2). Only then do you press the print button. This tells the processor to send the text to the printer, which then prints out the final document on paper. If you might want to use the text again, you press another button to save it. This records a permanent copy of the text in magnetic form, so that you won't ever have to key it in again. Thus the complete process has five stages: enter, edit, format, print and save. Because each stage is done separately, the author is free to concentrate on one thing at a time.

In traditional office practice, business typing is assumed to originate from one sort of person (an executive or professional) and be transcribed by another (a typist or secretary) from a longhand script, shorthand notes or a tape-recording, or perhaps even from an amended draft of something previously typed. It would be considered unusual for a secretary – and exceptional for an executive – to compose letters or reports while sitting at a typewriter. On a typewriter, authors would have to plan what they were going to say, choose their words and make their fingers pick the right letters all at the same time – knowing that it won't be easy to correct and disguise mistakes if they change their minds. Word processing makes it possible to question the unthinking continuation of labour-intensive office practice. By implication, it also raises questions about traditional job boundaries and whether keyboard familiarity should be confined to professional typists.

None of this should be taken to suggest that wp displaces

secretaries. A good secretary does a great many jobs which cannot sensibly be attempted by computer, many of which are vital to the smooth running of the business; copy typing is not one of them. The advent of wp has simply made copy typing an obsolescent skill – a fact which should make secretarial and administrative ability all the *more* highly valued. Copy typists who lack the ability or inclination to tackle other work – and their employers – will have mounting problems once this is more generally realized.

The keyboard remains the main access route through which words become printed text. There are various ways in which it might present a less formidable barrier than at present:

- Computer systems could change so that keyboards are less necessary.
- Keyboards could change so that people can learn to use them faster.
- Attitudes could change in business, training and education so that learning QWERTY is seen as an extension of basic skills, like using a pocket calculator.

There are some signs of all three of these at present, and it is anyone's guess which will happen faster. The kind of sophisticated operating systems which Apple and Xerox have pioneered (see pages 164–9) were developed specifically to combat supposed 'keyboard resistance' among executives. Whether the price of dispensing with the keyboard by this method is too high will emerge in the next few years. Once voice recognition systems have become simple, reliable and cheap, they will supersede such approaches, at least for text input.

Another possibility is the use of alternative keyboards. The QWERTY arrangement dates back to when typewriters were so primitive that the keys would jam if the typist went too fast; the arrangement of keys still unthinkingly incorporated into the latest product of the electronic age was actually designed to *slow down* human typists. The Maltron keyboard is an alternative arrangement, ergonomically designed to assist input, with logical groupings of keys to cut learning times and comfortable contours to make the keyboard fit the reach and shape of fingers.

142 *How can computers help business?*

Although the Maltron keyboard has proved itself faster and easier to learn in practice, the vested interests in manufacturing, promoting and training in QWERTY are formidable. Teachers of secretarial studies and skilled typists are understandably not enthusiastic about *unlearning* QWERTY!

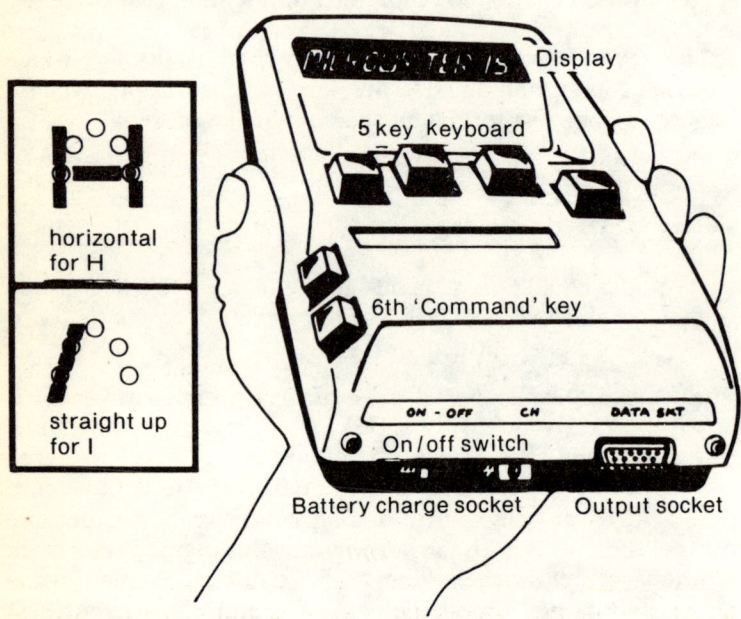

Figure 38. Microwriter: a hand-held word processing input device. Inset: two examples of letter codes

There is also a one-handed version of the Maltron keyboard. A different approach to one-handed operation has been adopted by the designers of Microwriter, a hand-held word processing input device (Figure 38). The user has to learn a set of codes for pressing combinations of the six keys to represent all the possible letters and characters: some examples are illustrated. The sixth key is actually used for commands to edit the text, re-format it and send it to a full-size printer and various other output devices. Microwriter has appeal to executives on the move as it can be battery-operated, has its own built-in memory and can be connected to televisions (for a full-size display) or telephones (to transmit text). It allows a traveller to phone in the text of a memo or order and have it printed out at the other end. The great sensitivity of the keys also makes it a valuable device for disabled adults and students. With practice, quite respectable speeds can be built up, though not nearly as fast as a touch typist experienced in QWERTY.

Alternative approaches like Maltron and Microwriter may be attractive to people who have no commitment to QWERTY. However, because they are innovative, they have not achieved a mass market and thus seem expensive compared with QWERTY keyboards. So a final possibility is that learning QWERTY – with all its faults – will be accepted by education and training as the going price for communication with affordable computers, and that acquiring QWERTY familiarity becomes an early priority. Given the ubiquitous presence of computers in British schools, this approach seems to be gaining ground at present.

Who needs it?

It is hard to generalize about the kind of organizations and people who will benefit most from wp; the facilities offered by different software vary as widely as DBMS software (see Chapter 5), and indeed large-scale systems combine the features of both.

Perhaps more important than the capabilities of the software, however, is the question of the attitudes and skills of those who are expected to use it. The qualities of the word processor are irrelevant if the business depends on a secretary who is passionately attached to her manual typewriter and resists the idea of learning a new system. Even if there are others in the business who are able and willing to use the system, all sorts of questions are raised about profitable use of time and the wisdom of installing a system unless all the relevant people learn to operate it.

It is usually assumed that organizations most likely to benefit from wp have a lot of material, like minutes or reports, which go through several drafts, or letters which are easily assembled from standard paragraphs, or 'personalized' mail shots. This is only partly true, as my own experience illustrates. Ever since I got hold of a £40 ROM chip which plugged into my BBC micro, I have used wp every working day and cannot now imagine doing without it – yet none of my work fits the above description. Although my books and articles are revised, many of the changes are made as I go along, most before I print out anything on paper. Other changes are made by various editors, usually 400 miles away, prior to typesetting. What is published thus seldom corresponds precisely to the text stored on my disc. Soon it may be feasible for final text from my disc to be sent directly to a printer – indeed it is theoretically possible at present. But the publishers who commission me are not geared to work in this way, which would have profound implications for employment as well as for technology in publishing.

Why, then, do I find word processing so indispensable? The main reason is that it emancipates my writing from the limitations of my typing skill. I can think freely onto the keyboard in a way which the uncompromising finality of a typewriter does not permit. I can polish my sentences, rearrange my paragraphs and delete circumlocutions – all without ever needing to retype or proof-read. Because I no longer need a typist to come and decipher the heavily amended longhand which I used to produce, I can produce finished results faster.

Secondly, nearly everything I write has to conform to length limits. The inevitable increment of the word count each time I hit the space bar raises my consciousness of this wonderfully. In one heavily illustrated book, the length limits were stringent: I had 27 characters per line and up to 41 lines per full column, or perhaps only 20 lines if a half-page illustration was to be used. By making the line length 27 characters on the screen, I could see at a glance when I was over-running without having to count letters and spaces. On a typewriter, I would never have found out till too late.

There are many incidental benefits. When interviewing someone by telephone I can tap the gist of what they say directly into the keyboard (not stopping for mistakes or linking words in order to keep up) and clean up their comments afterwards, incorporating them into an article. I can produce speech notes in jumbo type and sticky labels for the people I write to most. I am encouraged to try out draft versions of things like the quiz below on colleagues, often revising things in the light of their responses. (In the old typewriter days I was less likely to do this because of the chore of retyping and rechecking.)

Self-check

The quiz below tries to take account of these less conventionally recognized aspects of wp; and to help an individual or organization assess its own ripeness for wp. Try to answer it for yourself or for an organization you are familiar with. Alternatively, you could guess how I answered it, based on the above description of my work. The scoring key is at the foot.

Quiz for those wondering whether to embark on word processing

Note: this quiz is designed both for individuals and organizations. 'Your typists' should be taken to mean a pool of professional typists, a secretary with many other duties, or yourself, as appropriate. 'Documents' can mean anything from memos, letters, reports, minutes, articles, booklets to books.

1 What proportion of your typists' time is currently spent on non-typing duties (e.g. filing, phone-answering, administration)?
  a more than half **b** quarter to half **c** less than quarter

2 What proportion of your typists' time is currently spent retyping or amending documents that they typed previously?
  a negligible **b** up to quarter **c** more than quarter

How can computers help business?

3 What proportion of documents are currently proof-read (checked) for mistakes (typographical errors, mis-spellings, errors in transcription/retyping)?
a negligible **b** a minority **c** most or all

4 What proportion of your documents could be assembled from standard 'personalized' letters or combinations of standard paragraphs, provided that no evidence of 'cut-and-paste' were visible?
a negligible **b** up to a quarter **c** more than a quarter

5 To what extent might those who originate typing be able or willing to compose documents at a keyboard (instead of writing longhand or dictating)?
a negligible **b** possibly/a few **c** probably/a number

6 How would you rate the average skill level of those who would use a word processing facility if available?
a fast and accurate **b** moderate speed or accuracy **c** low speed and accuracy

7 Assuming you have no photocopier, how often might it be useful to produce fast cheap copies of documents that you originate? (If you have a photocopier, score **a**.)
a never **b** occasionally **c** quite often

8 How often do you produce documents in which word lengths matter, or where it is important for the text to fit an exact number of pages?
a never **b** occasionally **c** quite often

9 Would it be useful to be able to produce documents in a form which allowed them to be printed professionally without an intermediate stage of typesetting and proof-reading?
a no **b** possibly **c** probably

10 How often would near-silent keyboard operation be useful (e.g. for taking spoken instructions or dictation from the telephone)?
a never **b** occasionally **c** frequently

11 Easy production of error-free revised versions often results in more documents being produced in draft form for comment. Would this be a welcome by-product?
a no **b** possibly **c** probably

12 How would you rate the present attitudes to computers of those who might use word processing?
a hostile **b** apprehensive **c** interested

SCORING

For all questions, **a** = 0, **b** = 1, **c** = 2.

ANSWERS

I cannot guess what your answers were, and it is dangerous to recommend whether wp is suitable without knowing much more about you than a simple quiz can reveal. But tentatively I would suggest the following interpretation:

Below 7: it sounds as if typewriters are adequate, at least for the present.
From 7 to 13: word processing may be worth considering, but proceed with caution, especially on the issues where you scored 0 or 1.
Over 14: it sounds as if you should seriously consider word processing. A useful first step might be to see whether the other people who would be affected answer this quiz the same way you did – especially question 12!

In my own case, my answers were as follows:

c, **b**, **c**, **a**, **c**, **b**, **a**, **c**, **b**, **b**, **c**, **c**, so I scored 2 **a**'s, 4 **b**'s and 6 **c**'s (16 points).

What hardware is needed?

Although wp can be done on *any* computer which has suitable software, if a system is bought primarily for word processing, certain features of the hardware become particularly important.

The processor of almost *any* microcomputer is adequate, and the size of its internal memory is unimportant unless it is really tiny. My own micro, which has only 32 K of RAM (generally considered too small for a business micro) can hold 4,500 words (the length of this chapter), which may well be as many as you want to deal with *at one time*. You store the rest of the text on disc anyway. Although a disc system is vital for speed, a twin drive is not essential for wp (though it makes the taking of back-up copies faster and easier and may be essential if other software is to be run). Systems which need to store and edit really long documents use 8-inch floppy discs or even Winchesters. The whole of this book (and everything else I have written in the last couple of years) was produced using a single disc drive; the full text occupied half a dozen 100 K discs, with longer chapters stored as two text files.

In the early days of wp, systems designed for several wp operators tended to be **shared-logic**: a single processor supported several vdu's and keyboards on a time-sharing system. Nowadays, microprocessors are so cheap that better performance can be obtained more economically by giving each operator her own processor; there is little point in economising on a processor costing a tithe of the price of the vdu and keyboard (which are indispensable anyway). Indeed, for two or three operators it may be simplest to have two or three free-standing systems. However, if a Winchester disc or high-price printer are in use, the operators' systems can be networked in order to share these expensive resources (see Figure 23, page 89). Most business computers nowadays can be networked economically, but it is important for the purchaser to anticipate the maximum number of users and what transmission speeds are acceptable.

More important than the processor, oddly enough, is the quality of the keyboard. The best way to test the 'feel' of a keyboard is for you – or whoever will be using it most – to try it out personally. Keys should be sculptured, not too slippery and with a positive action and full travel. Unless entering numbers is likely to be unusual, an additional group of numeric keys is highly desirable, as this is much faster than using the row above QWERTY for all-figure entries.

Before settling on a hardware system, you should consider whether you want to buy your wp software on disc or as a ROM. A word processing ROM has to be designed specifically for a particular kind of microcomputer; not all machines can have them fitted. ROM-based wp has the advantage that it is at your fingertips a split second after switching on; you can switch instantaneously from normal computing to word processing; and it may leave your RAM space available for other purposes. It has the potential disadvantage that it is installed semi-permanently, perhaps by a dealer; if you may want more elaborate facilities in the future, this might be restricting. For example, if you want a spelling checker facility, it should be on disc, so that you can update the dictionary, e.g. to 'teach' it new words.

Whatever format the software is in, check carefully that it does everything you need in a manner that you (or whoever will operate it) find easy to use; even if it is on disc, you probably won't be able to modify it (except in trivial respects like adding to the dictionary). Find out how many keystrokes are required for commonly-needed operations, like saving a document or correcting the transposition of two letters as in htis. For Wordstar, perhaps the most famous of first-generation wp software, the answers are respectively four and twelve keystrokes, with both hands needed; it shouldn't be hard to improve on that! Decide whether you want facilities like automatic page-numbering and running heads (headings repeated automatically at the top of every page). Check if there is a search-and-replace facility; this scans text, looking for one string of letters, and automatically replaces it with another, so that you can turn a letter to 'Jane Smith' into one to 'Joe Bloggs' at a stroke.

The finished product

The final appearance of the processed words depends on the choice of printer, the attention given to layout and the choice of paper.

Printer

Printers vary widely in speed and quality. The choice made of printer and accessories will determine how much a wp system is used and to whom the business feels able to send its processed words. Since communicating with the outside world is essential to any business, false economy is a serious mistake.

Unfortunately, there is a trade-off between speed and quality, especially in moderately priced printers. Dot-matrix printers are faster and more flexible, but daisy-wheel printers are still unbeaten for producing ultimate quality, although the gap is narrowing. The ideal solution (adopted by Outer Temple, see page 88) is to have both, using the dot-matrix as a draft-quality printer for fast production of all internal documents, drafts and screen-dumps (e.g. of a spreadsheet, histogram or graphic) and the daisy-wheel only for finished versions, letters to the outside world and documents to be reproduced.

A printer cannot be chosen in isolation. The choice must be coordinated with that of software, because the two must work in partnership to produce effects like boldface, underlining, line feeds and even £ signs. It is essential to try out the complete system before you buy; otherwise you may be dismayed to find that you can't underline things properly, that you have to key in # whenever you mean £, or that you have to key in '*FX6,1' before printing if all the lines are not to end up superimposed on each other. If you want **proportional spacing** *and* right-edge **justification**, check whether the system can cope; many combinations can manage either but not both!

Most businesses sometimes have their printed materials typeset professionally, because the document requires greater authority, legibility or compactness. If this arises at all regularly it is well worth checking how easily and cheaply typesetting can be produced directly from the wp system, i.e. without any rekeying of text. This requires compatibility between the originator's wp and the printer's system. Ideally, they would both use the same standard code (e.g. **ASPIC** or **MUSIC**) for inserting codes for heading styles, typefaces, etc. The printer can then simply put the originator's disc into his typesetting machine, press a button and out come perfect printing masters.

Layout

Wp systems make it easy to try the effects of different line lengths, spacing and character sizes. You can see the effect on lay-out of some sample **control codes** by comparing Figures 39 and 40. These were reproduced directly from my own system's dot-matrix printer. With different wp software or a different printer, the codes would also have been different, and the choice of effects available might also have been different.

```
lm18 ll45 oc27, 71

oc14 A  sample  piece  of  text
        This paragraph is to show you the appearance
        of the same piece of text with various
        formatting commands.  The codes shown are
        taken from Wordwise, the ROM-based word
        processor which was used to prepare the
        manuscript of this book.  Although the actual
        codes vary from one system to another, the
        general principle is the same.
```

Figure 39. First version of paragraph with simple format commands

As originally printed, this paragraph had a left margin of 18 characters. The maximum line length is 45 characters. Codes beginning 'oc' control printing effects; for example, 'oc27,71' gives blacker-looking type by making the printer print each line twice.

Self-check

See if you can use the information above to work out which code controls:

1 the left margin
2 the line length
3 jumbo (enlarged) typeface

152 How can computers help business?

ANSWERS
1 lm18
2 ll45
3 oc14

Incidentally, because the left margin is defined by the *number* of characters left blank – rather than the space in inches – it has to be adjusted when you change from one size of typeface to another. This is illustrated in Figure 40, along with a few other format and printing effects.

```
         lm18 ll75 oc27,71 ls2
oc14     A sample piece of text
         oc15 lm31 jo

         This paragraph is to show you the appearance of the same piece of text with

         various  formatting commands.  The codes shown are taken from Wordwise, the

         ROM-based word processor which was used to prepare the manuscript  of  this

         book.  Although  the  actual  codes  vary  from one system to another, the

         general principle is the same.
```

Figure 40. Second version of paragraph with more elaborate format commands

Self-check

1 List as many changes as you can between the appearance of Figures 38 and 39.
2 See if you can guess which codes are responsible for them.

ANSWERS
1 a More characters per line.
  b Double spacing between lines.
  c Small (condensed) typeface.
  d Justified (right margin straight).
2 a 1175 (maximum of 75 characters per line)
  b 1s2 (1s3 produces triple spacing and so on)
  c oc15
  d jo (stands for Justify On)

There are many other codes involved in automatic centring (e.g. of headings), indentations, underlinings, running heads and foots, tabulations and a host of other effects. For rapid production of an internal newsletter or bulletin, a daisy-wheel printer can produce very cost-effective results.

Paper-handling

Printers may have **friction feed**, **tractor feed** or both. Friction feed means that the paper is held in place by friction against the roller, just like a typewriter. It is essential for feeding individual sheets of paper (e.g. letterheads). However, sheet-feeding means that the printer needs continual attention; any business doing large printing jobs on to sheets would have to think seriously about an automatic paper feeder. Unfortunately, these can cost as much as the printer itself.

Tractor-feed printers are designed for **fan-fold** paper: this is manufactured as thousands of sheets joined by perforations end-to-end and folded in a zig-zag. There is a row of holes down each side of each sheet, variously known as **sprocket-holes**, **tractor-holes** or **pin-holes**, into which pins on the tractor mechanism engage. This pulls the paper through the printer automatically and with precise control. Tractor-feed thus permits unattended printing, which is a great time-saver. Not many organizations wish to send documents out with sprocket-holes down each side. Paper can be supplied with perforations along the column of holes so that they can be detached; this might cost £5–8 per thousand sheets, depending on volume purchased. At a slightly higher price, clean-edge fan-fold looks almost like a cut sheet, once separated. Special machines called **bursters** can be bought to split fanfold paper en masse. The pre-printing of fanfold can be surprisingly expensive, so it is worth assessing the volumes involved before ruling out an automatic feeder. Also, if you need frequent changes of letterhead, or to alternate with plain paper, fan-fold can be very inconvenient.

Despite much idealistic talk about the paperless office, the reality is that computer printers devour paper. The faster the printer, the more paper it devours. Also, the more perfectionist the wp operator (and the more prone the author to correct and overcorrect successive versions), the more repeated print-outs of any document may be expected. A business embarking on word processing can expect to spend substantially more on paper than in the days of the typewriter. Furthermore, if its output is confidential in any way, it may have to consider another printer accessory – a **shredder**, for safe disposal of all that waste paper!

7 Software options

Business software is by no means confined to the kinds of software packages described in the last three chapters. Accounting, DBMS and word processing were allocated a chapter each because, together with payroll (see Chapters 10 and 11), they account for a very large proportion of the business software packages currently available. This chapter looks at extensions and alternatives to the traditional package approach.

For some businesses, a package can be a very cost-effective solution. It can be reasonably priced because the same overhead (the labour-intensive process of designing the package, debugging and refining the program and providing the documentation) can be spread across a customer base which may number hundreds, thousands or even tens of thousands of users. Thus a package which cost (say) £20,000 to develop can be sold profitably at just £100 if 400 users buy it, even allowing 100 per cent margin for marketing, production and distribution. Furthermore, if the business happens to conform to the way the package was designed (or if there is built-in flexibility), there can be a very close match between the needs of the business and the facilities provided by the package.

It is obvious that a large customer base benefits the designers, in that it makes for profitable software. Less obvious but more important is the way this benefits the users. There is safety in numbers, and consumer bargaining power is strengthened. It is more likely to be worth the designers' while to provide updates and correct any errors which may emerge. It is essential not to underestimate the need for software support of this kind; it is quite commonplace for bugs to emerge in the first few years of the life of new software (and even firmware), even if it has been extensively tested and apparently works correctly under normal circumstances. Furthermore, if the designers/distributors go into liquidation or discontinue the product, there is more hope of interesting another firm in the plight of users whose businesses may be dependent on continuing support.

Leaving these gloomy possibilities aside, there are many positive benefits to be gained from other users, both directly and indirectly. It is common for users to be able to help each other, sometimes more effectively than the computer professionals. User groups and newsletters exist for some software products and provide a direct source of help. Less direct, but of more general application, is the existence of an identifiable market for publishers of books and magazine articles about the use of the package. The same applies to the possibility of other software being designed to link with, extend or improve upon the original package.

Thus there are considerable benefits in being part of a secondary market consisting of purchasers of a popular package as compared with the vulnerability and isolation of someone who commissions software as a one-off exercise. Why, then, does anyone pay the many times higher price of having software written especially?

Self-check

Try to think of two reasons why off-the-shelf packages may be found unsatisfactory.

ANSWERS

You may have thought of additional ones, but here are three possibilities:

1 a business may have specialized needs or idiosyncratic ways of doing things;
2 a number of different operations may need to be carried out on the same data (e.g. a customer file or list of transactions) and using a separate package to carry out each one is likely to involve the time-wasting and error-prone process of keying in the same data again;

3 if a business constantly uses several programs, it is tedious and time-consuming to keep having to reload the same software, and if the user has to keep switching between conflicting conventions from different manufacturers, the process may be error-prone.

The first problem may partly be overcome by packages with a measure of built-in flexibility: on the first occasion of use, they have provision for 'customizing' their operation to the particular mode of operation of a business. If this is an extensive process, it may be better done by a dealer, rather than the user, but the process can go some distance to reconciling the standardization of the package with the idiosyncrasies of the individual.

Problems 2 and 3 may be met by the development of integrated packages. **Integrated software** became a buzz-word in 1983, when sales of software designed to combine all the commonest business functions started to take off. 'Integration' is a term which covers a variety of meanings: at one end of the spectrum, it may simply mean that the output of a spreadsheet can be displayed and printed directly in pictorial form without any need to re-key the data. At the other extreme, it may mean a sophisticated and comprehensive software combination which allows the user to switch between spreadsheets, database management, graphics and word processing without re-loading any programs or text, and using standardized commands for all functions.

Looking beyond the package approach will take us in two different directions along the software spectrum (Figure 41). Moving to the left takes us into the realms of systems software; first let us investigate the other approaches to applications software shown to the right.

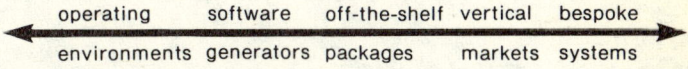

Figure 41. The software spectrum

Vertical markets

Traditionally, packages have been designed to have widespread appeal to a great range of businesses by performing certain universally necessary functions; they cut across the market 'horizontally'. The **vertical market** approach to software is the exact converse: a particular group of business or professional users is identified as a vertical market and software designed specifically to meet their needs. Ideally, all the software the users might need should be packaged together and integrated in a form which makes it easy to switch between applications. It is usually beneficial for users – or their representatives – to be involved in the design and documentation of such packages.

By 1983, an immense number of specialized packages were already available. So many had been produced for obvious markets like estate agents, solicitors, newsagents, engineers, insurance brokers and medical practitioners that they are often not listed separately in the directories. One magazine regularly lists over a thousand specialist software packages, with a range of markets which defies summary. Here is a sample – a dozen examples chosen at random – simply to illustrate the variety already available:

- Animal performance monitoring
- Architects
- Courier/motorbike despatch
- Fish farming
- Greyhound racing
- Kitchen design/manufacture
- Pig farming
- Portfolio management
- Pubs
- Schools administration
- Slide show presentation
- Solar heating predictions
- Sports stadium seat bookings

No matter what your business, it can only be a matter of time before someone brings out a package which caters for it. Potentially, such packages *may* have considerable advantages over more generalized approaches.

> *Self-check*
>
> Can you think of the possible disadvantages? Consider the case of a standard package that has had minor adjustments as well as that of a truly specialized and integrated package.

ANSWERS

- Producing genuinely specialized and integrated software for a vertical market is immensely time-consuming. In order to be profitable, there must either be a very high price-tag or a very large prospective sale.
- If producing such software is not profitable, the designers/distributors are unlikely to stay in business, with obvious bad effects on the prospect of long-term customer support. Even if the product is profitable, it may not be worth their while to invest much effort in a small group of users with little bargaining power.
- If the software is basically a standard package with only minor adaptations to suit the market it is aimed at, it may not be worth the extra cost and/or loss of the 'safety-in-numbers' factor.
- Most specialized software is available only for certain hardware and certain operating systems. In some cases, choice of a certain package might dictate the hardware to be bought. It is important to think twice before pre-empting this choice.

Much depends on the experience, skills and attitudes of whoever is going to operate the software and also on how specialized the business's needs really are. In some cases, it may be better to make minor adaptations to business procedures or terminology than to become trapped into a particular software/hardware set-up. In other cases, the vertical market option may be a short-cut to a working system; potentially it can save a lot of time and headaches.

Bespoke systems

A **bespoke** system is one which is commissioned by the user to match his needs exactly. When it is supplied in such a complete form that the user need only figuratively 'turn a key' to start it running, it is sometimes called a **turnkey system**. (The term has no connection with security.) Often the supplier takes complete responsibility for hardware, software, documentation, training and support. This kind of approach implies an immense investment of effort in setting up the system and sustained support to ensure that it is kept up to date with prevailing legislation and business practice. If a software package resembles an off-the-peg suit, and vertical market software a tailor-altered version of the same, the turnkey system is the ultimate in bespoke tailoring: made-to-measure and very expensive.

Bespoke systems are normally supplied by a hardware vendor, software house or firm of consultants to a specification agreed by parties who must be knowledgeable both about the business in question and about the capabilities of computers to benefit its operation. It is impossible to generalize about their costs, but certainly such systems can be expected to fall in a much higher price-bracket than the vertical markets software. Because the exercise is 'one-off', there is no one with whom the user can compare notes, nor share expensive manpower costs. £5000 might buy straightforward turnkey software, but £10,000 would not be at all unusual, and £100,000 not inconceivable. In short, if you are contemplating such a system, you need to be very sure that your needs cannot be met more simply. Unless you already know a great deal more than is contained in this book, you should certainly take professional advice, preferably from a well-qualified and independent consultant, before becoming committed to such a course.

Apart from the sheer expense of this approach there is also the problem of the future. Future-proof hardware simply does not exist. Even if it did, future-proof software is even more improbable. Unless the business can readily anticipate its future requirements *and* its likely future hardware purchases, it will be impossible for the suppliers of turnkey software to provide for all eventualities. Thus when the business finds it has outgrown the existing system, or that legislation changes its method of handling paperwork, or realizes that more of its information systems can be integrated, the supplier will have to be brought in again to provide specialized modifications of the software. Not only will these be expensive, but the business is unlikely to be able to argue with the asking-price, since it would be even more difficult (and expensive) for anyone who was not familiar with the original system to carry out the modifications. Thus the business is likely to be trapped into dependency on the supplier who designed the original system.

It should be recognized that many turnkey systems are admirably suited to their purposes and the providers often work to high standards and provide first-class documentation and maintenance. Nevertheless, prospective users should ask themselves whether the computer system will generate enough extra profit (or save enough running expenses) to offset such a large initial commitment. They should also recognize that it is very likely that the software as supplied will, like the commercial packages mentioned earlier, contain errors of various kinds and users should expect to make an agreement with the supplier over software maintenance costs, bearing in mind that obscure errors in little-used branches of a program may take months or years to surface. Some procedure must be agreed in advance for negotiating additional payments for variations requested by the user during the design process. Such changes are almost inevitable as the user increases his comprehension of what the system will mean in practice. However, by definition, if the user could anticipate the extent of such changes, they would not be necessary.

A major imponderable in the bespoke approach is the extent to which costs can be anticipated. It is unlikely that a supplier could even quote a firm starting-price for originating the software without doing a lot of preliminary work – which will itself have to be paid for. It is like expecting an architect to give a precise cost for building a custom-designed house; without doing detailed drawings, it is impossible for him to give the client a firm estimate. Future costs are even harder to predict without a

How can computers help business?

reliable crystal ball. The user should recognize the possible dangers of an open-ended and long-term commitment to a particular supplier – especially in a field of tumbling hardware costs and rapid and radical innovation.

In any event, some awareness of the high costs of commissioning turnkey software is a useful reminder of where the real investment in a business computer system lies. No matter how apparently expensive the hardware, a greater sum will usually be involved in the skilled manpower costs of adapting the computer to the business systems (or vice versa). At one end of the spectrum, turnkey systems display this cost in their typically high price tags; at the other, a self-employed person seldom properly costs his or her own time in adapting to and installing a package-based computer system, and may instead reckon only the cost price of the hardware and software. Between these two extremes, businesses who buy in outside help may be reminded of some of these costs by consultants' fees, though they are still unlikely to cost their own time investment rigorously. Whichever way costs are reckoned, it is vital to ensure that the main time investment in adaptation to the computer is once-and-for-all, so that whatever the future may bring, the process does not have to be repeated afresh each time there is a hardware expansion or software modification.

Self-check

Did any of the businesses described in Chapter 3 use a bespoke system?

ANSWER

The example of Beau Brummel closely resembled a bespoke system, with the important reservation that by sharing with other retailers, Julian Dapper split both the risks and benefits eight ways. Good Wheel and Rothespierre Wines both have customized elements in their systems, but they do not appear to have gone for a complete turnkey solution.

Software generators

Referring back to Figure 41 (see page 157), it is time to explore the other software options shown to the left of the package approach. The first grouping is labelled **software generators** or **code generators**. These are super-programs which generate (write) software in response to instructions fed in by the user. They thus resemble compilers (see page 61), in that they are program-writing programs. However, code generators work by a systematic process of constructing a full specification (in effect, a detailed flowchart) by interaction with the user. Afterwards, the specification is translated automatically into lines of coding.

Thus software generators are intended to help the user or programmer to generate their own software more easily than writing it by conventional means. The approach has great attractions for anyone who repeatedly needs to produce programs which share common features: having familiarized himself with the software generator and set up one program, the chores of actual coding (writing the program line-by-line) and debugging (taking the mistakes out) can be speeded up dramatically, and the resultant program code will be error-free.

Naturally, however, if the original specification contains logical or procedural errors, the program will not work as intended. If the programmer's main tasks are initial design – as will be the case if applications are very diverse – or making modifications to software written by conventional means, a code generator will be of little use. Those who are not professional programmers should know of the existence of such tools, but until you have direct experience of programming it is easy to overestimate the value of software generators. Coding, although often tedious, is in some ways the *easiest* part of computer programming.

> *Self-check*
>
> What do you suppose is the hardest part?

ANSWER

Planning precisely what the coding is to achieve and how it will do it. Software generators are less helpful with this than with the actual coding.

Indeed, a code generator can only assist the user by limiting the options available to some extent. Some work through a question-and-answer interrogation of the user, others assume some sort of model of how the program will work. In some situations, these restrictions may turn out to be a handicap rather than a time-saver; a novice user is unlikely to know enough about the alternatives to judge. And for a real novice, it may be quicker to program a given application scratch than first to learn how to use a software generator and then go through its own design sequence. So, despite over-ambitious claims made by some advertisements (for example, that their product 'will be the last program you'll ever buy'!), code generators are *not* a panacea. Nevertheless, in the hands of someone with programming skills and experience, they may be a valuable accessory. Before making a commitment to any particular system, it is worth evaluating the range of other software tools and utilities – often cheaper and sometimes much more flexible – which might be obtained at lower cost.

Operating environments

1983 marked the introduction of microcomputer systems combining integrated software with an operating system and special hardware. **Operating environment** is a convenient label for this development; it represents the first major innovation in operating software for microcomputers since the arrival of CP/M (see Chapter 2) brought portability.

With reference to Figure 16 (see page 64), an operating environment can be seen as 'sitting on top' of specially-designed hardware. Although it incorporates many facilities which would previously have been provided by applications software, additional programs can also be made to run 'on top of' the operating environment. Some of the attractions of such combinations will become clearer if we look at a specific example: Apple's LISA.

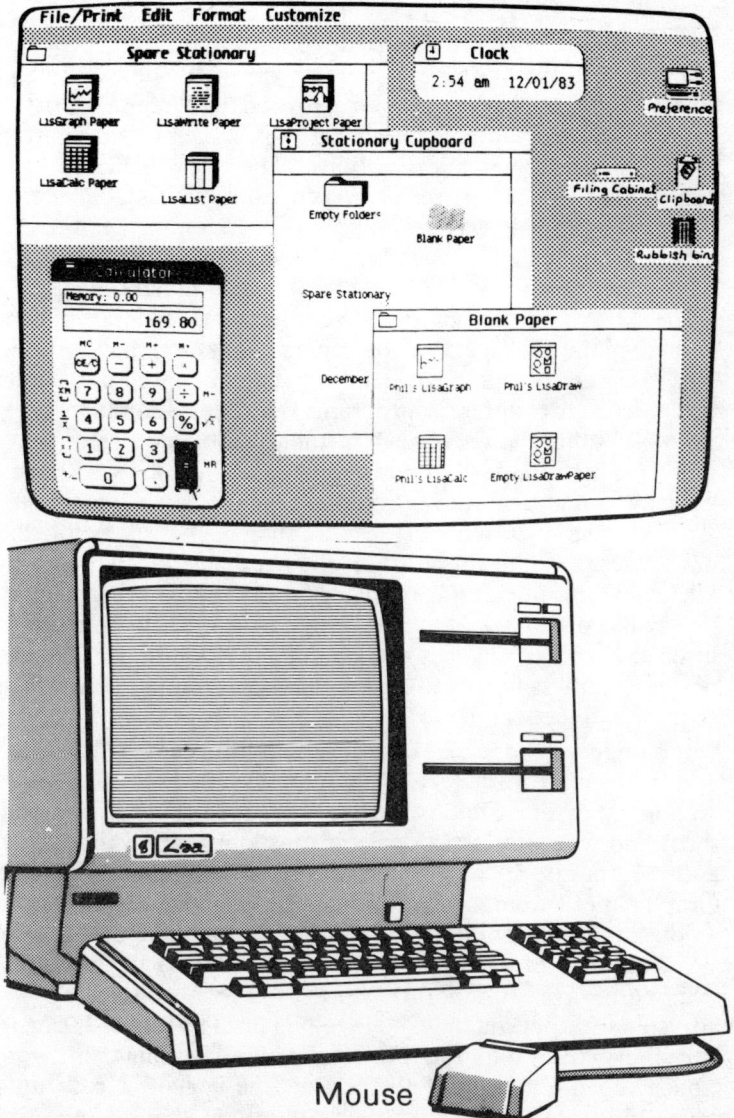

Figure 42. Apple's LISA system with overlapping windows shown on the screen and 'mouse' input

Figure 42 illustrates Apple's LISA microcomputer system. Although there is a conventional keyboard, the 'mouse' provides an alternative means of input. By rolling this little box around on his desk-top, the user controls an arrow on the screen. When the arrow points to something he wants to select, he presses a button on the mouse to activate the choice. The effect is like using a light-pen or a touch-sensitive screen, only without having to stretch. The mouse was developed to overcome alleged resistance by (largely male) executives to using keyboards – believed to have an excessively secretarial (and largely female) image.

The LISA's high-resolution screen is another important ingredient in the package. Previous operating systems have offered a 'split-screen' function, which allows the same monitor to show results from two different programs operating simultaneously. LISA takes this approach much further by showing a great many options in pictorial form (known as **icons**). Thus, the screen may seem to resemble a conventional executive's desk-top (Figure 43), with overlapping papers. By pointing to the calculator, the filing cabinet or the rubbish bin, the user can calculate, file or delete. When an option is selected, a 'window' opens up to display its contents, and the relevant part can be zoomed out to fill up the screen. Choices can be made by pointing (using the mouse) at any feature and making choices from a menu which 'pops up' on the screen.

It is important to realize that the integration provided by LISA is of a different order from 'integrated software' of the kind mentioned earlier. Suppose an executive is working on a spreadsheet and wants to display part of it as a histogram (bar chart) and incorporate it in a report. Pointing to a 'sheet' of LISA Graph paper automatically calls up a program which will display an outline histogram next to the data. This can be printed and saved as part of the report. Moreover, by placing it on the 'clipboard' icon (temporary storage), the histogram can be adjusted in scale, shading and labelling until its finished appearance is exactly as required. For example, by pointing to the word 'shade' on the margin of the screen, the executive calls up a menu illustrating thirty-six different sorts of shading; pointing and pressing the mouse button automatically fills in the shading

Software options 167

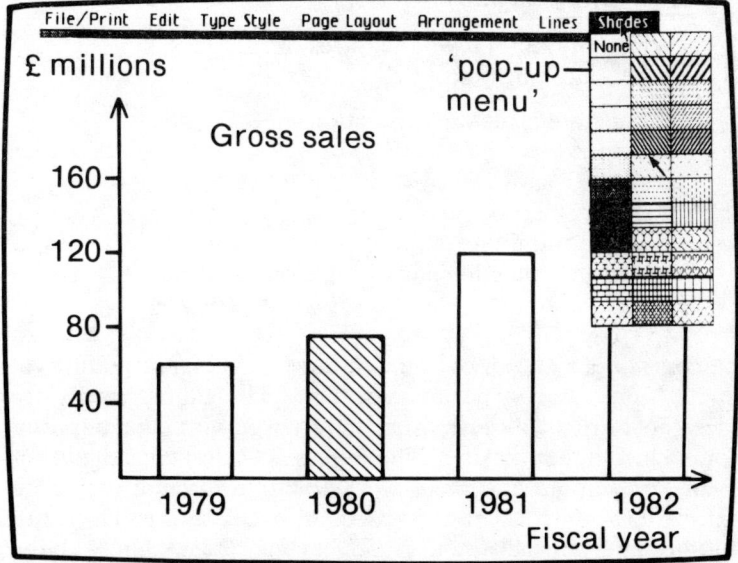

Figure 43. If the user chooses 'shades', a menu offers 36 options for shading the 1980 bar

in the style chosen. Typestyle and page layout can be adjusted in a similar fashion.

LISA software also allows the user to process drawings and produce PERT (Program Evaluation and Review Technique) charts to show critical path analysis. A range of processing functions can be carried out on text and numbers without having to break off and reload another program or find one's place afresh. Switching between functions becomes as easy as push-button changing of channels on a television set. Furthermore, LISA has a variety of friendly features to prevent the unwary from making serious operating errors. There is always the option of 'undo last change' at any stage. It automatically saves the latest version of your data before allowing you to remove a disc or to 'switch off'. (Actually, it is never really switched off, as internal batteries conserve vital system information even if it is accidentally disconnected from the mains.)

How can computers help business?

Self-check

Which of the following features of the LISA system seem to you most attractive?

- **a** integrated software operation
- **b** mouse input
- **c** system easy to learn
- **d** high resolution screen
- **e** icons resembling familiar desk-top
- **f** built-in protection against user operating errors.

ANSWERS

Of course it's a matter of opinion, but I would value features **a**, **c** and **f** most highly, rather than the much-vaunted mouse. In fact, most users will *have* to come to terms with a keyboard of some kind sooner or later. The mouse is of dubious benefit for some applications and a positive liability for others: if you are setting up a spreadsheet, it is just a nuisance continually to have to alternate between mouse and keyboard. Personally, I see little point in the fake familiarity of the icons. Why go to elaborate lengths to try to make a computer screen look like a desk-top when computer systems operate in a completely different way from paper and rubbish bins? To my mind, it is the design of LISA's software, rather than its hardware gimmicks, that make it important.

Sophisticated operating environments are by no means unique to Apple; Xerox and VisiCorp have both produced systems with these sorts of features, though the details vary. What they share is a strong bid to be easy to learn: a common claim is that a naive user can begin to work the system in thirty minutes, as compared with thirty hours for a 'normal' system. The innovation of a manufacturer like Apple actually trying out prototypes on groups of users and revising their plans in the light of reactions is also noteworthy in an industry which has traditionally paid little attention to the needs of the user.

Unfortunately, these systems all make heavy demands on the hardware and – when first announced – had a high price tag. For example, the LISA is a 16-bit machine with 1 Megabyte of memory (of which applications programs occupy 200 to 300 K) and cost around $12,000 in 1983. Initially, at least, this particular software option pre-empts a number of hardware decisions and demands a major investment.

Part 3
Computers in business practice

8 Acquiring software

Of all the decisions set in train when a business decides to computerize, the most crucial by far is the acquisition of software. This issue should be considered in detail *before* any decisions are made about the acquisition of hardware (which is discussed in Chapter 9). Not only does the business need to decide what kind of software it proposes to use and for what purposes: it must also make strategic decisions about what proportion of its activities it proposes to computerize, what level of integration is appropriate, who will use the system and what training they will receive, what level of programming expertise the business has at present and how it intends to develop in the future.

All these may be difficult matters to foresee in any detail. However, no consultant or dealer can help the business to make wise choices unless the business itself has thought through the management implications of a major change in its operation. In the absence of clear guidance from the client, such outsiders can hardly be blamed for falling back on their own preferences and recommending safe, familiar or profitable solutions which may be quite inappropriate to the business in question.

The business must take these strategic decisions from the inside; after all, if management cannot decide its own strategy, no one else can. Some tactical issues must then be tackled. For example, whether the software should be standard or custom-written depends on how comprehensive and integrated the software needs to be. And even if a business has decided, say, to buy a vertical markets software package to cover its main operations, the question remains of how to choose a particular package from the many available. This chapter starts with the strategic questions and finishes with a brief discussion of tactics.

Strategic decisions

Extent of computerization

Businesses vary widely in the extent to which they are suitable cases for computer treatment. Among those that are ripe for computerization, some will wish to hand over total control of all their transactions to a computer system, others will find that only a small part of their activity is suitable for computerization. Decisions about software must be influenced by how total the commitment to the system will be. In general, businesses with little routine, a tendency to the unpredictable and heavy dependence on human interaction are unlikely to be suitable for extensive computerization.

> ### Self-check
>
> Looking back over Chapter 3, pick any two businesses and note some of their activities which are *not* suitable for computerization.

ANSWERS

Most of Jenny Bruno's time is spent on activities which require uniquely human qualities (e.g. handling the animals, answering the telephone); only her paperwork systems are suitable for computerization. Some of DTU's activities (like salaries negotiation and individual discipline and grievance cases) depend on skills of human relations, conciliation and advocacy, where others (like membership and subscriptions) are eminently suitable for computer processing. Just about all of Beau Brummel's paperwork could easily be computerized, so that a comprehensive turnkey system allows Dapper to concentrate on his purchasing strategy and personnel management, and leaves the sales assistants free to concentrate on selling.

Such considerations naturally influence the methods by which these businesses chose to acquire their software. Jenny Bruno could never have justified buying an expensive vertical markets package for kennel-owners, much less commissioning a turnkey system. In any event, her training and inclination encouraged her to write her own programs. Equally, Dapper knew better than to try to write his own software: his problem represented a largescale task for a computer professional and was no place for an amateur to dabble. The future of a computer-based business depends on the efficiency and reliability of its software.

Level of integration

A highly computerized business sometimes requires a high level of integration in its software – but not necessarily. A business might engage in a number of diverse activities, each of which is sufficiently routine to be worth computerizing but which are costed and paid for in different ways, so that there is little merit in trying to integrate the software that deals with each of them.

Self-check
Can you think of an example?

ANSWER

A landscape gardener or garden centre might be involved in sales and small contracts and would thus fall into this category. Its clients might include individuals, firms and public sector agencies; it would have a different pricing structure for retail and trade sales; and it would use different models for estimating for regular contracts and one-off landscaping jobs. A small computer system might be very helpful for all of these activities, but a variety of standard packages might be the most cost-effective solution: the marginal advantage of integrating all the software systems might be too slight compared with the cost in money, time and trouble – especially if the business is evolving and changing its clientele.

There is another kind of integration to be thought about: how far is it desirable for the computer system to be integrated with other computers and other office equipment? For some businesses, this may seem to be an issue as unreal as the elusive 'Office of the Future'. However, making good software decisions demands some willingness to think about the future. The question is pressing for any firm that operates from more than one location, regularly makes long-distance telephone calls to the same destinations, or uses or wants to use telex, photocopiers, fax, viewdata, teletext or electronic mail. Clearly, this line of thought is linked to decisions about hardware (see next chapter), but since writing communications and networking software is most unlikely to be within the repertoire of the amateur programmer, it is relevant here as well.

Any business which depends on inter-office and intra-office communications should be asking critical questions about the capacity of any software to cope with its present and likely future requirements (see also Chapter 15). To ignore this is to invite excessive expenditure on a proliferation of desk-top appliances which usually prove incapable even of talking to each other. Some anticipation of what is imminent in the next few years may even suggest that, for some businesses, it is sensible to defer computerization. In the interests of avoiding *two* major office reorganizations where one will be bad enough, it may be better to wait until communications software and hardware has progressed a little further and to use the intervening period for staff and management training.

Who will use the system?

Anticipation of who will use the system, and, in particular, consciousness of the users' previous experience of and attitudes towards computers is vital. Not only will this affect the likely success and acceptability of applications software; more fundamentally, it indicates how important friendliness in the operating system is to the acceptability of the installation. If the main users are expected to lack keyboard familiarity, this could be an argument for considering one of the more sophisticated operating environments treated in the last chapter. Alternatively, if the users will not need to alternate between different software packages, this may simply argue for very careful selection of applications software. It may be possible to 'wrap up' the system's mechanics in such a way that the user is blissfully unaware of the complications. For example, a microcomputer can be made to behave like a terminal to a remote mainframe without the user having to realize that he or she is dealing with a different operating system at the other end. This approach obviously runs into difficulties whenever things go wrong, but in between times it may sustain a lot of conviction.

How much computer expertise does the organization possess?

Some medium-sized businesses already have full-time professional programmers in-house; many large ones have fully-fledged data processing (DP) departments. This is in many ways a great advantage when it comes to dealing with obscure manuals and salesmen who spout technospeak – but there are drawbacks too, and these are discussed in Chapter 12.

Small businesses are more likely to be embarking on computers for the first time, and for them the question is who in the firm needs computer expertise, to what level and how to acquire it. This is discussed in Chapter 14, where I argue that in *any* organization which uses a computer, at least one person should have some knowledge of elementary programming. (The rationale is given on page 268.) For the present purpose, the issue is whether a programmer within the business can or should learn to write useful programs as an alternative to buying in software or commissioning it specially. Clearly, the answer depends on the nature of the business as well as its size, but, in most cases and for small operations, the answer is no, *unless* the firm has other reasons for wanting to invest in training professional programmers.

In other words, for most businesses, the value of having some programming skills in-house is not for the purpose of software production but for general familiarity and possibly for adapting or customizing commercial software. It may prove valuable even for such apparently simple activities as setting up a spreadsheet or matching a printer to a word processing program. The decision made about the level of programming capability to be aimed at within the business will not only affect decisions about the purchase of applications software; it will also determine what systems software is needed and, especially, what programming languages and utilities. It would clearly be wise for whoever is to learn computer programming to be involved in the choice of both kinds of software, because he or she will be the one 'at the sharp end' when things go wrong.

It is preferable, but not essential, that this person learn something of the language in which the applications software is written. It is highly desirable that whatever language he or she learns is at least available on the computer chosen, so that simple routines can be tried out and the person can keep in practice. Most beginners' courses offered in the UK are in BASIC, of which some dialect is offered on virtually all microcomputers. So management should not underestimate the person's need for further training if applications software is purchased in some quite different language (which may nevertheless be a wise decision). Nor should the value of **software tools** and utilities be underestimated if any serious program modification is to be undertaken.

What is the likely future of the computer?

The business which is only just thinking about whether to buy its first computer may be reluctant to think about the second or subsequent purchases; but to avoid a series of expensive mistakes, it is vital to anticipate. I will deal with hardware upgrades in the next chapter, but the question of commitment to software may be more important. In a world in which hardware costs are falling rapidly and manpower costs rising, having to discard an outgrown microcomputer system after a few years may be a catastrophe, not so much because of writing off the initial £3000 or so spent on the hardware, but because of the much greater manpower investment in learning to use the system and transferring all the business's records to data files. After what was said about disc operating systems in Chapter 2, you will realize that, in general, a disc from one micro will not be readable by another micro. You may also have guessed that, even on the same hardware system, data files produced by one program will not generally be usable by another. Although there are ways of overcoming this problem, some of them depend on getting help from people who are knowledgeable about both the hardware and software involved. If you are just changing from one supplier to another, the supplier whom you are abandoning may not see any great incentive to help you even if he is still in business. In the past, unhappy experiences of this kind have caused many microcomputer purchasers to regret their early decisions.

> ### Self-check
>
> The raw material cost of a 5¼-inch floppy disc is around £2–£3. Suppose that it is densely filled with vital customer information which would otherwise have to be re-keyed by hand and then laboriously checked. What is the value to the business of being able to reproduce that disc in the necessary format automatically? Choose one of the figures below to indicate the order of magnitude:
>   **a** £2.50
>   **b** £25
>   **c** £100
>   **d** £1000

ANSWER

Admittedly, you haven't enough information to calculate precisely: you would need to know how much data was on the disc (100 K or 800 K?), how many keystrokes the operator did per minute, how much he or she was paid, how many mistakes he or she made, how long it took to check the work and what were the cost consequences of any undetected errors. However, the point of the exercise was not to test your mental arithmetic but to check whether you had an order-of-magnitude feel for what was at stake. If you said **b**, you need to refresh your memory on disc capacity or rethink your ideas about the speed at which keyboard operators can work (and if you answered **a**, you need to re-read the question!). Either **c** or **d** could be plausible, depending on the circumstances: a 600 K disc could hold all the text in this book (around 80,000 words) and might take a typist who could sustain 50 words per minute for 27 hours as little as a working week to retype. However, even a week's wages is far too low an estimate, as this makes no allowance for errors, proof-reading or corrections. Conscious errors made while keyboarding are estimated at around one per 250–350 keystrokes, and *unconscious* errors at around one per 1000 to 3000. So even to replace text on a disc could easily cost in the order of £100 or more.

However, text is the easiest and cheapest form of information to replace: it is *much* quicker for the typist to enter than numerical data and code letters, and typographical errors usually change only the spelling rather than the meaning. In the compressed coding used for account information, on the other hand, errors may be impossible to spot by inspection and much more damaging than a mis-spelling if they slip through. Sophisticated verification procedures are essential and the cost of residual errors may be high. Thus, somewhere between £100 and £1000 is by no means improbable as the economic cost of replacing a *single* disc.

This imaginary costing exercise should help to underline the value of software which transcends the limitations of the first hardware system that you buy. The point stretches much further than the mere replacement of data files, of course. Any software used by a business – no matter how friendly or easy to use – takes a certain commitment of time and energy to learn to use it and usually a much greater investment to gain the most from it. On top of this, there is an unquantifiable but very real cost attached to adjusting the business's method of operating to suit the way the software operates (from the redesign of stationery to the overhaul of paperwork systems).

For example, learning to use word processing software may take a secretary anywhere from a week to a month (or much longer if one includes knowing all the finer points). To buy cheap wp software which is machine-specific and cannot be adapted to a more powerful system is to waste that investment. If transportable software is available – even at a much higher price – it could be a better buy, other things being equal. More extreme examples are afforded by accounting systems and data base systems which may be more intimately identified with the operation of

Acquiring software

the business. They only emphasize the general point – that commitment to a software system can only sensibly be made with a view to the future of the total system. In the long run, obsolescent software is a greater risk than obsolescent hardware.

Tactical decisions

Once the issues above have been thought through and discussed internally, there are a number of secondary decisions to make. The first is perhaps where to obtain the software: Figure 44 shows some of the options.

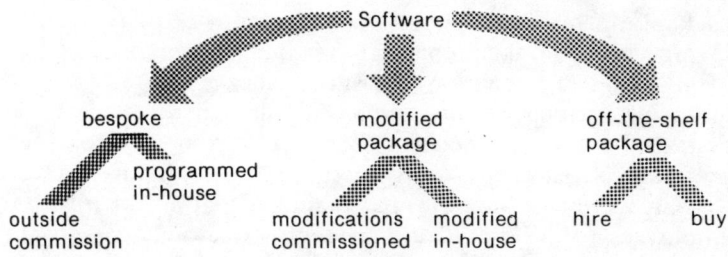

Figure 44. Some options for acquiring software

Clearly some of these options may be pre-empted by strategic decisions already made. Let us look at two examples, following the left-most side of Figure 44 first. If highly integrated software is required to cover all areas of a business's activity, there may be no alternative to a bespoke system. And unless there is extensive professional programming expertise in-house, there may be no choice about commissioning it from outside. Having come to that conclusion, the business should not necessarily rush out and commission, of course. A sober weighing-up of the likely benefits of computerization may suggest that they will not justify the costs involved. There is no shame in deciding to wait until the business can afford the system it needs – or until new developments allow what it needs to be provided more cheaply. This may be much wiser than rushing into a compromise which is half-baked and fails to satisfy.

Pursuing the right-most path down Figure 44, a business may decide to use a computer experimentally for a number of separate and discrete applications for which low-cost packages are known to be available, to build up its computer expertise without incurring major expenditure. This is a perfectly defensible strategy as long as the risks identified above are borne in mind, and as long as the capabilities of the system are reviewed regularly before an unjustifiable effort is invested in a system which may have a limited life.

Choosing a package

Because of the high proportion of readers who may decide that packages form part of the solution to their needs, it is worth saying a bit about the preparatory work needed before deciding to buy. (Indeed, the option of leasing a package before or instead of buying it should be considered if it is an expensive one.) The first step is to write down a list of your own requirements, preferably separating those you regard as essential from those that are optional. Suppose, for example, that a firm with 100 employees (of whom 70 are paid weekly) wants a software package to deal with its payroll.

> *Self-check*
>
> Write down three features that you would regard as essential and two which are desirable.

ANSWERS

Essential
1 Can store details on at least 150 employees (allowing 50 per cent margin for turnover and expansion);
2 Uses a master file with employee details loaded separately, so that standing information never has to be re-entered (except for changes);
3 Can cope with monthly-paid and weekly-paid employees in same operation and prints out payslips automatically;
4 Can carry forward tax and national insurance totals to end-of-year and print out necessary paperwork.

Optional
5 Can calculate Statutory Sick Pay (SSP) automatically;
6 Can do coin analysis for cash payments.

You may have given quite different answers here: **6** is redundant if no one is paid in cash and **5** might be regarded as essential. The point of the exercise is to illustrate the *sort* of features that should be specified by the business. This list will be invaluable, whether the next step is to ask an independent consultant for his advice, to consult a dealer or to send for details of packages which you have seen advertised or reviewed in magazines. It not only focuses on what the business actually wants, it provides a valuable reference point for comparison. By conveying to the dealer or consultant that you know what you want, it also makes them more likely to check their facts before assuring you that any particular product will provide it.

Comparison of the claims made for the packages with your own list of requirements should help to narrow the choice to a manageable number, and you will then be ready to see some of this software in action. Buying by mail order is not to be recommended unless you are confident of the source and have managed to see the program in action, perhaps through a colleague, a local college or a 'reference sell' (a satisfied customer who allows the supplier to give his name to prospective purchasers – whose motivation *may* be perfectly above board). In general, the ideal reference is someone in your own line of business who is actually using the package in the way you intend. It is worth going out of your way to contact such a person and find out what problems have been encountered.

Let us assume, however, that you are going to visit a dealer having done the necessary groundwork. Don't just watch a demonstration, ask to operate it yourself. Take with you data of the kind you would hope to process and ask how easily it can cope. Take an employee, associate or anyone you can enlist with you; while one of you is occupying the salesman, the other has a breathing-space to try out the package, size up the staff and remember the questions you might otherwise forget. Ask to see the manuals and try to decide if you'll be able to understand them unassisted. Ask about support: who will install the software, set it up the first time around (often the hardest part of all with packages that have to be customized), train the users and deal with problems when they arise? How flexible is the package and how easily could you or someone who knew its programming language modify it? Can it be listed and copied (**backed-up**)? If not, how many copies are supplied and how can they be replaced if damaged or lost? Will it work with your particular printer and, if so, will it control its special facilities (such as bold printing or underlining) easily? Can it be linked to any other software you might need?

Needless to say, the answers you should expect depend on, among other things, the price of the package (which influences how much profit the dealer has to finance customer support and training). Even so, it is important to word your questions carefully. Avoid questions beginning, 'Can it do . . .?' because the answer will almost invariably be 'Yes.' This is not dishonesty on the dealer's part but reflects the fact that, in the computer world, almost any system *can* be made to do almost anything if a skilled programmer spends enough time on it. The dealer may overestimate your expertise and you may underestimate the amount of work implied in the 'Yes'. It is better to ask questions like, 'How much would you charge to change . . .?' or, 'How quickly could you train someone who is frightened of computers like me/my secretary to . . .?'

Remember also to ask about the future: if tax or SSP law changes, who modifies the package and who pays? Some packages are designed to help the user to modify them as necessary and are well-documented for this purpose. Others are deliberately made impossible for the user to modify or copy and may have a maintenance charge of so much per annum. Depending on the scale and quality of the package, this may not be a bad sign: it at least indicates a continuing commitment to updating which is in the consumer's interest. If the package is newly on the market, and if it is protected so that it cannot be listed, ask about an 'escrow' contract: this means that the coding is lodged with a bank and released only if the suppliers go into liquidation.

Finally, should you decide on the middle path shown in Figure

44 (modifying a standard package), be warned of the heavy responsibility borne by the documentation. If a software house or dealer does the modification and everything works perfectly – don't relax! Make sure that you have exhaustive and comprehensible documentation for all the changes, otherwise grave and perhaps insoluble problems will arise when an error emerges – perhaps in several years – or when an external change means that further modifications are essential. If the package is modified by an in-house programmer, there is an even greater risk of continuous small changes being made which may never be fully documented unless it is someone's job to insist on it. Programmers are fallible human beings: they may forget what they did or move on to another job. If your business depends on modified package software, you cannot afford to be left with an undocumented mystery on your hands. Whatever the attractions of having modifications made to standard packages, there are also considerable risks unless it is properly managed.

9 | Acquiring hardware

Although I have emphasized the importance of choosing software before hardware, the two are obviously interdependent. This chapter looks at some strategic decisions, suggests a procedure for identifying the principal requirements and then proposes ground-rules for those who intend to buy a microcomputer system.

Strategic decisions

Buy, lease or bureau

Traditionally there are different ways of acquiring a computer, depending on its size, price and supplier. Before the arrival of the new generations of mini- and microcomputers, leasing used to be much commoner: for many small firms, it was the only means of access to computing power other than the bureau option (considered below). Price trends have worked against leasing: not only has outright purchase become much cheaper (both in relation to the value of money and computer performance), but leasing rates have also increased dramatically. For example, the rental charge on an IBM 360 increased more than six-fold in only ten years. If you contemplate leasing a system, compare costs and also check carefully how long you will be committed for: you might end up paying excessive rates for obsolescent equipment.

If you need access to more memory and processing power than you can afford to buy, there are two other options. One is to investigate a secondhand purchase. Needless to say, this can be a high-risk path, and the cost saving must be major for it to be worthwhile. The risks can be reduced by going to a major supplier or broker, getting a comprehensive maintenance agreement and thoroughly checking your entitlement to, and ability to benefit from, new software releases. It would also be advisable to get an independent assessment of the hazards and hidden costs from a consultant: some computers might be too expensive even if they are *given* away. Although some used machines have given their second owners years of reliable service at a give-away price, this is not an area for novices.

Another option is to use the services of a computer bureau. You may remember that this was an option used by the DTU (see page 79) on a batch-processing basis. The bureau had proposed that the DTU should install a terminal and use the bureau computer on a time-sharing basis, getting immediate results down the telephone line for local printing. Although this would have cut down the postal delays involved in the batch arrangement, costs would have been still higher and DTU would still have lacked control over the priority assigned to their work.

Self-check

In general, what are the advantages offered by the bureau solution to set against these problems?

ANSWERS

The client needs very little knowledge of computers; all the responsibility rests with the bureau, which has to sort out all the problems and deliver results to the client's satisfaction. The client does not have to make a capital investment in computer equipment or accommodation, nor does it have to spend time on investigating hardware and software options, nor staff straining. (Bear in mind that DTU – in common with an increasing number of modern organizations – had other reasons for wanting to develop its own computer expertise.)

It is easy to locate bureaux – for example, through a classified telephone directory or a computer users' yearbook in the public library. It is harder for the beginner to assess their quality, charges and experience. Factors like geographical convenience should carry some weight, because visits may be needed in the early stages and if things go wrong. Assessing what the likely charges will be is almost impossible without a trial run, since the user is unlikely to know how many computer units will be needed to run his job. If a bureau wants an initial payment for setting the job up, or insists on a minimum period for the contract, take independent advice on whether they are likely to give good value for money. At the very least, ask for reference users and visit them.

Where to buy

This section assumes that you have decided to buy a new microcomputer system. Where do you start? There are three main possibilities:

- Original Equipment Manufacturer (OEM)
- Systems house or software house
- Microcomputer dealer

OEMs are the major established names in the computer industry who manufacture, service and market their own hardware and software. Check the location of their nearest local office and compare their prices with those of local dealers. Service and sales staff are likely to be knowledgeable on the OEM's own products and should give good service. However, the purchase price is likely to be high and you may end up tied into OEM products when there are cheaper and better alternatives. For example, IBM customers were locked into the use of expensive and slow printers long after better printers were sold much more cheaply by independent suppliers.

Systems houses and software houses may provide a complete hardware and software service tailored specifically to a client's needs. Some offer a consultancy service which can be costed separately. Until recently, most dealt only with minicomputers and mainframes. Some have adapted very quickly to the microcomputer world, others share the attitude of ignorance and disdain that is all too common among computer professionals. Check whether their experience with your scale of business is adequate before committing yourself. You should expect a high level of professional experience in software systems, and the purchase price may reflect this.

Microcomputer dealers vary extremely widely. Some are superbly professional, take a pride in being abreast of new developments in software and hardware from all sources, provide excellent support to their customers and have considerable expertise in software development. They deserve to survive, and usually do. Others are basically dealers of some other kind (perhaps in office equipment or hi-fi) who have just decided to diversify (cash in) and may know less about computers than you do. There is no law against this, and unfortunately only about half of such dealers go out of business each year. You would probably be safer buying from a chain store or hypermarket, where there are no pretences. If you do not trust your business acumen to distinguish between these two kinds of dealer, you had better seek a supplier elsewhere.

Independent advice

The value of independent advice to a first-time user cannot be over-emphasized. It is sometimes difficult to convince a businessman who would never dream of consulting anyone before spending several thousand pounds on a company car or photocopier to hesitate before spending a lesser sum on a microcomputer. Nevertheless, computers *are* different; for many people, coming to terms with them requires rapid mastery of a whole new vocabulary, foreign concepts and an unfamiliar sub-culture. Second, the low purchase price of many microcomputers is deceptive. If a system is not powerful enough to deal with the business's needs, it is worse than useless. However cheap it was, it is unlikely to justify the effort that has to be invested in making it work at all. A poor choice of photocopier may give disappointing copy quality, but it doesn't take long to learn to press the right button. Furthermore, it's unlikely to make the business grind to a halt every time it breaks down.

At the very least, a business or profession should seek advice from within its own circle of contacts. There is bound to be someone who has relevant recent experiences, and usually colleagues are only too willing to share their discoveries and horror stories. Such people are helpful in that they are likely to know from the inside how you operate, but they may not know a great deal more than you about computer systems. What is really dangerous is when they don't know how much they don't know! If you have an accountant, find out if he or she has specialized in computers or can recommend someone you should talk to.

However, to get professional computer advice you are likely to have to pay – perhaps by the hour or by the day. You may pay surprisingly little for advice which can save you a great deal of money and a lot of wasted time. There are various sources of such advice: computer consultants, local college or university contacts and government agencies. Consultants may operate on an individual basis or as part of a firm. Find out about their qualifications and ask for previous client references. Ask whether they have any connection with any manufacturer, publisher or dealer: some 'consultants' offer their services free and instead take commission on systems sold.

Self-check

What is the disadvantage of such an arrangement from the client's viewpoint?

ANSWER

The advice is biased from the start. Such a person could hardly recommend a system from a different source, much less that you should not buy a computer at all – irrespective of what you really need.

If in doubt about a consultant's status, ask for a written assurance of independence. Find out how he or she charges for their advice and then ensure that you get good value by careful preparation (see section below on *Stating the requirements*). Advice from a well-qualified and professional consultant should be both authoritative and tailored to your own situation.

Another possibility is to contact a local college, polytechnic or university. Many have units which specialize in giving advice to business and industry. In any event, you may wish to assess whether they offer a programming course which might suit you or an employee. Many colleges encourage staff to collaborate with local businesses, and if computing is a major interest there may be expertise you can tap among the staff – who may look on your experience as valuable case-study material. A college offering diplomas and degrees in computer studies might suggest that your business accept a student on placement; the student gains real-life experience of applications of business computing, and you gain the student's programming and operating experience.

Various government agencies can direct enquirers to sources of help: the Department of Industry's Microprocessor Application Project CONsultancy scheme (MAPCON) encouraged manufacturing businesses to use a professional consultant by refunding consultancy fees under certain conditions. The DoI also maintains a list of authorized consultants, as does the National Computing Centre, an industry/government non-profit-distributing agency.

During 1982–4, a network of over 150 Information Technology Centres (ITeCs) was established jointly by the Manpower Services Commission and the DoI. Each ITeC is sponsored by a company or a group of companies and collaboration with local businesses is an integral part of its operation. ITeCs help unemployed young people to find jobs by training them in information technology; their staff usually have a good range of experience in business and industry and each ITeC has a considerable collection of computer equipment. More than half operate some sort of open access, so it would be worth visiting one to see whether there is scope for cooperation. (See Appendix 1 for contact addresses for all of the above.)

Multi-user, networked or stand-alone systems?

Small businesses may find a single micro adequate to their needs initially, but they need to think about the future when several users may need access to computing facilities at one time. Other businesses will want to start with a multi-user configuration. Either way, there is a strategic decision to be made about how to go about it: is it better to provide central computing facilities, in the form of a powerful mini or mainframe connected to a number of terminals, or a network of micros sharing resources like hard discs and good printers? Or is it better to provide a number of complete **stand-alone** microcomputer systems and handle the communication between them by non-electronic means when the need arises?

Clearly the answer depends on the kind of work being done. If users regularly need access to large common data files, or to communicate with each other, there may be attractions in the centralized solution. If the applications are diverse and there are advantages in local and immediate control over processing and print-out, a number of stand-alones may be preferable. If minimizing the cost of each station while maintaining fast response time within each program is the criterion, a network of micros with shared additional resources may be preferred. It all depends on the trade-offs between different features, and professional advice should be sought for each case. The decision taken has implications for policy on back-up and maintenance and other management issues discussed in Chapter 12. It is related to the general question of how the system will develop in future: there are limits on the number of users that each system can cope with before performance deteriorates and an upgrade is needed. The next section discusses what the professionals like to call the **upgrade path**.

The upgrade path

The system's ability to expand in future is vitally important, since it allows you both to recover from early mistakes and to adapt to changing circumstances. To buy a system with no upgrade path is to buy into a dead-end: it is a guarantee of obsolescence. Cheap micros often fall into this category, and thus may be more expensive than they seem in the long run. Others may be able to have both their internal and external memories increased dramatically and can also increase their processing power, perhaps by connection to a second processor or even a mainframe. The ability to add communications interfaces may also be important for any business which will develop its telecommunications.

Once the business has decided which way it is likely to grow, an expert can lay out the hardware options and their pros and cons. The position taken on decentralization (raised above) will be one ingredient in the decision. In thinking about possible upgrades, put out of your mind any inhibitions based on current costs. Hardware which only a few years ago was unthinkably expensive is now commonplace in shop windows. Let your imagination be restricted only by what your business is likely to need, not by what it might cost.

Stating the requirements

Before anyone can help you, you will have to help them with a written statement of your requirements. If a large system is being contemplated, this might require a lengthy document running to hundreds of pages. Even for a small system, a crisp summary under each of the headings below will help your thinking and save a lot of time and false starts.

1 Brief statement of nature of your business (with special mention of information flow or problems, e.g. between different offices);
2 List of major items of existing office equipment (e.g. telephone system, photocopier, telex);
3 Role foreseen for computer system (who will use it, for what purposes, how often, etc.);
4 Immediate and future applications envisaged (e.g. spreadsheets and word processing immediately, possible electronic mail in mid-term future).
5 Some details on present applications:
   - data to be stored and method of coding used at present
   - indication of volume and frequency of processing
   - reports required: size and frequency
   - any non-standard features (e.g. export customers, mixture of VAT status).

Ground-rules for microcomputer systems

Although I have recommended the use of professional advice and the adoption of a systematic approach to acquiring hardware, the last section of this chapter recognizes that some readers simply won't have enough time or money to follow this path in full. They are overwhelmingly likely to be microcomputer purchasers. It is hardly likely that anyone would contemplate buying a minicomputer or mainframe without taking professional advice.

However, at a time when department stores, chains of retailers and stationery suppliers are selling microcomputers in sealed boxes, as if they were ordinary consumer durables, many small business people may be tempted to start on computerization by this route. Since it is at the stage of their first purchase that people most need advice, some pointers are given below on the memory and processor requirements. These rough guidelines are in no sense a substitute for specific advice from someone with detailed knowledge of your business.

The initial selection of input and output devices is less critical than the memory and processor, since upgrading can usually be done in stages and without disabling the whole system. For example, a better-quality monitor may simply be plugged in to replace the original choice as long as the memory and processing capacity is there to drive it. However, if future applications might involve any of the less common forms of input or output – like voice recognition or graphics tablets – it is vital to mention this possibility at the outset.

Internal and external memory

The basic rule here is to buy as much as you can and at least twice what you estimate you currently need. If the system can easily have both its internal and external memory expanded, the consequences of being wrong are obviously less disastrous. But any system upgrade is liable to mean disruption of the business, and any computer system that is working well is likely to breed expansion. So err on the generous side – you will never regret it!

Acquiring hardware

No rule of thumb can substitute for a careful review of requirements, but here is a helpful starting-point for a firm supplying goods on credit (provided by the National Computing Centre):

> For a rough estimate of the minimum number of characters for your files, add up the following and multiply the total by 3:
> Number of customers times 150
> Number of suppliers times 150
> Number of different items supplied times 90
> Number of supply lines actually stocked times 50

Self-check

Suppose that Rothespierre Wines have 4000 customers, handle wine from 8 different sources and supply 30 different wines, of which 16 are in stock at any one time.

1 Use the above formula to estimate the minimum number of characters for their files;
2 Convert this into a storage requirement in K;
3 What does this tell you about their memory requirements for **a** their mainframe computer and **b** their reps' microcomputers?

(If you don't want to do the arithmetic, you may want to consult the answer given to **1** before proceeding to **2** and **3**: but try to make an order-of-magnitude guess first.)

ANSWERS

1 Following the formula, we have:
```
  4000 × 150 = 600,000
     8 × 150 =   1,200
    30 ×  90 =   2,700
    16 ×  50 =     800
              ─────────
                604,700
                    ×3
              ─────────
              1,814,100
```

2 To store nearly two million characters would require at least that number of bytes, i.e. 2000 K, or 2 Megabytes.
3 Not a great deal! One of the problems of such rule-of-thumb formulae is that they have to be based on assumptions about how the software is organized which may not apply to individual cases. For example, Rothespierre's mainframe needs to calculate monthly commission for their ninety sales reps, so there must be a storage allowance for that, including some provision for carrying forward total for tax purposes, and perhaps also a sales performance profile for management purposes. You would have to know more details to estimate this properly.

The above calculation highlights the fact that the number of customers is the dominant factor in determining storage requirements. Thus, it is important to look carefully at what customer details really need to be stored in the computer and how compressed the coding could be without making them too difficult to interpret. By contrast, there is little point in economizing on storage of the other information since it consumes such a small proportion of the total.

The formula says nothing about the reps' micros, of course; these might need to store only prices and product codes for thirty wines, together with the rep's identification code. If the rep entered the customer code from a pre-printed customer card, the micro would not need to store customer details at all.

The NCC formula is bound to have limitations: it tries to give a simple answer to a complex question. Nevertheless it provides a useful starting-point for this kind of estimation and should help you to see why you need some idea of what the software has to do in order to make any realistic estimates of what hardware you need. Obviously if you are committing yourself to a system with no easy upgrade path, you should allow a generous margin (at least 100 per cent) if you want to avoid the trauma and expense of having to replace the whole system once your business has outgrown the storage space.

The processor

The choice of processor is less important than you might think, because it is the part of the system least likely to affect the user. In interactive use, much of the time the processor is waiting for user input or dealing with output or retrieval from disc. The speed of these operations is more important in determining the overall performance of the system than is the bench-test figure which says how many thousand or millions of instructions the processor can do per second.

Thus, although you might think that the arrival of 16-bit processors in the early 1980s made micros based on 8-bit processors obsolete, you would be wrong. With suitable software, an 8-bit machine may be able to out-perform a 16-bit: the first 16-bit machine (the ACT Sirius) actually ran MBASIC at around one quarter the speed of an 8-bit machine, because the processor spent so much of its time disentangling the systems software, which had been adapted from that of an 8-bit system. Many 16-bit systems have disc operating systems which are no faster than the old 8-bit DOSs, thus negating the advantage of faster processing.

Nevertheless, 16-bit machines can address more RAM: typically, 256 K in place of 64 K. For this and other reasons, it is likely that 16-bit machines will prevail in the future. But no one with a satisfactory 8-bit micro (or a good working system of any kind!) should rush lemming-like for the latest innovation. For a start, there is a vast library of tried and tested business software available for 8-bit micros – an area where it may take 16-bit micros some time to catch up. First-time buyers who want to hedge their bets should consider buying a twin-processor micro which can run both 8-bit and 16-bit software (preferably with a combination of operating systems that allows both kinds of software to be mixed on a single disc).

Self-check

After a general look at the strategic issues, let's have a look at a concrete example. A freelance architect is about to buy a computer to do his accounts and routine letters. Eventually he thinks he may use it to help him design house extensions as well. He has shopped around in local stores, combed the advertisements in the computer magazines and come up with a shopping list, which he shows you:

- Rairsinc microcomputer with 1 K RAM £50
- Microvitesse high resolution colour monitor £350
- Laski stereo cassette recorder £60
- Lorivetti daisy-wheel printer £490

He says: 'All this stuff is brand new, so it'll be covered by guarantees and the prices are pretty keen. But, look, you know more about this than me. Am I buying the right things? But don't tell me to spend a penny more. £1000 is my ceiling.'

What advice would you give him?

ANSWER

This kind of problem has no clear-cut answer and advising people about choice of equipment is a specialist (and often thankless) task which you may be better to avoid unless you know a lot more than this book contains. Nevertheless, even on the basis of what you've read so far, you can help him to avoid the worst mistakes.

In the first place, you might try to persuade him that buying piecemeal on mail order is a high-risk approach and that, if he values his time at above tuppence ha'penny an hour, it is also a false economy. Commend the value of establishing a good relationship with a reputable dealer, both to guarantee the initial purchase (and to simplify the process of getting the system to work) and as an insurance against future difficulties.

If £1000 is really his ceiling, the system he is proposing could not even be switched on. Just for the cables to connect this lot he would need another £40 or so, not to mention paper for the printer. Furthermore, even if he is going to write all his own programs, he will need blank cassettes to store them. However, he would do better to save until he can afford a disc system, as he will soon discover while waiting for cassettes to load and save. In

Acquiring hardware

practice, unless he wants to give up architecture and go over to computer programming (at which he may or may not be able to earn a living), he should budget to buy commercial software, anyway.

The microcomputer he has chosen might be all right for a child learning to program, but it is totally unsuitable for his needs. 1 K is far too little RAM, and a machine at this price is unlikely to be upgradeable or to work with the accessories he will need, like printers which can cope with full-width paper. It certainly would need additional memory before it could support medium or high resolution graphics, and since it cannot produce colour, the expensive monitor would be a waste of money at this stage. A monochrome monitor (or even a television) would be a better choice.

If he is determined to rely on cassettes as external memory, a stereo cassette recorder is less likely to be suitable than a cheaper mono machine. He might also consider economizing on the printer. Although a dot-matrix will not give him quite the standard of a daisy-wheel, a good one can give presentable results, will save him money and can print much faster when quality does not matter. Furthermore, if he ever gets around to the design work, a good dot-matrix can produce working drawings of serviceable quality.

Here's an alternative shopping-list for him to consider. The budget does not permit a CP/M system, but the Rico has been chosen because it is easily upgradeable to CP/M at a later date. There really isn't enough allowance for buying software in this list, but £150 might buy a simple word processing program, a low-price spreadsheet and a graphics package. This would allow him to start getting useful work out of the system, and he could add more software later:

- Rico microcomputer (48 K RAM) £150
- Cate single disc drive (100 K) £200
- Monochrome monitor (or tv set) £100
- Soneps dot-matrix printer £300
- Cables, discs and paper £100
- Software £150

10 A taste of programming

The purpose of this chapter is very simple: it tries to give you an idea of the *kind* of activity involved in computer programming. It does this through two actual examples of programs in BASIC. Even if you've never seen or understood a computer program before, don't skip this chapter. First try the self-assessment quiz below. It should dispel any myths you may have heard about what it takes to make a programmer. Whatever your score, it is worth having a good look at the rest of the chapter, even if you decide not to do all the self-checks. At least then you will know what's involved and this should help you to decide (a) whether you want to persevere with programming and (b) whether there's anyone else in your organization who might make a suitable person to develop this skill.

Let me first emphasize some of the things that this chapter does *not* attempt to do. It does not try to teach you to program. Nor does it try to explain the minor changes you would have to make to adapt these two programs (which are written in BBC BASIC) to suit any of the hundreds of other micros which you might have access to. Nor does it develop these programs into a polished form to make them conform to standards for good software; this issue is discussed further in Chapter 11. The programs are not important in themselves as end-products; it is the *process* of putting them together and taking them apart that is valuable. They were written specially for this chapter, to give you a taste of programming.

Self-assessment quiz

The quiz below is not meant to be taken too seriously. Don't be put off if you get a low score: if you are really keen to learn to program, you can take a proper aptitude test which will be more

A taste of programming

reliable than a quick self-test like this. But the quiz has been tried out extensively; usually people who get high scores find that they enjoy programming.

1 Can you tell if a word is spelled correctly just by seeing if it 'looks right'?
   a no
   b sometimes
   c yes

2 If you needed the answer to a long arithmetic calculation, are you more likely to
   a use a pocket calculator?
   b work it out using pencil and paper?
   c try to get someone else to do it?

3 Do you like to find out how household gadgets work?
   a usually
   b sometimes
   c hardly ever

4 If you read a report or article where the same word is used repeatedly, would you notice if it sometimes had a capital letter and sometimes didn't?
   a yes
   b perhaps
   c no

5 Do you consider that you approach problems logically and systematically?
   a no
   b sometimes
   c yes

6 Do you spend time doing crosswords, puzzles or playing games like Bridge or chess?
   a no
   b occasionally
   c yes

7 Look back at the self-check on page 53. Did you
   a write down answers and check them afterwards?
   b look ahead at the answers?
   c skip the self-check?
   (If you didn't read Chapter 2, score **c**.)

8 Do you tend to leave tasks unfinished
  a only if interrupted
  b sometimes
  c often

9 Are you known to your friends and colleagues as someone who keeps on pegging away at a problem until you have solved it?
  a yes
  b maybe
  c no

10 Are you interested in how a program actually works?
  a not really
  b moderately
  c yes

Scoring

Question:	1	2	3	4	5	6	7	8	9	10
Your answer: a	0	2	2	2	0	0	2	2	2	0
b	1	1	1	1	1	1	1	1	1	1
c	2	0	0	0	2	2	0	0	0	2

Give yourself points for each answer as shown in the table above. If your total was under 6, it does not sound as if programming is likely to appeal to you. Between 6 and 12 points, you are probably well enough suited to programming if you have the time and inclination. With 13 points or more, you sound like just the kind of person who might enjoy programming.

Although the quiz doesn't claim to substitute for a proper aptitude test, it is based on sound evidence. You *don't* need to be good at maths to be a good programmer; good spelling is more relevant than your arithmetic. A logical mind helps, and you *do* need a lot of patience and persistence. You definitely do *not* need a university degree or any academic qualifications – although if you're going to produce business software you should certainly take a recognized course, preferably one leading to a qualification. It is perfectly all right for an amateur to dabble in programming for his or her own satisfaction. But if you are going to *use* your programs for serious purposes, it is important to develop a professional approach and get into good habits right from the start.

The rest of this chapter is devoted to two working programs. The first is a very simple wages calculation program, which we will build up in stages, each version being an improvement on the last. The second program is introduced in more complete form; it generates computer jargon with which you can confuse your colleagues, and can also be adapted to other subject-matter. Thus you can get a taste of programming both 'from the bottom up' and 'from the top down'.

The WAGES program

Suppose that you wanted to instruct a computer to calculate wages for an employee who had worked, say, 36 hours times £2.40 per hour. To make the processor multiply, you use * instead of times (×). The PRINT command causes the result to be displayed on the screen. Thus

PRINT 36 * 2.4

would give the result

86.40

telling you that the sum due is £86.40. Here you are simply using the computer as a pocket calculator. It is not a program; the calculation is done immediately and the instructions are not stored.

Each line of a BASIC program starts with a line number, and the processor executes (acts on) these in numerical order. You don't have to type them in the right order, and you can leave gaps between numbers. It is usual to number the lines in tens, so that it is easy to add intermediate instructions when making changes to programs. The first line of a program normally contains its title and perhaps a remark to describe its purpose.

REM is an instruction to the processor to ignore whatever follows on the same line, so REMs are a convenient way of leaving messages for humans without upsetting the computer. Here is a complete program:

WAGES

    10 REM WAGES: a program to calculate wages
    20 PRINT 36 * 2.4
    30 END

Line 20 does the calculation and line 30 tells the processor that the program has finished. To write this program you could type the instructions in any order and you could have called the lines 5, 10 and 15 (or 100, 200 and 300) if you preferred.

However, it is important to realize that the processor simply stores the instructions ready for action; nothing would actually *happen* until you typed RUN. And unless you had only just typed the program in, you would first have had to load it from tape or disc. That means typing LOAD 'WAGES' (since WAGES is the name by which the computer knows the program) followed by RUN. In practice you could have worked it out for yourself more quickly! However, we can now set about improving this very simple program.

Let's make a new program called WAGES2 to print the employee's name alongside his or her pay. First there will have to be a PRINT command: this sends everything enclosed in inverted commas to be printed on the screen, including spaces and punctuation. Line 20 will prompt the user to type in the employee's name. Line 30 uses an INPUT statement; this takes whatever is typed at the keyboard and stores it in a box. INPUT can be used to read in numbers or letters, but you need a different kind of box in each case. INPUT n would put a number in a box called n, but to store a string of letters you'd have to call the box something like n$ (pronounced n-string). Line 30 actually calls it name$ (name-string) to make it clear what the box is for. Line 40 then calculates the wages and stores it in a box called pay.

Finally, line 50 prints a sentence in four parts. There are two sections in inverted commas: 'This week's pay for' and ' is £', and these will be displayed exactly as they are shown, *complete with blank spaces*. The other two parts of the PRINT instruction are variables which will be different each time. name$ contains whatever the current name happens to be and is enclosed between semi-colons simply to prevent it from being printed on a new line. Finally, pay contains the current value of wages (86.40 in this case) and is printed immediately after the £ sign.

WAGES 2

```
10  REM WAGES2: a program to calculate wages
20  PRINT 'What is employee's name?'
30  INPUT name$
40  LET pay = 36 * 2.4
50  PRINT 'This week's pay for ';name$;' is £'pay
60  END
```

'Boxes', like pay and name$, which can have different contents each time the program is run are called **variables**. In technical language, pay is an example of a numeric variable and name$ of a string variable, i.e. the processor stores numbers and letters in different ways. Many dialects of BASIC limit you to single capital letters for variable names (e.g. P or N$); in BBC BASIC it is easy to choose names for each variable that show what they mean.

A program that couldn't deal with different pay for different employees wouldn't be much use. So let's see how the program could be made to deal with deductions. To keep things simple, we'll ignore income tax and national insurance at the moment and just consider union dues as an example. Suppose there is just one union and that all employees who belong to it contribute 40p per week. We'll need a question to ask whether the employee is a member or not. If yes, deduct £0.40; if not, by-pass the deduction.

WAGES3 (below) shows how this can be done. Lines 10 to 30 are as before, but then I've re-numbered line 40 (because I'm planning to add more in the next version). After the new line 80 is another REMark, to explain what lines 100 to 130 do. The answer to the question in line 100 is stored in a$ ('a-string', another string variable). Line 120 tests the contents of a$: if it's N (for no) the program jumps to line 140, thus by-passing the deduction for union dues. If it's Y, line 130 reduces the value of pay by .40 and then proceeds to the same print statement in line 140. (NB. When testing the contents of a string variable, you need the quote marks shown around the 'N'; similarly, if you wanted to put the word 'employee' into e$, you'd have to say LET e$ = 'employee', using quote marks.)

WAGES3

```
10  REM WAGES3: a program to calculate wages
20  PRINT 'What is employee's name?'
30  INPUT name$
80  LET pay = 36 * 2.4
90  REM deductions
100 PRINT 'Does s/he belong to the union? Type Y for yes or N
      for no'
110 INPUT a$
120 IF a$ = 'N' THEN GOTO 140
130 LET pay = pay − .40
140 PRINT 'This week's pay for ';name$;' is £'pay
150 END
```

Self-check

Suppose that you have just typed in this program and are running it for an employee called Fred Smith, who is a union member. Write down everything you will see on the screen from the moment you type RUN.

ANSWER

For clarity in the answer, I have shown what the processor sends to the screen in lower-case letters and what you would type in capitals. In practice, the processor would display name$ in whatever form you typed it.

   What is employee's name?
   FRED SMITH
   Does s/he belong to the union? Type Y for yes or N for no
   Y
   This week's pay for FRED SMITH is £86

This is still a very inflexible program, because it assumes that all employees work for the same number of hours and get the same rate of pay. So let's see how WAGES4 could ask for the hours to be keyed in and cope with the results. A PRINT statement could ask for the number of hours to be typed in and stored as a variable – let's call it hours. If there is a standard overtime rate of 'time-and-a-half', we must multiply overtime hours by £3.60. So we need a test of whether 'hours' is greater than 36 and, if so, **GOTO** some new lines which multiply the excess by 3.6 and store the result in a variable called, say, overtime. Pay can then be calculated as the standard amount plus overtime.

WAGES4 can be developed from WAGES3 simply by adding extra lines. Here is one way of writing lines 40 to 70 with the test for overtime in line 70. (This is known as a conditional jump, because it is not always obeyed; the jump happens only if the condition 'hours>36' is true).

```
40  PRINT 'How many hours did s/he work this week?'
50  INPUT hours
60  Check for overtime entitlement
70  IF hours> 36 THEN GOTO 160
```

Self-check

See if you can write down instructions to calculate pay with overtime and then return to the deductions bit of the program. Start with line 160.

ANSWER

One way of doing it is:

```
160  LET overtime = (hours − 36) * 3.6
170  LET pay = 36*2.4 + overtime
180  GOTO 90
```

There are many other ways you could have done it which would still work. You could have combined lines 160 and 170, or put in a remark at line 160, or let line 180 say GOTO 100 instead of 90, for example. Try to satisfy yourself about the effect of what you have written. It is important for the program to proceed to the deductions section whether overtime was applicable or not. Line 180 is an unconditional jump, which means that lines 90 to 150 are obeyed in any case.

WAGES 4

```
10   REM WAGES4: a program to calculate wages
20   PRINT 'What is employee's name?'
30   INPUT name$
40   PRINT 'How many hours did s/he work this week?'
50   INPUT hours
60   REM Check for overtime entitlement
70   IF hours > 36 THEN GOTO 160
80   LET pay = 36 * 2.4
90   REM deductions
100  PRINT 'Does s/he belong to the union? Type Y for yes or N
     for no'
110  INPUT a$
120  IF a$ = 'N' THEN GOTO 140
130  LET pay = pay − .40
140  PRINT 'This week's pay for ';name$;' is £'pay
150  END
160  LET overtime = (hours − 36) * 3.6
170  LET pay = 36*2.4 + overtime
180  GOTO 90
```

Self-check

Suppose that Fred Smith worked 48 hours this week (and is still a union member). Let's work out the dialogue that

A taste of programming

would appear on the screen as in the last self-check, but this time add program line numbers in the order they would have been obeyed on this particular run. Using the same convention as before, but with brackets around the program line numbers, the sequence would start:
(20) What is employee's name?
(30) FRED SMITH

Using the same conventions, see if you can complete it.

ANSWER

(40) How many hours did s/he work this week?
(50) 48
(60, 70, 160, 170, 180, 90)
(100) Does s/he belong to the union? Type Y for yes or N for no
(110) Y
(120, 130)
(140) This week's pay for FRED SMITH is £129.20
(150)

This program is beginning to do something useful now. In practice it would be irritating, because it ends after dealing with just one employee. You would have to type RUN every time you wanted to make it accept another employee's details. See if you can work out how to make it return to the beginning again.

Self-check

If we change line 150 to read
　　150 PRINT 'Another employee? Type Y or N'
can you suggest what the next three lines would be?

ANSWER

151 INPUT a$
152 IF a$ = 'Y' THEN GOTO 20
153 END

It is unlikely that you will have written your answer in exactly this way; try to work out whether the discrepancies matter or not. For example, you could call the variable where you store the answer to the question whatever you like, as long as it's the same in both lines 151 and 152. Again, it doesn't matter if you gave the lines different numbers, e.g. 153, 157 and 159, as long as they have not already been used, like lines 160, 170 and 180.

If you wrote out the complete WAGES5 program, it would be over 20 lines long. Even WAGES5, however, would be of no practical use to a business.

Self-check

Write down several reasons why not. (Some were indicated on page 205.)

ANSWERS

- Employees are paid at different hourly rates;
- Employees sometimes work less than 36 hours; WAGES5 pays them the full rate regardless;
- Very important deductions are not allowed for (e.g. tax and national insurance, other unions, etc.);
- Rates of pay change, and there may be different overtime rates for different employees;
- A wages program is of little use if you've got to type in all the information each time;
- Some or all employees might be paid monthly.

There are various other criticisms that could be made. Some can be overcome by minor changes, others need a major reorganization of how the program works. We will consider this further in the next chapter. Meanwhile, this should give you an idea of how a simple program can be built up.

In practice, adding enhancements in piecemeal fashion is a poor way to develop a long or complex program. It is much better to decide at the outset on all the facilities to be built in. Each section should then be worked out in detail and tested. The process is like making a ship out of watertight compartments: the result ought to be unsinkable! This approach is known as structured programming.

The JARGON program

To make a change, this section introduces a longer program that processes words not numbers. First we'll look at an introductory mini-program that simply picks an insult at random. Don't worry about the line numbers; they were chosen to correspond with the JARGON program that comes afterwards.

```
10  REM INSULT: a mini-program to introduce JARGON
20  REM First we reserve space for 5 words in an array called a$
30  DIM a$(5)
60  REM Then we supply the data i.e. the first set of words
70  DATA cranky, mean, devious, sly, stingy
100 REM Next, we use a loop to fill the array
110 FOR x = 1 TO 5
120 READ a$(x)
130 NEXT x
340 LET p = RND(5)
380 PRINT a$(p)
430 END
```

As line 20 explains, line 30 just tells the processor to make room for five words in an array (set of boxes) called a$; the boxes are called a$(1), a$(2), a$(3), a$(4) and a$(5). DIM is short for dimension – we're simply warning the processor how big the array will be. Line 70 provides the insults as DATA which will be read in by the READ instruction in line 120. Line 100 introduces a useful device called a loop. Often a programmer needs to make the processor obey certain lines over and over again. One way of doing this is to use a counter; in this case we've called it x, the letter that always seemed to stand for a variable in school algebra. It causes lines 110 to 130 to be obeyed 5 times over, filling each a$ box with a different insult. Line 340 uses the RND instruction – a handy way of picking a random number: RND(5) chooses a number between 1 and 5 and stores it in p. Finally, line 380 prints whichever a$ box was selected by the number p.

Computers in business practice

Now we're ready to look at JARGON; it's shown in its entirety opposite. Don't be put off by its appearance! See how much you can guess about how it works by comparing it with corresponding line numbers in INSULT. Look for overall patterns, too: lines 60 to 90, 140 to 170 and 210 to 240 all start with a remark that explains their function and then consist of a list of words. Other remarks are scattered through the program and may help you to get the gist of what is going on. Once you turn the page, all will be revealed.

This program contains quite a few new ideas, so don't worry if you don't follow it yet. We'll work through the main sections in order.

LINES 30 TO 50

These tell the processor to make room for 13 words in each of three arrays; they are called a$(1), a$(2), a$(3) . . . a$(13); b$(1), b$(2) . . . b$(13); and c$(1) . . . c$(13).

LINES 60 TO 90

These provide the first 13 words as data.

LINES 100 TO 130

This loop is obeyed for each value of x from 1 to 13 (i.e. 13 times altogether). As before, it reads one word from the DATA list into each of the a$ boxes.

Self-check

1 Which program line reads words into the c$ boxes?
2 What change should be made to line 110 if there were only 9 words to be read in?

ANSWERS

1 260
2 FOR x = 1 TO 9 (NB. 'for x = 1 to 9' would not work; the capitals are important.)

A taste of programming

JARGON
```
 10 REM JARGON: an instant computer jargon generator
 20 REM First, we reserve space for the words in three arrays
 30 DIM a$(13)
 40 DIM b$(13)
 50 DIM c$(13)
 60 REM Now supply the first set of 13 words for the a$ array as 'data'
 70 DATA multi-user, state-of-the-art, high-resolution, resident, menu-driven
 80 DATA user-friendly, ephemeral, hierarchical, on-line, serial-access
 90 DATA downwards-compatible, random-access, high-level
100 REM Next we use a loop to fill the first array
110 FOR x = 1 TO 13
120 READ a$(x)
130 NEXT x
140 REM Lines 150 to 200 repeat the procedure for the b$ array
150 DATA operating, integrated, sophisticated, communicating, animated
160 DATA dedicated,logic-seeking,electronic,screen-orientated,real-time
170 DATA relational,stand-alone,multi-tasking
180 FOR x = 1 TO 13
190 READ b$(x)
200 NEXT x
210 REM Finally put remaining words in the c$ array (lines 220 to 270)
220 DATA environment,system,procedure,application,database
230 DATA microcomputer,emulation,firmware,network,language
240 DATA graphics,protocol,routine
250 FOR x = 1 TO 13
260 READ c$(x)
270 NEXT x
280 REM Now we're ready to generate some jargon!
290 REM First, let's find out how many phrases the user wants
300 PRINT 'How many phrases? Please type a number.'
310 INPUT n
320 FOR k = 1 TO n
330 REM Repeat n times; choose 3 random numbers
340 LET p = RND(13)
350 LET q = RND(13)
360 LET r = RND(13)
370 REM Now print one random word from each array
380 PRINT a$(p);' ';b$(q);' ';c$(r)
390 NEXT k
400 PRINT
410 PRINT 'Do you want another set of phrases? If so, type Y'
420 IF GET$ = 'Y' THEN GOTO 300
```

214 *Computers in business practice*

If you've followed this much, you can probably see how the process is repeated to fill the b$ and c$ arrays. This means that you've understood more than half the program (to line 270).

LINES 280 TO 310

The user is asked how many phrases s/he wants, and the answer is stored in n.

LINES 330 TO 380

Here's a more sophisticated loop than we've met before: the number of cycles is a variable, n. So line 320 says that lines 330 to 380 are to be obeyed n times, with n taking whatever value the user just gave it.

LINES 340 TO 360

RND(13) is used to pick three random numbers between 1 and 13 (p, q and r) so as to take one random word from each of the three arrays. This might choose, say, a$(5), b$(12) and c$(2) on one occasion and a$(9), b$(1) and c$(13) on the next.

LINE 380

This looks complicated but it's just a PRINT instruction to make all three words come out on the same line with a space between each word. Without the semi-colons and spaces enclosed in quotes, each word would automatically have appeared on a new line, spoiling the effect of a phrase.

LINES 400 TO 420

PRINT by itself in line 400 just forces a new line. Line 410 is to save the user having to type RUN whenever s/he wants another phrase. Line 420 uses GET$ to get whatever is typed at the keyboard and repeats the process if the answer was Y.

high-resolution relational procedure
downwards-compatible electronic network
random-access integrated application
on-line operating language
multi-user communicating database
resident stand-alone emulation
high-resolution animated firmware
resident operating protocol
multi-user relational routine
menu-driven sophisticated protocol

Figure 45. Sample of output from JARGON program

Figure 45 shows a sample of the output from the program. (If you look at some computer magazines, you may find a surprising number of these phrases in active use!) Figure 46 illustrates a mechanical device for achieving the same purpose. You turn each of the cardboard discs until three words are lined up and then read off the phrase. This doesn't give you the sense of effortless power you get when they appear at the touch of a button, but it achieves the same sort of result without a computer. (You could also use random number tables to choose words from three lists.) The inner circle corresponds to the a$ array, the middle one to b$ and the outer to c$.

216 *Computers in business practice*

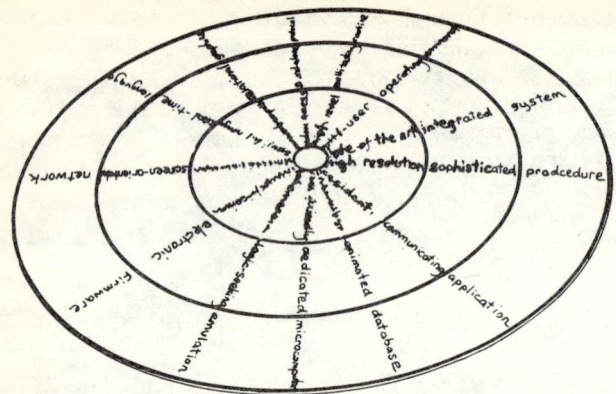

Figure 46. A cardboard disc jargon generator; each disc corresponds to an array in JARGON

Self-check

1 Which program lines correspond to turning the discs?
2 Suppose you wanted to increase the choice of words to 39 instead of 13. You could modify each disc by writing two new words in the space between the existing words (if you could write small enough). What corresponding changes would you need to make to the JARGON program?
3 Suppose you replaced the outer disc by a disc containing a different set of words altogether. What lines in the JARGON program would have to be replaced to make it correspond?

ANSWERS

1 340 to 380
2 **a** replace 13 by 39 in lines 30 to 60, 110, 180, 250, 340 to 360.
   b add another 26 suitable words to each of the DATA sections.
3 Lines 220 to 240.

A taste of programming

In practice, it is normal to collect DATA statements at the end of the program. As long as there are enough items of data (separated by commas) in the right order, the arrays will then be filled up in order. A more general program could read the words from a separate file of data which was not built into the program at all. That way, the same instructions could be made to produce random insults or compliments, or even nonsense poetry.

Self-check

What is the major limitation of the present program for more general use and how could you overcome it?

ANSWER

At present, the number of words to be chosen among (13 or 39) is built into the program and changing it means making lots of alterations (see answer **2a** above). To cope with different numbers of words you would have to start by asking how many words were to be used and store that as a variable – say W. Then all you would have to do is to replace 13 by W in all the lines identified in **2a** above. The program would then work with any number of words, as long as the data file provided enough to fill the arrays.

If you wanted a universal jargon generator, you wouldn't want to be limited to having three words in each phrase. This change takes a lot more thought, as it involves setting up a variable number of arrays, loops and random numbers.

However, you have now met enough of the basic ideas of programming to get some idea what it is like. Some people find it a fascinating challenge, others a boring chore. Either way, it's essential to know that getting it right takes lots of work and painstaking accuracy.

11 Serious software

If you found the WAGES program in Chapter 10 easy to understand, you may be tempted to think you can write your own business software. Think again. There is much more to serious programming than is obvious at first sight. Even if you have the necessary qualities, the amount of time it takes to produce robust and efficient programs takes many people by surprise. Writing long and complicated programs takes disproportionately longer than writing short ones. Furthermore, there is a much greater danger of unsuspected – and potentially catastrophic – errors. Even sorting out the ones you know about may prove a mammoth task. Time spent on programming and debugging is time taken away from managing the business, or whatever you did before you became involved with computers. This chapter underlines the differences between amateur programming exercises (useful for increasing your understanding of what is involved) and serious software (vital if you are going to depend on a computer to help run the business). This will take us some distance towards what has traditionally been known as data processing. If you have access to Roger Carter's Breakthrough, *The Business of Data Processing*, you will find greater detail on the points covered in this chapter, especially in his Chapters 4 and 5.

WAGES revisited

The employee's viewpoint

The WAGES program developed in the last chapter was a long way from being of any possible practical value. Some of the reasons were identified on pages 205–7. Others follow from the list of essential and desirable features compiled in Chapter 8 (pages 182–3). The next self-check asks you to consider the issue of a computerized payroll system from the point of view of the employee.

> *Self-check*
>
> Imagine that you are one of 100-odd weekly-paid employees in a business that is rumoured to be going over to a computerized system. You have no confidence in, or liking for, automation or computers and fear that in the longterm management may use the new computer as an excuse to reduce manning levels. List the qualities of the computerized system that management will have to convince you of before you are ready to accept a change from the familiar trip to the cash room.

ANSWERS

- *Privacy and security*
  Wages information should be confidential, and employees have the right to expect that sensitive information is protected from accidental or deliberate misuse. This may involve using a system of passwords for access to the software. Systematic maintenance and secure storage of back-up copies of data files is clearly vital.

- *Absolute reliability*
  Wages are a vital part of the contract between employer and employee. Unless they are paid on time and accurately, week in and week out, the system will not only get a bad reputation, but also lead to a rapid deterioration in industrial relations. To blame mistakes or delays on the computer is usually a pathetic attempt by management to shelter from its own mistakes. No one is likely to be deceived by it for long.

- *Flexibility*
  Computer programs inherently tend to be inflexible, unless special measures are taken to build flexibility into their operation. This is vitally important in any system where human

welfare is at stake. If employees have been in the habit of drawing holiday pay in advance and at odd times of the month, they cannot be expected to give up this privilege lightly. Employees in their first or last week of employment will rightly expect to be treated with the same promptness as other employees. No workforce will welcome a computer program that is said to be incapable of dealing with 'exceptional' cases like these. Similarly, if employees are accustomed to being paid in cash, they are unlikely to take kindly to having cheques forced on them by any computer system.

Practical payroll

Once you start to think about the practicalities of the system, there are a number of further requirements that make considerable demands on the program. Some examples are given below:

Minimum human intervention The program must be designed to deal with as many as possible of the foreseeable events which require human intervention. For example, the printing of hundreds of payslips could be a lengthy task and will normally be done on special stationery. What happens if the paper runs out part-way through the run? The operator who is supervising the print run should know how to change the paper supply, but is unlikely to have foreseen the problem or to know enough about the program to deal with it. So it is vital that the programmer builds in safeguards to make it very easy to restart an interrupted run and very difficult to omit or to repeat any employees' payslips in the process. It is unlikely to reassure a wage-less employee to know that his payslip was printed into thin air!

Automated inputs and outputs If a firm is to go to the trouble of computerizing their payroll, it will want to automate inputs and outputs to the system, as far as this is feasible. Large firms using clock cards for time-keeping may use a machine-readable type; smaller firms may be content with manual input from specially-designed time-sheets. Whatever the size of the organization, however, it is likely to want the system to produce payslips and other output automatically.

Self-check

Give some examples of 'other output'.

ANSWERS

Output might include cheques or credit transfers for employees with bank accounts, or coin analyses for employees paid in cash. In addition, the system might produce payroll reports for management – perhaps allocating overtime to different projects or departments. At minimum, records of payments made must be kept (either on disc or paper or both), in case of queries by employees or by Inland Revenue.

Validation and error reports At every stage of input and output, it is essential to provide checks on the validity of the data, to detect errors such as result from mis-keying of data from time-sheets or problems in processing (e.g. associated with an interruption as above). There is a whole variety of techniques for doing this. One of the simplest is to use a 'hash total': a nonsense total found by adding up all the digits relating to one employee, disregarding the fact that some are dates, others sums of money and others tax codes (and ignoring any letters that may occur). In the example below, the hash total can be worked out by adding up the sub-totals shown on each line in brackets. It comes to 50. If the hash total of the data after input is still 50, it is likely to be correct (though the possibility of two errors cancelling each other out cannot be eliminated this way).

- employee number: 24014 (11)
- date of birth: 24.02.48 (20)
- National Insurance: YM 340120 A (10)
- Hours worked: 41 (5)
- Tax code: 220L (4)
- Hash total: 11+20+10+5+4=50

Another validation method is to use **check digits**. These are digits which carry no useful information themselves, but are calculated from all the other parts of the entry and are thus likely to show up errors in any of them. International Standard Book Numbers all incorporate a check digit as their last digit. The way it is calculated is best shown by a worked example. The ISBN of the paperback edition of this book is 0 330 28448 7. Ignore the leading zero, which appears on all books published in Britain. Multiply 9 times the first digit, add 8 times the next, add 7 times the one after and so on until you get to 1 times the last digit. Divide the result by 11. If there is no remainder left over, the ISBN number is valid. Thus 27+24+0+12+40+16+12+16+7 = 154, which is 14 times 11 exactly. Thus a book with the previous ISBN (0 330 28447) would need a final 9 instead of the 7 to make it valid. (You can check this without recalculating the whole sum just by looking at the last two digits: $2\times8+7=2\times7+9=23$.) A final X is used instead of 10 when necessary. The publisher actually calculates the last digit from the rest when first assigning ISBNs. Whenever ISBNs are put into a computer, the program verifies them and automatically rejects any which do not check out.

Whatever technique is used for data validation, it is essential that someone responsible is available to deal with error reports. For example, a time-sheet claiming, say, 100 hours might be rejected as excessive for a single week, but could be valid if it represented hours carried over from a holiday weekend or included a multiplication factor for overtime.

Accommodating change within the program In Chapters 8 and 10, we mentioned the importance of keeping changeable data separate from the structure of the program. No business wants a program that has to be altered every time there is a wage rise, change in tax codes or new agreement on overtime rates. Equally, the bulk of the employee information will be fairly constant, and no one wants to have to re-enter the same names and addresses each month. The solution is have three separate entities:

    a the program itself, in which everything possible is treated as data to be read in separately;

b a master file of all the employee information, much of it invariant but including cumulative totals for tax, National Insurance and sick pay;

c an earnings input file that contains all the data needed to calculate wages for this week/month.

Unless the processor is to waste a lot of time matching up the data in **b** and **c**, the earnings input file must be sorted so that the employees are in the same order as in the master file. This sorting (e.g. into ascending employee number) is usually done as a separate operation – a kind of pre-processing of the earnings input file. The main stages in the processing of data are shown in Figure 47.

In practice, each of these might be subdivided further. In addition to the main payroll program, there might be several additional programs: one to provide a demonstration for first-time users; one to do jobs which only need to be carried out once a year, like printing tax certificates; another to customize the software to the requirements of that particular firm and the printer/stationery in use. The employee master file might be separated into information relevant to earnings (like rates of pay) and parts relevant to output (like bank account number), with cumulative information in a separate file again.

Enabling changes in the program Notwithstanding everything said above, software must be designed with awareness of the inevitability of change. No matter how well-designed the program is, unforeseen alterations in legislation may make software modifications mandatory. It is most unlikely that the original programmer will be on hand to make these modifications, so it is vital that another programmer has access to comprehensible and detailed documentation. Meticulous technical documentation – both within the program and on paper – can play a major role in enabling changes to be as painless and reliable as possible. Without a well annotated and complete listing of the program, the process of trying to make modifications can be endlessly difficult. That is why an 'escrow' contract (see page 184) may be advisable with an off-the-shelf package from a company that might go out of business.

224 *Computers in business practice*

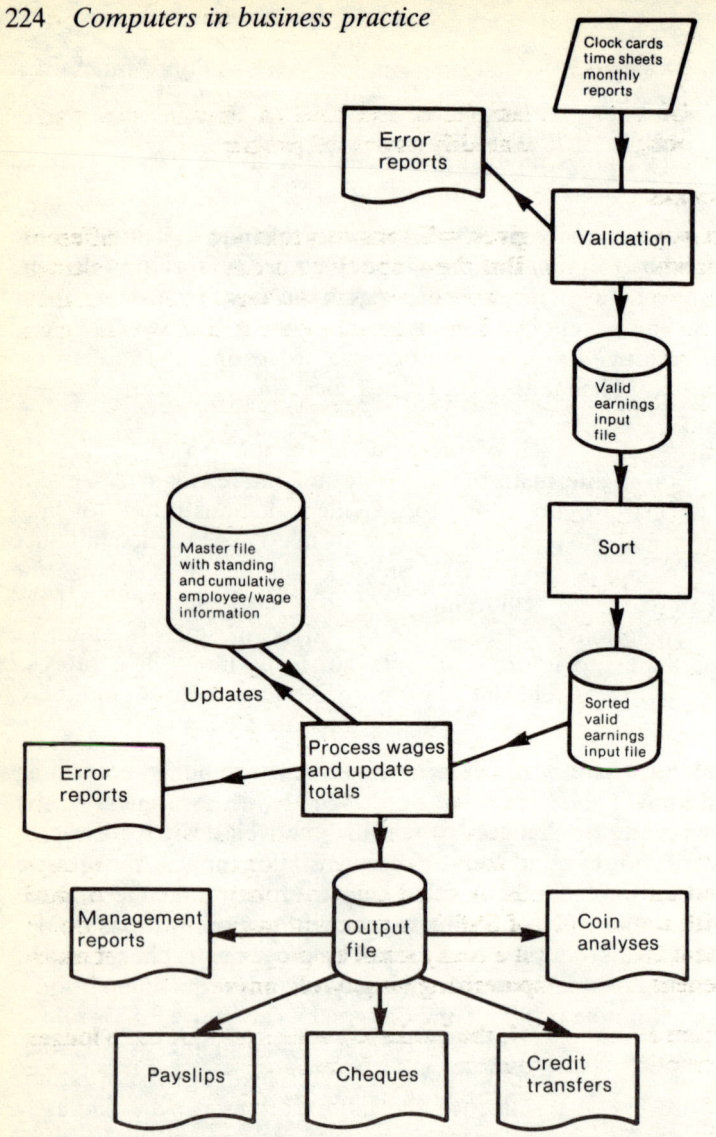

Figure 47. Flow-chart showing processing of data in a payroll program

Self-check

Give three examples of the kind of changes that might oblige a firm to modify its payroll program.

ANSWERS

You may well have given valid answers that were quite different from what follows. But there are three areas of recent change which you may or may not already know about. In any case, they are so important that I have given rather fuller answers than usual below:

a The Statutory Sick Pay (SSP) legislation that came into force in April 1983 demanded changes in payroll software to cope with it. Employers could be liable to fines if they do not keep proper records. Depending on the package, quite major re-writing might be needed, because employees' entitlement depends on average weekly earnings over the eight weeks prior to the last pay day before the incapacity began. Some software does not store the information in the necessary form, especially if the qualifying period spanned two financial years. Although many suppliers were offering SSP upgrades at extra cost, some of these were based on a mistaken interpretation of the legislation and many did not do more than 20 per cent of the SSP paperwork. For example, some packages could not cope with the hardest part of the regulations (dealing with those that do not qualify for SSP) and others expected the employers to do all the work of identifying the qualifying days and linking periods. A small employer may not have to deal with many cases of SSP in a year and might not mind doing them by hand. But a really small employer may not get much benefit from computerizing his payroll, anyway!

b From January 1984, the banks' clearing system was no longer accepting credit vouchers in the form in which payroll software had hitherto produced it. One of the strong attractions of computerized payroll had been the ease with which an ordinary computer printer could produce batches of old-style bank giro credit forms ready for direct processing by the banks.

From 1984, these were no longer acceptable without a computer readable code line (detailing the account number, sorting code and transaction code).

Machine readability requires a special typeface, either MCR or OCR. Few printers can handle magnetic ink for MCR, and the dot-matrix printers in widespread use with microcomputers cannot achieve high enough resolution for OCR. Even with more expensive printers, the positioning of the code line on the form is so critical that it would probably not be worth setting up other than for very long runs. There are various ways around the problem: employers can revert to paying by cheque; they can go over to the banks special credit input forms; or they can take a high-technology option with electronic fund transfer, using BACS (the Banks Automated Clearing Service). Whichever they choose, they will need modifications to the section of the payroll program that dealt with printing the giro credit forms.

c The 1983 Data Protection Bill, is expected to become law during 1984. It will oblige every business that uses a computer to store information about people, other than their names and addresses, to register itself. Although the Bill is principally designed to prevent misuse of data by large organizations, once it becomes law at least 1,300,000 companies and many clubs and charities will fall under its scope. They will be obliged to pay a registration fee and notify the Registrar what data they hold, how it was collected and how it is used. Changes in use will also have to be notified, incurring further charges. Failure to register properly can involve various penalties: fines of up to £1000, seizure of data and searching of premises. The same penalties apply if the employer fails to supply users with a copy of the data held on them within forty days of receiving a written request. Employers can also be punished if they fail to take adequate precautions against personal data being tampered with or falling into the wrong hands – for example, to be used for a purpose not disclosed both to the registrar and to the employees.

Clearly this legislation has implications both for the design of payroll software and the conditions under which it is used. The ease with which individual records from the employee file can be printed out is clearly important. Although a responsible employer should have little to fear from these provisions, they are a reminder that the days of unregulated computer data banks are over.

A real-life example

Just to underline the difference between serious software and the WAGES kind of program, have a look at a sample from a real-life program called Gemini Payroll (Figure 48 below). Don't worry about the details of what each line does – the extract is from the middle of the program, anyway. However, notice that most lines seem to combine a string of instructions; even so there seem to be an immense number of program lines (actually 12160 in all). This is a piece of serious software which took a skilled and experienced programmer around 600 hours to develop and test: this extract is from the 27th internal revision of the program – the form in which it was released.

```
8678IF A$="F"THEN GOTO8680
8679PAYE=PAYE-E(Z%,7)
8680IF PAYE<-50 THEN PRINT" "E$(Z%,0);"IS ENTITLED TO A " " TAX
REBATE OF"PAYE-2*PAYE:PRINT"ENTER Y_ TO CONTINUE OR N"'"TO GIVE NO
REBATE ":REPEAT:PROCI(22,1):UNTILI$="Y"ORI$="N":IFI$="N"THENPAYE=0
8690RETURN
8700P%=INT(P).FOR N=.25TO1STEP.25:IF P-P%>N THEN P=P%+N
8710NEXT:PAYE=P*T%/200:GOTO8675
9000DEFPROCPAYSLIP
9020DATANAME  :,REF NO  :,DATE  :,TAX CODE  :,STANDARD  :,OVERTIME 1
:,OVERTIME 2 :,OVERTIME 3 :,NONTAXABLE ADJUSTMENT :
9030DATATAXABLE ADJUSTMENT :,GROSS PAY  :,GROSS PAY TO DATE  :,TAX
:,TAX TO DATE :,EMPLOYEE'S N.I. :,EMPLOYEE&ER N.I. :,SSP :,TOTAL SSP
TO DATE :
9040RESTORE9020:READA$,B$,C$,D$:VDU2:PRINT':VDU1,27;1,69:PRINTTAB(30)
"PAYSLIP"'TAB(28);STRING$(11,"*")''':PRINTA$;NAME$TAB(40)B$;A$(2)''C$;D
ATE$TAB(40)D$;A$(4)':READA$,B$,C$,D$
 9045@%=&100090A:PRINTA$;NH;" Hrs @ £";E(Z%,0);TAB(40)B$;OT1;"  Hrs @
£";E(Z%,1)''C$;OT2;"  Hrs    @    £";E(Z%,2);TAB(40);D$;OT3;"  Hrs @
£";E(Z%,3):@%=&2020A
```

Figure 48. Excerpt from Gemini Payroll, an example of a piece of serious software

Gemini Payroll runs on my own micro (a BBC with only 32 K). One reason that the program **listing** is difficult to read is that unnecessary spaces and words are left out, and several instructions combined on one long program line, so as to save precious internal memory space for employee data. Even so, the program can only cope with 40 employees at a time. Part of the art of programming for small microcomputers is to make the best use of the memory space available while still keeping the program user-friendly. The Gemini program includes a demonstration data file, and makes effective use of the BBC's function keys to select options presented in a menu. Furthermore, by allowing you to list the program and telling you which lines to modify, Gemini actually encourages you to modify the program – for example, to customize the print-out routines to your particular printer.

This program is clearly meant for smaller businesses. Nevertheless, it includes all the major features such as tax, national insurance, standing and one-off adjustments to pay, holiday pay, end-of-year calculations, pay-slip and employee details print-out, payroll reporting and SSP recording (but not automatic calculation). It is easy to use and incorporates extensive safeguards against operating errors. Yet it costs only £40. In relation to the effort it would cost an amateur programmer to produce anything remotely comparable, serious microcomputer software is now available remarkably cheaply.

The process of programming

If you embark on the process of producing a program of any length or complexity without a clear plan and a systematic approach, you will very quickly find yourself in a terrible mess. No one should imagine that serious software can be typed straight in at a keyboard given a mixture of inspiration, intuition and good fortune. Serious software requires serious thought, careful preparation, frequent pilot testing and a systematic approach.

Professional programmers generally work on the following principles:

Serious software 229

- Global planning should precede detailed decisions;
- Decide what variables you are using before you begin to write the program;
- Build up the program in self-contained sections, with plenty of remarks (you can always remove some of these later if space is at a premium);
- Test each section individually before you try to test the whole thing;
- Draft the documentation long before you are near to finalizing the program;
- Test the program thoroughly before you try to persuade others to use it;
- Try it out on friends and colleagues first, then on strangers;
- Revise the program and the documentation often, in the light of comments, especially those from users typical of the group for whom the program is intended.

Self-check

Here are eleven different stages involved in designing a piece of serious software. See if you can arrange them in a sensible order. (You may want to use some letters more than once.)

  a Persuade strangers to try out program
  b Revise documentation
  c Write each section of program
  d Plan program in detail
  e Persuade friends/colleagues to try out program
  f Revise program
  g Decide exactly what program does
  h Plan overall flow of program
  i Write documentation
  j Make a list of variables and variable names
  k Test program as a whole
  l Test each section of program

ANSWERS

g, h; **d, j**; **c, l, f**; **k, i, f**; **e, f, b**; **a, f, b**.

Naturally there is no single best route for all occasions; the best path to follow depends slightly on the application, on the programmer's personal style and on whether he is starting completely from scratch or has a clear model in his mind or a written brief supplied by a client. Nevertheless, there is a fair degree of consensus on the general sequence given above.

I have separated the main blocks of activity by semi-colons. Within each block there would typically be some back-and-forth between the elements. In practice, the process of revising the program and documentation overlap and may be almost continuous. Furthermore, if a program is to be distributed or published, the process of trying it out on likely users and revising it in the light of their reactions (**a, f, b**) must be repeated many times over until all the known faults are eliminated.

Various forms of diagram may be helpful at the software planning stage. Most programming books advocate the use of program flow-charts. These show the main processes and decisions in boxes of various shapes linked by arrows, similar to the data flow-chart shown in Figure 47. Before trying to produce a program flow-chart of your own, look back at Figure 47 and notice that four different shapes of boxes are used.

> ### Self-check
>
> See if you can guess what process each shape represents. You have the following four to choose from:
>
> - data file
> - processing
> - output on paper
> - general input or output

ANSWERS

Figure 49 shows each shape labelled according to its function, and adds two shapes that were not used in Figure 47 (a data flow-chart) that might be needed in a program flow-chart.

Serious software 231

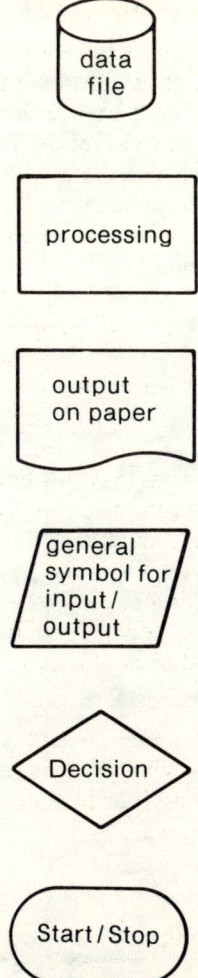

Figure 49. Some standard shapes used in data and program flow-charts

232 Computers in business practice

Self-check

So now you have met all the symbols you will need to draw a program flow-chart. Look back to the JARGON program on page 213 and see if you can rough out a flow-chart for it. Since its data is built into the program, you only need to show the different stages of processing.

ANSWER

Figure 50 shows one way of doing this. Don't worry if you showed less detail than this, or arranged the boxes differently, as long as you have shown processes that correspond to what the program does. I have added program line numbers to help you to see the relationships, but this is not customary.

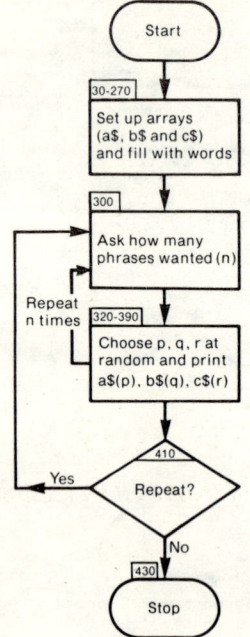

Figure 50. Program flow-chart for JARGON (shown on page 213). The numbers in the 'boxes' are program line numbers

Serious software 233

Finally, although flow-charts are appropriate for some programs, they can become unwieldy and hard to follow if they have to be split over a number of pages and have lots of arrows weaving back and forth. Some people prefer a structure chart in which each box spells out the details of the box in the level above. Structure charts are always read from the top down. Figure 51 illustrates a structure chart for the same program. You could go on spelling out each box in more detail until you reached the level of lines of program; I've just indicated how the third level might look. Whichever you prefer, some sort of diagram can be a great asset to following how a long or complicated program works.

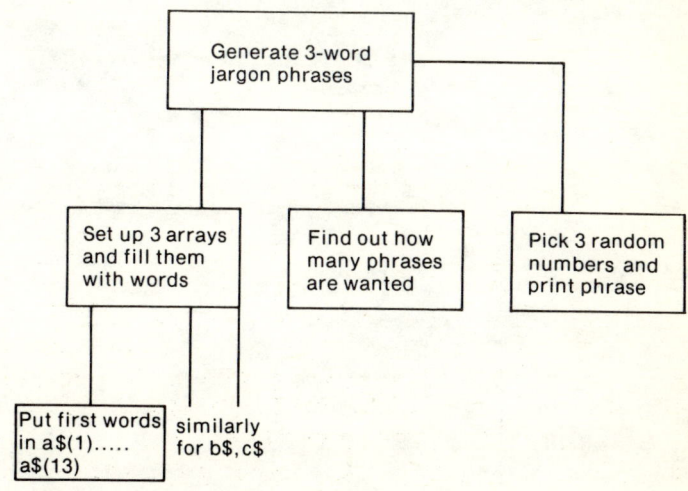

Figure 51. Structure chart for JARGON (compare Figure 50)

Part 4:
Computing and the organization

12 | Managing the computer

Introducing computers into a business is not a move to undertake lightly. Many first-time users find it a stressful and hazardous process and many 'experienced' businesses perpetuate their original mistakes (or make fresh ones) when upgrading and replacing their equipment. The case study summarized below documents a real-life example. If you have access to Roger Carter's Breakthrough, *The Business of Data Processing*, you may like to compare this with the case study (of a first-time user) that he presents in his Chapter 7.

Roberts's book club

What follows is a diary of the main events in the installation of their third computer by a large international mail-order book club. The organization started with a number of advantages: its staff were well-educated, the firm had satisfactory previous experience of computing, its office manager was a trained accountant, there was a clear and limited objective for the role of the computer and a single supplier was engaged to provide hardware, software and training. Although minor details have been altered to avoid recognition, on all significant points the diary is an accurate contemporary record. None of the problems has been exaggerated or invented.

Background

Since 1980, Roberts had used a leased computer for all its membership records and accounts. The typing pool had no dealings with the computer, producing mailings and all other documents to a high standard using electric typewriters with memories. The machines were reliable and the staff skilled in their use. However, Roberts's maintenance agreement with the suppliers was near to expiring, and the office manager felt that it would be more cost-effective to replace both the existing computer and the memory typewriters with a modern minicomputer. He engaged a systems house to recommend and supply both hardware and software. They proposed a shared-logic system with five vdu's, a fast daisy-wheel printer and several dot-matrix printers for drafts. These were to be installed initially all together in the pool, until staff had mastered the system. Afterwards, three secretaries would be moved out to departments to provide 'typing puddles', each equipped with a vdu and a dot-matrix printer 'to provide a better service to departments'. In the longer term, it was envisaged that these local terminals would provide departments with direct access to management information held on the computer. The agreement specified that the software house would install the system and provide initial training for as long as necessary. The diary begins two weeks after the new computer was delivered.

DAY 1

Memory typewriters disconnected and suppliers told to collect them. (Existing computer continues to do membership and accounts). Word-processing minicomputer system first switched on and tested by systems house.

DAYS 1 TO 7

Typing pool engaged in full-time word processing training provided by systems house. Urgent typing done on manual machines in departments. Mounting backlog.

DAY 8

Pool start work on backlog. Need for special pre-printed computer stationery discovered; talk of three-week delivery time minimum. Typing turnaround at least 100 per cent slower than before. Management complain about first products: dislike of typeface, complaints about layout and paper quality. Pool unable to produce indented margins, much paper wasted because name and address now appears on every page of long letters.

DAY 9

Production of 'carbon' copies impossible, so secretaries have to photocopy originals – a time-consuming job because paper wrong shape. Systems house offer to investigate customized multi-part stationery. Office manager rejects this on receipt of estimate, which he considers extortionate.

DAY 10

Typing of envelopes said to be impossible. (These were produced automatically under old system.) Secretaries looking wistfully at memory typewriters, still awaiting collection. Most junior member of pool persuaded to type envelopes while kneeling on floor using a spare manual typewriter for which there is no desk-space.

DAY 11

Letters now coming from pool on green-striped wide paper with sprocket-holes. Managers complain about lack of connection between priority attached to work when sent to pool and turnaround time achieved. Pool claim that it is 'impossible to predict' in what order the print-out will happen. Systems house consultants still spending all day, every day at Roberts, looking increasingly worried and starting to talk about pressure from 'other important customers'. Managers start having any 'prestige' correspondence typed by departmental secretaries, using pool only as last resort and for internal documents. Office manager looking increasingly unhappy.

DAY 12

Pool beginning to make inroads on backlog, largely because flow of incoming work reduced to a trickle. Secretary begins to tackle the filing of pool output, only to discover that computer print-out won't fit existing files. Everything starts to be photocopied on to true A4 paper prior to filing. Secretaries joke about getting fitter because of running up and down stairs to photocopier all the time.

DAY 14

Senior member of pool asked to begin work on the annual amendment of the membership leaflet and Christmas catalogue. Text all stored on magnetic tapes on previous typewriters. Systems house consultants nowhere to be found. Eventually one is located by telephone, but he declares task of transferring the text on to floppy discs 'impossible', though had been optimistic about compatibility when asked prior to

240 *Computing and the organization*

installation. Office manager chagrined to find he had not stipulated this as a condition in the contract. Laborious task of re-keying all standard documents on to floppy discs commenced. Pool typists allocated this job overheard muttering sarcastically about computers relieving humans of routine drudgery. Fitness no longer joked about; one secretary enters for marathon.

DAYS 15 TO 17

Typing pool closed down again for further training in layout, printer control and disc management.

DAY 18

Office manager checks photocopier usage and finds running costs have tripled since the arrival of the computer. Issues secretaries with scissors and instructions to trim print-out before filing. Contacts stationery supplier and is horrified by estimated cost of renewing files and other storage.

DAY 19

Things seem to be going well. Layout has improved, the green-striped paper has been replaced by plain white and managers can now detach their own sprocket-holes. Managers invited to visit the computer. Suggested that they might meet the consultant from the software house and 'think about' what other tasks they might like the computer to perform.

DAY 21

Most junior pool member complains of swollen knees and refuses to continue typing envelopes. This chore farmed out to departmental secretaries, who have taken to sarcastic jokes about artificial intelligence and computers that 'can't do addresses'.

DAY 28

Managers discontented after two cases of letters produced by pool ending up in wrong envelope typed by departments. Also complaining that letters no longer go out on personalized letterheads (i.e. bearing the name of the originating manager), because of batch printing. Ambitious manager has filled paper feeder with batch of 'his' stationery, so everything now goes out bearing his name. Other managers support a complete redesign of stationery to suit window envelopes, also to abandon personalized letterheads.

DAY 30

Managers meet consultant to discuss other possible applications for the computer. Receive three-hour lecture on computing (reasonably intelligible, but mainly confined to history and theory of computing, little indication of relevance to their needs). Question-and-answer session reveals communication problems; managers have limited knowledge of computing, consultant has little understanding (and many preconceptions) about how Roberts operates. Willing to cooperate in finding uses for the new computer, the managers agree to build up a statistical data base, though no one seems clear about why this would be useful or why it could not be done on paper. Consultant goes off to draw up estimate for bespoke software. Office manager looks extremely worried. Managers quietly sceptical of whether machine will ever cope with word processing to former standards, let alone be able to handle extra work.

DAY 32

First attempt to move secretary out of pool and establish 'puddle' in department. Some internal dissension about which secretary should go, and some ill-feeling within receiving department. Puddle secretary initially delighted when plugging into the system proves impossible (plugs incompatible), though her pleasure fades over the next four days with manual typewriter while systems house try to sort out cables and plugs.

DAY 35

Work starts coming back from pool with occasional lines transposed, like a badly typeset newspaper, and with paragraphs repeated and odd bits of garbage text. Consultant puzzled. Starts to talk about a forthcoming and improved release of the software. Office manager no longer even asks for the estimate.

DAY 36

Typing puddle now wired up and keying in rapidly. Secretary proud of her morning's output, relieved to have remembered correction techniques for drafts (which, since all on dot-matrix, have to be printed again on pool daisy-wheel). Goes to pool at lunchtime to pick up final print-out, is appalled to discover pool staff completely unaware she had sent work for printing; her morning's output is irretrievably lost. Unpleasant scene involving mutual recrimination, argument about procedures recommended during training to avoid this.

Computing and the organization

DAY 37

Puddle secretary phones in sick; her mother says she is suffering from nervous strain induced by computer.

DAY 40

Pool still badly behind, even though much more typing work now done by departmental secretaries, with the result that managers are having to do more of their own filing and telephone calls. Office manager tells pool to stop proof-reading work before returning it to departments. Level of errors leaps from negligible to several per page, so that letters can no longer be sent straight out. Some documents still affected by mysterious garbage, especially just after machine switched on.

DAY 45

Word gets around that managing director has instructed his personal assistant to type all his letters personally and send none to the pool. Widespread discontent among managers, pool and personal assistant.

Three months after the new computer was switched on, all processing of accounts and membership records was still being done on the 'old' computer and the office manager had shelved plans to terminate its lease. The memory typewriters still had not been collected by the leasing firm, and they became a source of serious embarrassment, as demands for their retention were increasing on all sides. The productivity from the typing pool was still less than 60 per cent of its previous level, the output less attractive and the error rates higher. Departmental secretaries were still doing more typing than previously and managers were doing more secretarial work for themselves as a result. The reputation of computers at Roberts was at an all-time low. By then, the installation had cost £80,000, with a commitment to a further £330,000 over the next five years, excluding specialized stationery, new filing and storage and possible additional bespoke software.

Self-check

On the basis of the facts above, write a couple of sentences about each of three (or more) major mistakes that Roberts's management seem to have made.

ANSWERS

Because there is so much to choose from, I have written about five in some detail. It doesn't matter if you have grouped your answers differently, as long as you have identified the critical factors: lack of preparation and failure to consult the people affected.

1 In the first place, Roberts disregarded the cardinal principle of the football manager: never change a winning team. The expiry of a maintenance contract might be a reason to look around for other maintenance arrangements, or to monitor the frequency of breakdowns, or to consider buying extra interchangeable equipment as back-up; it hardly justifies a massive commitment to a completely different system, just because a new computer is thought to be fashionable. In practice, it is perfectly possible that the memory typewriters would have given years more service and/or been capable of being interfaced to a computer-based system had there been any unsatisfied demand for computer facilities.

2 Having made the dubious decision to go ahead, at an early stage (and certainly long before the decision about a system was pre-empted) the office manager should have started discussions with the secretaries about which word processing facilities they regarded as essential and which desirable. They are the people who actually know about the day-to-day problems and routines and a sensible office manager would have learned from their comments and questions. If he were unable to convince them that the new system had enough advantages to justify the upheaval, he should have reconsidered his plans. At the very least, the systems house should have been obliged to make a presentation to the secretarial staff, explaining exactly how their work would be affected, demonstrating the new system on samples of print-out paper and using the actual

typeface that was proposed. The problems over paper sizes, layout, filing systems and typeface would have arisen naturally during a question-and-answer session; had they been anticipated at an early stage, they could have been solved. The serious difficulty over incompatibility between the typewriter's tape memory and the floppy disc could also have been identified before it was too late.

3 If the office manager was at all serious about making computing facilities available to departmental managers, he should have consulted them – and that means starting discussions at least six to twelve months before the new system was to arrive, not a month after! As it was, the meeting was a classic case of a solution looking for a problem, and it is not surprising that an ill-considered project resulted. If the statistical data base went ahead in the same fashion as the word processing decision, it is likely that a very overpriced and under-used facility would result. In any event, the starting-point of this should have been a careful feasibility study. This would have examined questions like whether there was spare capacity on the existing computer, how its running costs compared with the proposed facility, whether there was a real potential demand for computer facilities by management and, if so, what was the most economical method of meeting it.

4 Whatever the previous mistakes, the office manager was clearly remiss in his dealings with the systems house. Had he provided them with a written list of the requirements, samples of the existing typewriter output and a clear outline of the work routinely performed – indicating the importance of compatibility with the existing system, for example – he would have been in a strong position to negotiate an agreement which gave them a powerful financial incentive to produce a system with superior performance to the existing one. As it was, his failure to do proper preparatory work resulted in a severe blow to the organization's efficiency over several months and irreparable damage to his own credibility. Thorough homework, although time-consuming, would have been a good investment as it would probably have taken less time than he was obliged to spend in sorting out consequent

problems with Roberts personnel, with the systems house and with stationery, etc.
5. Apart from the defects of the actual equipment installed, there is room for doubt about its configuration. If decentralized word processing was really necessary, why was shared-logic chosen? Half a dozen stand-alone microcomputers systems capable of running word processing on top-quality daisy-wheels would have cost less than one quarter of the £80,000 spent. Moreover, these would have provided finished work where it was needed, instead of the uneasy compromise of draft quality on-the-spot and time-wasting running back and forth to the daisy-wheel printer in the pool. In addition, stand-alone systems are simpler to operate (because there is no need for sophisticated operating procedures, for communications between vdu's or for elaborate systems for arranging jobs in the print queue), so there would have been less time spent on training. Stand-alone systems also usually give greater job satisfaction, because the secretary sees each document through from keying it in to the printing-out of finished work.

Plan and review

Expensive, inefficient and badly managed computers are much commoner than most people realize. Not surprisingly, the people in charge of them tend to be reticent about how long it all took and what the total cost was. Many businesses could not give a convincing explanation of why they needed a computer, and indeed would have been much better off without one. If some of the businesses that rushed into computing had instead spent half the time on a thorough review and streamlining of their office systems and paperwork, they might have achieved a far greater improvement in their efficiency at a tiny fraction of the cost.

Understanding and improving the flow of information in a business is certainly an essential preliminary to computerizing it. But if the basic systems are a mess, computerizing them is likely to make an almighty mess! And having gone to the trouble of sorting out better systems in preparation for the arrival of a computer, some businesses should stop and ask themselves whether the computer is still really necessary. It may be that what the business really needed was the radical rethink of its practice, rather than the electronic processing.

Let us assume, however, that the business does not fall into this category and that it has carried out the steps recommended in previous chapters. It knows exactly what tasks the computer is to perform, has drawn up its list of requirements, identified suitable software and hardware (perhaps with the help of a consultant) and even found a reputable dealer. Let us further suppose that it has learned from the mistakes of firms like Roberts and done a thorough job of consulting its employees and involving them in the specification and selection of a system. Before the business commits itself to going ahead with a computer, it must plan its budget carefully.

Counting the costs

It is often said that computers are cheap but computing is expensive. There are significant hidden costs, and they have a habit of escalating in an unexpected way. In early 1984, it was commonplace to see advertisements like: '16-bit microcomputer complete with £1200-worth of software, only £1099'. Doubtless some gullible people will conclude that the hardware is effectively free! Before deciding on any computer system, however marvellous or cheap it seems, it is essential to make sure that the business really can afford to run it.

> ### Self-check
>
> Draw up a check-list showing headings under which hidden costs may arise. Separate one-off items that might apply only around the time of installation (e.g. a large system might need air-conditioning) from running expenses (e.g. daisy-wheel printers constantly seem to need replacement ribbons). Assume that the business has already counted the cost of *all* the hardware components (including cables, interfaces and printer accessories, like paper feeders, shredders, buffers and bursters, if appropriate) and all the

software (including initial training courses, if necessary). Try to include items which relate to staff time, as well as items of equipment.

ANSWERS

Don't worry if your list is not as long as mine, but do make sure that you've noted all the major 'extras'.

Possible one-off 'hidden' costs

- lost productivity while staff become familiar with system (in addition to time 'lost' in formal training);
- cost of keying-in basic data files or transferring them from other media;
- electrical wiring (extra supply points, 'clean' or smoothed supply);
- office furniture (extra desks, specialist computer furniture, vdu operators' chairs);
- air conditioning (larger systems only);
- acoustic treatment (e.g. if printer noise unacceptable);
- replacement filing/stationery redesign;
- secure, dust-free disc storage (possibly even fire-proof safe).

Possible recurring 'hidden' costs

- wage increments awarded to 'sweeten' staff attitudes or in recognition of more demanding/tiring work;
- maintenance contract (could cost 10 per cent of system price, but varies according to response time);
- insurance (against damage and/or breakdown);
- software maintenance/upgrade/modification;
- consumables (discs, paper, ribbons, replacement daisy-wheels);
- rental of additional office space to accommodate computer equipment and to store print-out, back-up copies of software/data, computer supplies.

Although some of these items do not apply in all cases, most businesses find that hidden costs add between 10 per cent and 25 per cent to the purchase price of a system in the first year, and perhaps 5–15 per cent in each subsequent year.

The critical period

Suppose the business has done thorough preparatory work, estimated all the costs carefully and is ready to go ahead. Considerable thought must be given to the first couple of months of computer operation – a critical period in the life of any business. (For simplicity, I am writing about first-time users here, but most of these points apply, at least in part, to a computer upgrade or changeover.) The timing of the installation should be chosen carefully.

Ideally, the computer should be installed at the slackest time of year but, if this is impossible, it may be sensible to take on extra staff to cover the routine load, or even to close down for a short period. Obviously, these precautions cost money, but that should be weighed against the hidden cost of having harrassed staff unable to benefit from training and failing ever to master the new system. People cannot be expected to learn a completely new set of skills or procedures while continuing to produce work at normal rates.

For applications like stock control, there may be extensive amounts of data to be transferred on to computer files. Months previously, a thorough process of updating and verifying this information should have been done, getting it all prepared in suitable form for trouble-free input. The process of adding codes, printing and verifying the accuracy is lengthy and vitally important. The whole job can be done by an outside firm (most suppliers can arrange this); the extra cost may be well worth it.

Applications which are central to the business's operation may well require a period of 'parallel running' – running the computer in parallel with the manual system it is to replace, and comparing results. This would be essential for something like a payroll and may be advisable in other cases. Different systems will require different periods of overlap and different levels of safeguard.

Before you sign

There are two main sorts of contracts that a business acquiring a computer system may consider signing. One is for the supply of hardware and software, the other for maintenance. If the hardware is a standard system and the software consists of off-the-shelf packages, there may be no written contract for the supply, in which case the usual principles of *caveat emptor* (buyer beware) apply. The supplier or manufacturer may offer a warranty (often only 60 or 90 days) and the purchaser has normal rights under consumer legislation. In addition, it is important to establish how far the supplier is able and willing (a) to provide on-site staff training and (b) to answer telephone enquiries, and what costs would be involved: (b) should normally be free.

On larger purchases, the supplier may have a pre-printed agreement that the purchaser is expected to sign. Although the dealer will probably mention it dismissively as 'just a standard contract', purchasers should read all the small print very carefully and if large sums are at stake consult a solicitor, accountant or computer consultant. Too many purchasers are overawed by the apparent finality of a printed document. In practice, it is often possible to negotiate more favourable terms. The wording of a pre-printed document is by no means sacrosanct: it may be modified by handwritten amendments or by an exchange of letters. A supplier may even be persuaded to type out a fresh agreement, although he is unlikely to do so unless a really large order depends on it.

It is essential to scrutinize the contract, because once signed it will normally be considered to constitute the *total* agreement between the two parties at law, superseding any previous correspondence or assurances. Even if the purchaser's list of requirements clearly states that the system must be able to produce at least 100 payslips per hour, this may have no legal significance unless the contract specifically refers to the list. Bear in mind that contracts are seldom looked at when systems are working well; the whole point of a written contract is to clarify the position when things go wrong, so they should be read in a pessimistic frame of mind!

Furthermore, standard contracts seldom cover both hardware and software. This is unhelpful to the consumer, whose reason for going to that supplier may have been solely his belief that this was the route to getting guaranteed performance for the whole system. Separate contracts for hardware and software throw the burden of establishing what is wrong on to the purchaser. It is also worth checking that the dates for payment are appropriate; no one should have to pay for hardware that has been promised but not delivered, or switched on but unable to do anything useful for lack of software. In practice, the purchaser needs a period of approval – *at least* a week, and perhaps a month or longer – to establish whether software is performing correctly anyway.

Opinions are divided about maintenance contracts. Some people assume that they are indispensable; if a business depends heavily on a single computer system, then down-time could be very expensive in lost business. Businesses may pay 10–15 per cent of the purchase price per annum in exchange for preventive maintenance and a guarantee that an engineer will be on-site within hours of a breakdown. Maintenance service may be provided by the manufacturers, the supplier or an independent maintenance firm. Incidentally, if supplier maintenance is agreed at the time of the original sale, it is important to check that the supply invoice total on which the percentage calculation is based includes only legitimate hardware items (i.e. not software or consumables) and that payment begins only after the expiry of the standard warranty period.

Some experts say that preventive maintenance is generally unnecessary with the present generation of equipment and simply interrupts operations unnecessarily. Some businesses make no maintenance agreement at all and are willing to risk having to take equipment back to the supplier in case of breakdown – a perfectly defensible business decision if there are several identical systems, if immediate repair is not critical and if the business is capable of diagnosing which bit of equipment is at fault. Indeed, with hardware getting cheaper and more reliable, while engineers' time becomes more expensive, there is often a good case for buying surplus equipment for back-up. That way, a slower standard of repair service may be perfectly acceptable. Another option is to take out breakdown insurance; this compensates the business for the direct costs of computer breakdown (provided it is not due to operator error), but not for lost business.

Decentralization and large organizations

Large organizations which already have DP departments might be thought to be at an advantage when it comes to computerization. However, a DP department may present senior management with a problem that requires firm but diplomatic handling. This is the attitude of the DP department, and especially of the department manager, to decentralizing computing within the organization.

DP managers are liable to the common human failing of wanting to protect their empire. Sometimes this leads them to attack blindly anything which does not fit into their view of the world. In the early 1980s, many large organizations ignored microcomputers as a result; and only belatedly started to take them seriously after IBM launched its Personal Computer and thus gave micros a spurious respectability.

Even so, many DP managers maintain a view of microcomputers which combines disdain and fear. Their dislike of micros often has a rational component: there are situations in which the micro's limited memory and slower processing speed is a serious limitation. But some DP managers are simply ignorant of the flexibility and economy available in recent micros. Newcomers to computing often underestimate how fragmented and hidebound the computer industry is: the 'expert' who is really knowledgeable and has practical experience of all sizes of computer is a most unusual person!

The DP manager's fear of the micro is to some extent an understandable by-product of its subversive nature; the cheaper and friendlier a computer, the more it threatens the empire that the DP manager has carved out. Again, there may be a rational component: the DP manager may rightly suspect that, whenever a department gets into difficulties with a poor machine or a badly-written program, they will be expected to help out. If the organization has allowed autonomous departments to buy a chaotic mixture of machines, without regard for compatibility or communications, they will naturally resent these demands. However, an enlightened DP department can take the initiative, instead of blindly resisting the *idea* of decentralized micros, recognizing that they can play a valuable role in the education of other departments and in the development of competence within the organization by pointing out the possible advantages and recommending suitable systems for linking to the firm's mainframe, mini or telephone system.

Top management should remember that the DP manager probably regards himself as a computer professional rather than a businessman. His attitude to computers is akin to the enthusiast's attitude to Formula One racing cars: more interested in their engineering and racetrack performance than whether they make convenient shopping vehicles. In particular, because the computer installation is accessible for the DP department, he probably underestimates the obstacles (both real and imaginary) that make computing services less convenient for other departments than they should be. Consequently, he may underestimate the attractions that departments perceive in having control of their own microcomputer rather than being dependent on centralized computing services.

Offering microcomputers to departments is not always the best course of action, anyway. Much depends on the nature of the organization and the attitudes and skills of its staff. But if a business decides that this is the correct path to follow, the DP department can be a valuable ally – or a powerful foe.

13 | The employee's viewpoint

The last chapter was concerned with managing the introduction of computing to a business. Good management entails good industrial relations, yet writers frequently talk about the introduction of computing entirely in terms of the problems of management. This chapter tries to redress the balance by focusing on the attitudes and welfare of the employee.

For simplicity, I will assume that there are a number of employees, possibly organized into one or more trade unions, and that the business is introducing a computer for the first time. Some of the points apply with equal force to a one-person business in which the 'manager' is self-employed. Many points apply to large organizations which already have computer departments but which are decentralizing their computing to involve employees who previously had no contact with the computer. In what follows, to avoid stating the obvious, I have left you to consider these cases for yourself.

Attitudes to computing
Spreading understanding

It is a truism to say that ignorance leads to fear, yet many employers seem unaware that much of the general public's hostility towards computers stems from a lack of understanding of what computers can and cannot do. James Thurber, an American writer, wrote about his grandmother's worries about electricity: she went around screwing light bulbs into every possible socket so that none of the electricity could leak away and be wasted! Many adults who have come to terms with mains electricity still have misconceptions and fears about electronics that are as groundless as Thurber's grandmother's.

254 *Computing and the organization*

Self-check

1 List some of the fears that employees may have about the introduction of computers.
2 Which of them do you regard as entirely groundless?

ANSWERS

1 There are so many myths and half-truths that it is impossible to anticipate what you may have written. Here is a selection which have some currency (though no one is likely to entertain them all!):
 a Computers will take your jobs away;
 b Computers will be used to check up on your work;
 c Computers are all connected up together and used to compile dossiers of information about your private life and financial affairs;
 d Computers are bad for your health;
 e Computers can read your thoughts;
 f Computers are so clever that humans will no longer have to think about their jobs;
 g Computers are so stupid that they send final demands for £0.00;
 h It is all very well for management: computers will never make an impact on their jobs;
 i Computers are basically malevolent;
 j You have to be clever/well-educated/good at maths to work with computers;
 k Computers are always making mistakes.

2 By the time you have read this much of this book, you should be able to dismiss **e** to **k** without much hesitation. **f** is fundamentally mistaken, because the need for human intelligence is usually greater when operating a computer-based system, though concern for the effect that computers have on the content and skills of a job is entirely natural (see below). Although **g** and **k** are widely asserted, they are almost invariably an excuse for human errors of various kinds: computer hardware is incredibly reliable, and software is much more

likely to be to blame. **i** is nonsense: computers are morally neutral, it is those who control them that are benevolent or malevolent. **j** can be dismissed out of hand: many of the most talented programmers and systems designers have little formal education and no special ability at mathematics. For most people, the main barriers are more likely to be lack of motivation, experience and confidence (see below).

The rest cannot be dismissed so lightly, as they contain at least a grain of truth. A later section in this chapter is about computers and health, and the effect of computers on employment prospects is a matter for continuing debate. **b** may be valid to some extent, though a wise employer will not attempt to introduce performance monitoring in a secretive or unilateral way. **c** expresses a genuine cause for concern; see pages 129 and 226.

The best method of helping workers towards a more realistic assessment of computers is through a programme of education and familiarization. This need not be organized formally, and ideally might be planned in conjunction with a trade union. The purpose is to inform all the employees about the principles on which the system works and to encourage them to handle the equipment.

Many employers are aware that their staff know little about computers but draw the shortsighted conclusion that it is not worth trying to explain what changes are proposed. Others fail to realize that the introduction of a computer is of far wider significance than simply to those who will work with it, and thus confine their training and briefing to a small portion of the workforce. Such narrowness of vision stores up trouble and builds the foundations of alienation and hostility towards the computer. Apart from the general value of good industrial relations, it is prudent to remember that if a business is to depend heavily on its computer system, it will become particularly vulnerable to industrial action.

Without subscribing to stereotypes, it should be recognized that certain kinds of employees often have especial difficulty in identifying with new technology: those without much formal education, older employees and women of all ages. This means that extra help may be necessary. For example, it has repeatedly been demonstrated that if their initial diffidence can be overcome, women often make very good programmers and operators. Their problems more often stem from lack of confidence – frequently made worse by a lack of early experience with electronic devices – than any shortage of ability. Their male peers, who may have no greater skills, are more often willing to risk 'having a go'. There may even be a case for having women-only sessions for getting 'hands-on' experience of computers, because of the overwhelming danger that, in mixed groups, the men participate while the women stand by and watch. No one builds their confidence with computers just by watching.

Privacy and security

It is understandable that employees may be worried about the computer as a potential electronic Big Brother. They may imagine that vdu screens can act as television cameras and that their performance is constantly being checked on. If a computerized payroll is being introduced, they may worry that details of their salaries and circumstances could fall into the wrong hands. Dealing with these anxieties is an important part of the preparatory period. It may be worth stressing the employees' rights to know what information is held about them and to underline the employer's obligation to restrict access to it. Management should explain the precautions it proposes to take to safeguard payroll discs and paper output – perhaps it will use a shredder for the print-out – and invite employees to suggest improvements.

Job satisfaction

Employees will rightly be concerned to know how the computerized system will affect their working conditions and job satisfaction. If a computer is used to automate the boring and repetitive parts of a job, a competent and ambitious employee will usually welcome its introduction. Remember, however, that an insecure and overstretched worker may dread the removal of the only parts of the job he or she feels really confident about.

Some employers make the mistake of exaggerating the ease with which the new system will give results. This not only depresses morale when employees are confronted by a 300-page manual to master before they can make the system perform; it also underplays the employee's contribution to the success of the system. In practice, many computer systems demand both discipline and flexibility from those who work with them. Many employees respond better if the new job is portrayed as a challenge rather than as a soft option. They may also be persuaded that learning to master the new technology is an essential key to continuing employability and promotion prospects. If the workforce is strongly organized, the attitude of the trade union activists can make an enormous difference to how the computer is perceived. This reinforces the argument for early consultation.

Employment prospects

It is possible for a trade union to cooperate with the introduction of a computer into an expanding business, even if it means avoiding recruiting more staff. It is almost impossible for a trade union to acquiesce in the contraction of the workforce unless voluntary redundancy happens to be in demand. Sometimes the introduction of a computer tends to replace a large number of moderately skilled jobs by a very small number of highly skilled ones and a larger number of very low-skilled ones. In these circumstances, employees will naturally feel threatened and tend to resist the introduction of computers. The transition to the new wages structure may have to be gradual; finding ways of redeploying and retraining displaced personnel may be both difficult and expensive.

Money

There is a very simple but seldom-used short-cut to 'sweetening' employee attitudes to computers: pay them more. Everyone is pleased to get more money, and some of their pleasure will rub off in kinder feelings towards the computer. If a job working with the computer is more demanding or tiring than the previous job, it may be only fair (and may also be unavoidable) for management to recognize this. If the computerized system has resulted in a substantial change in the firm's methods, it may be necessary to review the grading of posts around this time, as the previous differentials may no longer be appropriate. Since no one is likely to accept levelling downward, this course can add very considerably to the costs of computerizing, and it does so as a recurrent expenditure item. If the reason for introducing the computer was to increase profitability and competitiveness, it cannot be allowed to trigger an uncontrolled and inflationary series of wage demands. The possibility of increased wage costs must be considered carefully by management at the outset, when considering whether or not to computerize.

Involving and consulting

There is a delicate balance to be struck in the process of consulting the workforce. It is management's business to manage, not to abdicate decision-making in order to court popularity. Nevertheless, the process of involving the workforce in the decision to computerize should be started early and carried out with sincerity. The reason is not any trendy belief in cosmetic 'consultation' for its own sake: it is simply a matter of enlightened self-interest. Management – unless it spends its time doing its employees' jobs for them instead of managing – simply does not know enough about the day-to-day working practice of its workforce to anticipate all the problems which a computer may bring in its wake. The example of Roberts's book club (see pages 237–42) makes this clear enough. Of course the workforce is more likely to commit itself to a system in whose specification it has been involved, and that is an added bonus.

In a stimulating book entitled *On-line Computing for Small Businesses: Silver's Wall*, Silver *et al* (1983) describe an interesting technique whereby the systems designer can enlist the employees' cooperation in a thorough critique of his proposed system: the Pound Note Game. Their book is about businesses that commission bespoke software for on-line computing. A meeting is arranged between the systems designer and the employees in each department at the end of the working day. The firm provides coffee and sandwiches and, if necessary, pays the employees overtime to attend. It also provides a pile of brand-new pound notes as prizes in the game that then begins. The systems designer has all the written details of the system in front of him and gives the meeting a short introduction to it. He explains how their work will be affected and what part they will be expected to play. Questions are then invited about how the system will handle different situations. Any employee whose question cannot be fully answered by the systems designer *by reference to his written systems specification* receives a pound note (and the systems designer notes the point carefully). Once money starts to change hands, employees tend to lose their reticence and apply some ingenuity to recalling unusual situations that will test the system. Although it obviously costs money to mount Pound Note Game sessions, it may cost much less than having to modify an on-line system once it has been commissioned.

A business does not have to be contemplating a full-scale on-line system to benefit from the idea of a meeting that gives employees a genuine incentive to think in detail about the effect of a new system. The presentation could be made by a dealer demonstrating an integrated software package, and the prizes might be for questions that could not be answered from the manual or additional written material prepared for the meeting. Alternatively, the prizes could be for identifying security precautions not specified, or wasteful print-out which will never be used. The advantages of such meetings are not only the way that they highlight difficulties before they arise, but also in the quality of preparatory work that they oblige management to undertake in advance.

Computers, comfort and health

The effect of the computer on the office environment needs advance thought and may demand extra expenditure. In offices where static electricity is a problem, the presence of a lot of vdu's

260 *Computing and the organization*

can make matters much worse, and potted plants can be a real functional aid, as well as helping to relieve the bleak, electronic atmosphere. The trend to smaller modern computers has reduced the need for air conditioning, but it may be worth taking the opportunity to explore employees' attitudes to having a non-smoking area. Cigarette smoke is undoubtedly a hazard to floppy discs (see Figure 53) and is often offensive to non-smoking employees, who have never previously liked to speak up about it. Clearly, this is a sensitive problem about mutual invasion of freedom for which there can be no general solution.

Vdu work-stations

Sitting at a vdu for hours on end is tiring and potentially uncomfortable, especially if the display is unstable, suffers from glare or reflections, or if the furniture is unsuitable. Following Sweden's lead in 1979, most developed countries have issued guidelines on vdu ergonomics and health, and these are beginning to have some effect on vdu manufacturers. For example, detachable keyboards that give the operator more freedom over posture are becoming more common. Expensive displays should be rock-steady, feature high resolution characters that are pleasant to work with and may even have dark characters on a light background (i.e. like ink on paper) to reduce problems from screen glare. A *very* few are, sensibly, shaped like A4 paper, thus reducing the need for scrolling during word processing.

Whatever the characteristics of the equipment, however, it is the employer's responsibility to ensure that it is properly sited and that staff are able to adjust both the vdu and the furniture for maximum comfort. Vdu's cannot just be plonked down where typewriters used to be. However, if proper consideration is given, even a cheap vdu can give prolonged comfortable service. Avoiding reflections from windows or overhead lighting may require furniture rearrangement.

A high-quality chair with adjustable lumbar support is essential. Trying to make do with a cheap seating is a foolish economy. Unless you have sat for long hours at a vdu you may underestimate the fatigue factor of the fixed geometry. (I write with feeling, having keyed in and revised the text of this book and

The employee's viewpoint

many other publications personally.) The vdu operator's claim to decent seating is as strong as that of the airline pilot or long-distance driver, though it is seldom backed by as much industrial muscle. In 1982, the Norwegian Labour Inspectorate introduced legislation covering health aspects of vdu work; it is noteworthy that they set an upper limit of four hours for continuous vdu operation.

If only one operator is to use the equipment, having an adjustable vdu screen and detachable keyboard may be a luxury. If there is a shift system and operators of different dimensions are to be accommodated, they could be necessities, making the difference between smooth operation and persistent complaints. Figure 52 illustrates some features of well-designed work-stations.

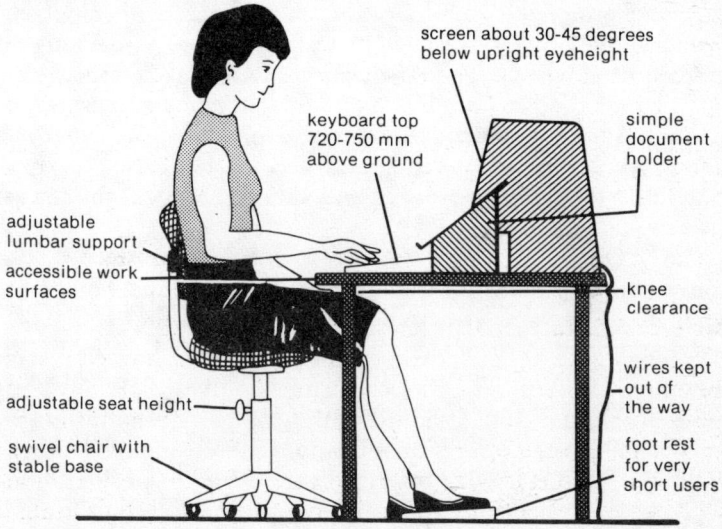

Figure 52. Some features of a well-designed vdu work-station

Although there are published standards for the screen display itself, they cannot be taken too literally, as many of the factors interact. For example, it is meaningless to specify a minimum **refresh rate** without also indicating what sort of **phosphor coating** is used. However, having seen the difference between an unstable display and a rock-steady one, most people can see whether apparent **flicker** will be a problem simply by looking really closely at the screen. The appearance of the screen display actually depends on a complex interaction between the processor, software and vdu, not just the hardware, so it is always safer to examine the combination personally.

Similarly, the standards that lay down minimum spacing between letters should not be taken literally, since technically they may preclude proportional spacing, although it is known to be easier to read than fixed spacing! A sub-committee of the International Standards Organization is trying to develop an approach based on impact on the user, rather than product design.

Meanwhile, there has been considerable concern about the effects of prolonged vdu operation on eyesight, with reported symptoms including headaches, red, stinging eyes, visual fatigue and disturbed vision. The Association of Optical Practitioners, in their 1983 report, *Vdu's On Site*, said that many of these were accounted for by inadequate operator training, poor environmental conditions and psychological factors. For example, they found that the more interesting and varied the work, the fewer the complaints.

The AOP study was based on their research since 1979, drawing on reports from trade unions and patients. The older types of vdu's were criticized for poor design, but often the positioning and prevailing illumination were even more to blame. They point out that vdu's do not damage eyesight, but often reveal eyesight defects of which the operators were previously unaware. For this reason, it is a wise precaution to have all employees' eyes tested *before* vdu's are installed. Otherwise, there is a real danger that the vdu's will be blamed for problems that they detected rather than caused. This is particularly likely for older operators, who may have difficulty in switching between focusing on documents close at hand and on the screen, which should be further away.

The AOP dismissed the idea that radiation from vdu screens could affect operators' health. Research both in Britain and abroad has found both infra-red and ultra-violet radiation levels well below safety limits. Nevertheless, employees may have heard rumours about the problem and it is sensible to keep up to date with the evidence if this is a cause for concern. In any event, the prolonged use of vdu's is a recent development and any wise employer will treat complaints seriously as they arise.

Industrial relations and profitability

A hard-headed businessman might well be asking himself what the cost of all this 'pandering' to the employees will be, and whether the introduction of the computer will still be worthwhile as a business decision. It is important to think about this carefully. A business with a highly organized workforce which is likely to resist computerization needs to be doubly sure of its rationale and budgeting before going ahead.

However, if the arguments for computerizing are still overwhelming, and increased profitability seems assured, it is only fair and sensible to spend some portion of the anticipated proceeds on the employees' health, comfort and education. After all, they are much more likely to make the system work if they believe in it and if they know that management believes in it sufficiently to invest in preparing for it. Although the costs may be less visible, there is a real penalty attached to poor industrial relations. The final self-check invites you to take a pessimistic view and identify some of the possibilities if things go badly.

Self-check

List some of the ways in which poor industrial relations in relation to computers could cost a business money.

ANSWERS

- Increased absenteeism;
- Higher incidence of self-certificated sick leave;
- Strikes, work-to-rules, 'go-slows';
- Demands for extra allowances and rest periods;
- Increased turnover;
- Inflexibility about changes in job descriptions;
- Demands for more expensive vdu's and furniture.

14 | Computers and training

Computers create major training needs: employees have to learn how to adjust to computers in the workplace, how to develop good operating discipline, perhaps even how to write or adapt programs. In addition, however, computers offer a major resource for training, both for computer-related skills and for general business competence.

This chapter considers in turn these two aspects: training for computers and computers for training. The distinction is not, of course, watertight. Computers offer an excellent medium for some kinds of training, including training about computers. For example, the word processing software which I use is supplied complete with a typing tutor program which makes good use of the computer's facilities (sound effects, automatic error counts and gradually increasing difficulty levels) to teach touch typing at the computer keyboard while keeping the trainee's eyes glued to the screen.

Nevertheless, it is convenient to look first at training needs related to computers before considering wider issues of computer-based training. The last chapter dealt with the case for general familiarization sessions for all employees prior to the arrival of the computer. The needs of the employees who will work directly with the system once it has arrived are more specific. Throughout this chapter I will use the word 'trainee' to mean anyone who needs training at any level, whether an employee, an owner-manager or a student.

Operating skills

'Training' can mean anything from a formal course provided by an outside body to some informal help from another employee who has had a bit longer to read the manuals or just more practice. No matter in what form the training is provided, the same basic principles apply. They may sound too prescriptive as listed below, but they have wide applicability and important implications for the organization of training sessions:

- Practice precedes theory: let trainees get their hands on to the equipment before giving theoretical explanations of what will happen;
- Theory precedes practice: once trainees have had 'hands-on', make sure they understand what was happening and why;
- Combine the above two principles to provide an alternation between practice and theory, so that practical experience makes the general principles come to life and knowledge of the underlying principles prevents practice from becoming superficial or mechanical;
- Never try to do too much at one time. Until trainees have confident mastery of one level, they will be unable to digest new ideas at a higher level. The kind of questions people ask is a good guide to the level they are operating at; if they are not asking questions, make few assumptions about how much they understand.

There is no necessary connection between possessing a skill and being good at passing it on. Computer professionals often make terrible teachers, because they make unconscious assumptions about the trainees' previous knowledge and frequently lapse into technical language without even realizing it. An employee who has only recently become proficient with a particular system may, if available, make an ideal tutor.

The manuals provided with the system may be useful for reference but are generally useless as training material, as you often have to be an expert operator before you can understand them. Unless specially designed training aids are available, a set of simple reference cards may be much more helpful for operator training. These should provide a check-list of the commands needed to load and run the software, to operate the printer and any other vital details. Although the procedures will soon be second nature to the person who uses the system daily, she or he may be absent for a while, and anyone who has to deputize will find a simple job aid an invaluable short-cut. It is surprising just how deeply buried in the manual most of the really vital information always seems to be. It must also be admitted that some of the requirements of computerized systems are so profoundly perverse that they are unlikely to become second nature to anyone!

Operating discipline

There is more to skilled operation than just knowing the controls. It is also essential to establish good working habits at an early stage and to document them and transmit them to everyone who uses the system. Let's take word processing as an example. Suppose that a trainee starts by knowing nothing about computers. If he has been taught how to load the software, how to enter, edit, format and print, what more does he need to know?

> *Self-check*
>
> List some aspects that should be covered by his training in operating discipline.

ANSWERS
- Basic procedures and precautions in disc handling, e.g. need to avoid touching or contaminating the exposed part (see Figure 53), how files are locked, how discs are write-protected, what to do in the event of a power cut, etc.;
- Awareness of the ease with which hours or weeks of work can be wiped out instantaneously unless systematic and regular back-up copies are taken (and possibly also print-out made);
- Methodical filing of discs and text with file-names written on to each document and a written catalogue kept with each disc;
- Systematic approach to disc house-keeping, with regular weeding-out of files that can be deleted, secure storage of master copies, separation of unformatted discs from discs in circulation, etc.

With operating discipline, as with operating skills, it is essential that specialist knowledge is not confined to only one employee and that the most important points are quickly accessible on some kind of reference card.

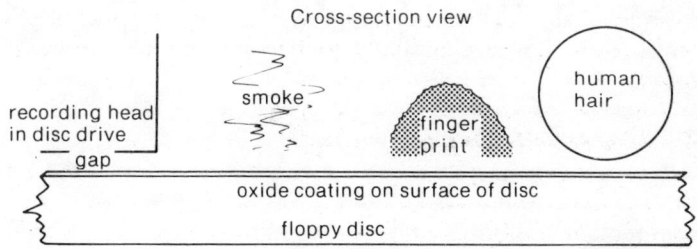

Figure 53. Some environmental threats to data on a floppy disc, showing relative sizes

Writing and adapting programs

Some familiarity with programming is rapidly becoming a hallmark of computer literacy. This does not mean that businesses should expect to write their own software, for reasons discussed in Chapter 11. But however small the business, and however unlikely it is to want to write or modify software in-house, someone – and if possible at least two people – should have a clear idea of what is involved in the process. Writing some elementary programs might be an excellent way of acquiring that knowledge.

To clarify the issue, let us consider the case of David Brown – the owner/manager of a small newsagent's business employing two assistants, one part-time. He is fed up with spending long hours on paperwork and wants a microcomputer system to be able to expand his customer base and perhaps apply to take over a sub-Post Office without having to take on more staff. He is of average intelligence, left school at 16, has no previous experience of computers and was never particularly good at maths. Should he learn how to program his microcomputer?

Self-check

Draw up a list of pros and cons which David should consider. You may want to review Chapter 10 to remind yourself of what programming involves.

ANSWERS

Pro

- Knowing how to program will make him less dependent on outsiders;
- Elementary programming will give him a better idea of what the computer can – and cannot – be expected to do, and help him to use programs like spreadsheets;
- Knowing how programs work may enable him to adapt commercial programs to suit his system by making minor changes;
- The ability to write simple programs is good for building confidence in handling the machine and in introducing it to his assistants;
- Investing some time and energy in computer familiarization is a wise move at a time when any future expansion – e.g. with the Post Office – is likely to involve contact with computer-based systems.

Con

- Computer programming is not easy: it takes careful planning, meticulous attention to detail and lots of time;
- Computer programming is not easy: it takes careful planning, meticulous attention to detail and lots of time;
- Computer programming is not easy . . . (repeat ad lib).

The repetition of the single 'con' is to emphasize the point, because most people underestimate it: almost everything to do with computers takes a bit longer than the enthusiast remembers, a lot longer than the dealer admits, and *ages* longer than you would ever have believed before you became involved with them! Time spent on programming does not contribute directly to the business, nor is it exactly leisure for most people. So although this is the *only* real argument against learning to program, it *is* a major one for a busy person. And if David Brown had not been busy, he wouldn't have decided to invest in a computer.

On closer reflection, what the 'con' really argues against is making an *unlimited* time commitment to programming. Most people will make significant progress on a short course of a few days – or, better still, ten sessions spread over a few months – or a clear contract for a self-study course (preferably with tutorial back-up). The 'spread-out' options are usually better for avoiding mental indigestion and fitting in with the demands of working and domestic life, but the intensive short course may have attractions for the person in a hurry.

None of these options will equip the trainee – however able or hard-working – to write efficient, robust and fool-proof software on which any business could depend. As long as the trainee is under no illusion about this, such courses can be very helpful, for the reasons indicated under the 'pros' above. What is dangerous is when such courses give formerly successful business people enough misplaced confidence in their own abilities to spend countless hours producing inefficient and error-prone software which is difficult for others to use and impossible to modify reliably because the programs are badly constructed and the documentation is poor or absent.

Computer-based training
System facsimiles

The advantages of using the computer as a training aid are perhaps most obvious when the content of training is something like the installation of a new computer system. Novices cannot safely be left to make their mistakes on a real-time system, such as an airline or credit company might operate, with live files and real customers at stake. A system facsimile is essentially a small-scale simulation of the real thing and provides a good solution to the problem. Essential features of the system are modelled, small imaginary data files created, and the trainee is gradually introduced to the operations that will be needed to work the real system without the anxiety of knowing that errors could be disastrous.

Ideally, the system would provide feedback on errors, 'help' facilities and progressive increases in the level of difficulty. It is relatively easy for the designers of a **real-time** system to provide such a training model as an offshoot of the main design, as long as this is built into the original statement of requirements, but as an afterthought it could be surprisingly expensive. Just as an airline pilot still needs supervision when making the transition from a flight simulator to a real aeroplane, the trainee whose experience has been on a system facsimile will need some support before he or she is ready to 'fly solo'.

The technique of building skills and confidence without risk can be applied on a smaller scale to systems that are not real-time. Initial training in using almost any software can be accelerated by the use of an introductory version with sample data files. If the software arrives without such an aid, creating an appropriate demonstration sequence should be a high priority for whoever in the business is responsible for introducing staff to the computer. Programming skill is unnecessary; what is needed is an understanding of what the novice's difficulties are and how to cross the different bridges one at a time, as well as a willingness to keep on modifying the sequence in the light of the trainee's reactions.

The computer as a medium

The computer has unique characteristics as a learning medium. Depending on the training needs of the organization and the availability of the hardware, it may make sense to exploit computer-based training (CBT) to the full. Small businesses are unlikely to do enough training to consider acquiring computers solely for training purposes, but once they have computerized they often find that a spare microcomputer can double as a training machine and a back-up.

In order to use CBT to teach skills unrelated to the computer, special software is likely to be necessary. For most applications, the production of this will be assisted by the use of an author language (see page 60). The availability of a suitable one may be an important factor in the choice of hardware. Authoring systems may include powerful editing and layout aids that help the trainer to produce and revise well-designed materials quickly and easily. These are sometimes sold outright and sometimes under licence. A good authoring system not only enables trainers who are not programmers to create training materials, but also increases the productivity of professional programmers when writing computer-based training materials. Although all author languages involve some loss of flexibility compared with programming languages, in a good system this is a small price to pay for a substantial reduction in the preparation time needed, for avoiding many of the problems that can arise when a trainer has to work entirely through professional programmers, and for limiting the costs of authoring CBT materials.

Investment in CBT will only be justified if the organization does a reasonable amount of training of a kind for which computers are suitable. To make a balanced judgement about this, let's draw up a list of the pros and cons.

Self-check

Compared with a human teacher and conventional classroom methods, what are the potential *advantages* of using a computer as a training medium?

ANSWERS

Here are seven; you may have identified some additional advantages as well:

- It never gets bored, impatient or sarcastic;
- It can be made available wherever and whenever the trainee is free (provided that the business has not fully committed all its computers for business purposes);
- It can give immediate and individualized feedback on mistakes;

- It can vary the pace and difficulty to suit the trainee;
- It can keep records of progress and test scores automatically;
- The trainee has to respond actively, rather than listening passively, so training can be intensive and motivating;
- Different styles of training can be provided to suit different trainees and different content.

The last point is important. Many people imagine – quite wrongly – that training by computer will resemble the old-fashioned kind of programmed learning, in which lessons were broken down into tiny steps, with frequent multiple-choice questions to be got right before you were allowed to go on to the next point. CBT covers a whole spectrum of techniques, including drill-and-practice, open-ended simulation, educational games, problem-solving tutorials and a range of others which there is no space to describe here.

Of course CBT is no panacea: the potential disadvantages can be serious. Human teachers can modify their teaching at short notice or even as they go along, whereas CBT is expensive and time-consuming, not only to develop but also to modify. (The development time for CBT is estimated at between 50 and 200 man-hours per trainee-hour.) Books can be read while the trainee is travelling or curled up in an armchair, whereas CBT requires suitable hardware and a mains supply. Some training objectives (for example, developing telephone skills or dealing with difficult customers) cannot be handled adequately by computers alone, since they require interaction with other trainees as well as the trainer.

Bearing these pros and cons in mind, here is an example of a company that has used CBT extensively. The next self-check asks you to identify what features of the company's training needs made CBT particularly appropriate.

Self-check

Barclaycard Ltd is one of the largest CBT users in Britain. This credit card company has over 1500 employees working from seven different centres in work-groups of eight or nine people. They have to operate around eighty different procedures to deal with all aspects of issuing and replacing cards, preparing and following-up statements, adjusting credit limits and so on. Until 1977, all training was by lecture/demonstration and classroom exercises conducted at head office in Northampton. The company then started preparing CBT materials, using an author language, so that all the routine procedures could be carried out using computer terminals; new entrants are now trained almost exclusively through CBT.

List the features of the company and of its training needs that made CBT appropriate.

ANSWERS

- Since the company is highly computerized, the operating procedures are unlikely to change at short notice. Thus, effective CBT, once developed, is likely to have a reasonable shelf-life;
- For the same reason, CBT has high credibility; the training medium resembles the real system that the trainees need to master;
- Because the company is decentralized, using CBT on location is likely to be both cheaper and more effective than removing trainees from their normal working environment and colleagues for residential training;
- Trainees are probably taken in with widely varying levels of knowledge of, and familiarity with, computer-based systems. CBT can adjust to their starting level individually and be sustained for longer for those trainees with more learning difficulties.

It does not follow from this that a company *has* to resemble Barclaycard for CBT to make a suitable training method. Quite small firms may find CBT cost-effective, if they have already acquired microcomputers for other reasons, especially if the trainees are dispersed and the subject matter reasonably stable.

Many firms already make extensive use of slides and videotape in training. Computer graphics cannot rival the definition of colour transparencies, nor can animation and synthesized speech compare with the realism of video film. Although various methods have been used for combining computer systems with visual aids, they are being superseded by the new breed of systems known as interactive video.

Interactive video

In Chapter 3, the example of Sandycare Ltd showed one way in which interactive video could help a business. The same basic equipment (videodisc player, microcomputer and television set) was used to provide an animated catalogue, customer education and entertainment and staff training after hours. Interactive video at its best combines the strengths of video (realism, high resolution, lifelike soundtrack) with the strengths of the computer (random access, high interaction, individualized routes). In the wrong hands, of course, it can provide the worst of both worlds!

Although videotape recorders can be controlled by computers, they suffer from the disadvantage that they are fundamentally serial-access, whereas a videodisc is random-access. A library of 55,000 slides can be stored on a single videodisc and any particular one found within seconds; moving and still sequences can be combined on the same disc, interspersed with CBT stored on the computer's floppy discs; text and graphics generated by the computer can be superimposed on the video picture; the possibilities are almost endless. Certainly it will be many years before trainers are able to exploit this new training medium to the full. Videodisc designers seem to find it hard to escape from the old traditions of passive video! Yet the implications of putting such a vast learning resource under the trainee's control are immense.

There are two different systems of videodisc at present, based on different principles and incompatible with each other. The technical differences are outside the scope of this book. Both are longer-lasting than videotape, store information much more densely and can be scanned to find particular frames very quickly. For these and other reasons, it is likely that the future of interactive video lies with videodiscs.

Their main disadvantage is the finality and expense of the process by which the disc is pressed. From the user's point of view, it is the difference between a gramophone record pressed at the factory versus an audio cassette that you can record and re-record for yourself. Firms that already have closed-circuit television equipment for training are unlikely to welcome the way in which videodiscs preclude the do-it-yourself option. Since a computer program can be altered with relative ease, for training purposes it is essential to put all the commands that control the videodisc into the computer software (although they can be recorded onto the disc for other purposes, e.g. exhibitions/catalogues).

Once a videodisc has been mastered, it represents a huge resource for training. At present, there is a great shortage of videodiscs that really exploit the potential of equipment which only became available in Europe in the early 1980s, and was developing rapidly at the time of writing. Experiments with interactive video in the US, where the medium has been available since 1978, suggest that it may transform methods of training *and* selling.

Self-check

a Give your imagination a free rein for this one! Now that you have nearly finished this book, here is a good opportunity to speculate about how the same content might have been treated as an interactive videodisc with appropriate computer software. You may find it helpful to refer back to Figure 2 (page 17) and/or the contents page. Just think how much more impact you could have given the same material if you were not – as I have been – confined to cold linear print and simple line diagrams. If you find this too difficult or time-consuming, just pick a couple of chapters instead of the whole book.

b To get our feet back down to earth, what would have been the disadvantages of this combination of media from the viewpoint of reader, author and publisher?

Computing and the organization

ANSWERS

a There are, of course, no right answers here, but for interest I have listed some ideas I'd like to have explored (given unlimited time, money and equipment!):

- The glossary would be replaced by a sort of animated visual encyclopaedia with cross-references. If you looked up 'floppy disc', for example, instead of just seeing colour illustrations of the various kinds, pointing out the write-protection notch, etc., you would be able to peel away the protective sleeve and see the magnetic material spinning away. You would be offered a short film clip to show correct and incorrect ways of handling a disc, which could fade to show a computer-generated graphic of the parts inside the disc drive. If you asked for information about formatting, graphics would show you the invisible sector markings, zooming in to illustrate the dense packing of information. An optional self-test section could ask you to identify hazards to discs in a film clip of an office environment. You would be directed towards other relevant entries in the encyclopaedia (like hard disc and videodisc), in case you wanted to follow them up.

- Part 1 would be replaced by a number of sequences explaining how software works and illustrating different items of hardware in action. Three-dimensional objects would be shown actually rotating, synthesized speech would be demonstrated, and programs could be interpreted and executed line by line. The case studies in Chapter 3 would be presented with realistic film, showing Jenny Bruno's cats and dogs, her equipment and her software in action.

- The software described in Part 2 would be presented with a combination of computer graphics, live users talking about their experiences and demonstrating their systems in action and – most important of all – scaled-down simulations of actual software in each category for the user to try out. The self-assessment quiz for word processing would, of course, be computer-marked, and the user would soon afterwards have been processing words, not just reading about doing it.

Computers and training 277

- The processes in Chapters 8 and 9 would be enlivened with realistic, filmed episodes of conversations between customers and dealers. Some might illustrate how misconceptions arise accidentally or are created deliberately; others would show how the benefit a customer gets from a session with a consultant depends on how well he prepares for it. The user would constantly have to identify the mistakes made, pinpoint the misunderstandings and respond in other ways. Chapter 10 would naturally give rise to the creation of a real working program, which the user would write, run and modify. Chapter 11 could hammer home its message with some dramatized scenes of a business going bankrupt because its manager becomes obsessed by programming and insists on doing it all himself.

- Chapters 12 and 13 would lend themselves to a case study treatment, in which the installation of a computer system in a business was followed through from two viewpoints, that of the manager in charge of the computer and that of an alienated employee. Perhaps two contrasting cases should receive this treatment: in one, the installation goes smoothly, in the other there is continuing industrial action and low productivity. The user has to identify the key differences in management style in each case and would receive feedback from the software on his or her responses. Chapter 15 would be represented by futuristic reconstructions of possible scenarios, possibly interspersed with clips from relevant movies and/or archive material of past predictions: the user might have to guess which came true and which were proved wrong!

b The 'readership' of this version of the book would be drastically reduced by the need to have the right videodisc equipment, the right computer and the necessary software and interfaces. You might also regret not being able to read in the bath, on the bus or wherever you are now! The author would be suffering from acute senility, because it would have taken at least 100 times as many man-hours to produce the book in that form. The publishers would either have gone bankrupt or changed the nature of their business: videodisc publishing will reach a large market, but one of a quite different kind from book publishing, needing different skills, immense budgets and very careful market research.

15 | Computers and business futures

This book is not about the social implications of computers, nor is it my intention to speculate about what life will be like in the 21st century. Instead, this final chapter takes a brief look at some of the trends which are already so strong that they could make nonsense of today's business decisions if not recognized.

Throughout the book, I have tried to stress how the impact of computers on human beings and organizations is much greater than their mere ability to process data quickly and reliably. As the first paragraph of the Introduction emphasized, the pace of change is so rapid that it is impossible to grasp all the implications. Let me suggest some principles that have emerged in the intervening chapters:

- No business can afford to make a decision to buy *any* computer – no matter how cheap – in isolation, because the computer will inevitably affect the organization of the business; it must look carefully at its total information-processing needs, present and future, to ensure that the anticipated upgrade path is suitable.
- The convergence of technologies in office equipment is now so rapid that the business's computing needs must also be considered in the light of its use of telecommunications (whether telephone, telex or fax).
- Hardware prices will go on falling for any product for which there is mass demand: for example, mass memory storage, processor power and printers that are both fast *and* high-quality. Software and training are unlikely to become significantly cheaper, and increasingly this is where the real costs of computing will be most visible.

- The spread of microcomputers in small and large businesses will continue; although greater memory and processor power seems inevitable, the concept of a single-user microcomputer will remain popular, especially with the same machine having multiple roles in a network, as a telecommunications and viewdata terminal and as a terminal to other mainframes.
- Operating systems will be developed that make more concessions to the first-time user, and hence more demands on the processor and memory. Effortless alternation between different tasks – and perhaps even simultaneous processing in parallel – is likely to be a high priority for many users.
- Although languages like BASIC and COBOL will continue to be popular because of the number of users already committed to them, their positions will be seriously challenged by languages of a new generation like SMALLTALK, PROLOG and OCCAM.
- Business software will increasingly display artificial intelligence in place of mindless obedience to pre-programmed instructions; managers will be able to compare their business decisions and forecasts with those of an expert system and ask it to explain its 'reasoning'.
- The impact of computers on *how business is transacted* is only just beginning to emerge. Each business must review for itself how its market, product, sales techniques and distribution is likely to be affected.

The importance of the last point is considerable. Unfortunately, there has been so much journalistic overstatement in recent years about the implications of microelectronics that our minds are in danger of becoming numb: who today believes in the collapse of work, the paperless office, the electronic global village, the demise of schools and the cashless society?

So far, progress towards the streamlined electronic office has not been impressive. Computers have proved capable of generating immense quantities of paper that nobody reads at higher speeds than ever before. Where formerly there used to be a single sheet of paper to file, today there is all too often a pile of awkward-shaped computer print-out *and* some magnetic media to store. The industry is miles from solving the problems of incompatibility between systems, and without much more compact and foolproof forms of back-up, paper will continue to be the only universal medium.

In the field of banking, it is significant that one of the most popular forms of computing has been the way that the high-street cash-point allows customers easier access to cash. Those who predict the cashless society seem to underestimate the convenience and anonymity of cash. Not everyone relishes the prospect of leaving an electronic trail of their movements, spending patterns and payments.

The universal home-based terminal seems unlikely to replace either offices or schools, although it may well change their nature and the hours they keep. Many people prefer to earn their living at least partly away from home and would not welcome a total merger of domestic and employment time and facilities. Many of the activities carried out in primary schools could not possibly be replaced by electronic devices, depending as they do on personal contact between children.

Although simplistic predictions like these seem quite improbable, I am in no doubt that our society is in the process of various subtler sorts of transition. Our notion of the pattern and distribution of full-time work is changing and must change further if we are to conquer the spectre of long-term mass unemployment. Career changes, job-sharing, self-employment, flexible opportunities for retraining and continuing education for all: these are some of the ingredients in a less destructive pattern which has yet to emerge. By job-sharing, I do not necessarily mean only part-time work, although I believe that this will appeal more widely in the future, but also the deliberate combination of two part-time commitments which might be quite disparate.

There are already signs of renewed interest in do-it-yourself home improvements and art and craft work; the demand for personal services like catering and child-minding is increasing; direct selling through mail-shots and viewdata appears to be taking off; there is a boom in products and services which have any connection with the new technologies. Society constantly redefines what constitutes education, what is work and what makes good business. Each enterprise must judge the implications for itself.

Self-check

Below is a list of a number of developments of potential significance to business. For each one, try to guess whether it is

    a unlikely to happen this century
    b imminent within the next five or ten years
    c possible at any moment
    d already available

1. A new medium for external memory allowing 5 Megabytes (5000 K) of information to be stored on a robust card exactly the size of a credit card.
2. A complete microcomputer and modem, costing less than £200, that give access to viewdata, telex and electronic mail, using any television; if a printer is attached, information retrieved from viewdata or electronic mailboxes can be printed out.
3. A journalist writing an article on location abroad using a hand-held computer, transmitting it down the telephone to an editor, who cuts and revises it on his screen before forwarding it to the phototypesetting machine; the text is never typed or printed on paper until it appears in the final newspaper.
4. A package comprising a computer, vdu, printer and modem that can automatically answer the telephone (using synthesized speech) and store and transmit messages, letters and telex, costing less than £1000.
5. A device that links a computer with a peripheral (or another computer) and exchanges information at 77,000 bits/second through a tiny fibre optic cable.
6. A point-of-sale device that reads bar codes and automatically not only prints a product description and price but also updates the stock control software, initiates a re-order, if appropriate, and debits the customer's account.

Computers and business futures 283

7 Computer programs diagnosing diseases, helping managers in brainstorming sessions and improving their performance as a result of experience.
8 A cable television network allowing subscribers to control what programs they view and also to vote on current issues and select interactive educational computer programs.
9 An electronic magazine available for 'readers' to call up as it was originally 'written', but also allowing them to see comments made by other readers on the usefulness and content of the articles.
10 A telephone with a 7"-screen, numeric keypad and concealed full alphanumeric keyboard, with built-in modem, automatic dialling of up to 81 telephone numbers and the ability to connect with British and European viewdata services, storing log-on codes and passwords automatically, and able to transmit computer data and speech simultaneously.
11 A touch-sensitive screen that can be fitted to a computer monitor, so that users can operate software by pressing their fingers against the screen instead of having to use a keyboard.
12 An unmanned computer, connected to a telephone, that can sell software to people who ring it up in the middle of the night; the software is sent down the telephone line straight into the memory of the receiving computer after the buyer has identified himself with passwords.
13 A high resolution monitor capable of showing text and graphics in overlapping windows with a choice of 'portrait' (like A4 paper) or 'landscape' (like a television set) formats filling the screen.
14 An internationally agreed set of standards so that a terminal can transmit text thirty times faster than telex, with the terminal able to do other work while sending or receiving, and catering for all languages using a Roman alphabet; the system could operate with a wide range of terminal devices (from a memory typewriter

upward) and would be compatible with the million-and-a-half existing telex subscribers' equipment.
15 A cheap, tamper-proof device attached underneath cars, so that underground sensors can monitor their movement through the city centre; the system enables tolls to be charged according to the roads used, the time of day and even the type of vehicle, so that urban congestion can be relieved. It could also allow homing devices to help a driver navigate in unfamiliar surroundings and avoid traffic congestion.
16 A videodisc presentation allowing prospective motor car customers to browse among a complete range, seeing all the body options, with various combinations of trim, colour and accessories. Road performance and mechanical details would be conveyed in still and moving pictures. The car 'showroom' might occupy only a small office space and portray thousands of different options.

ANSWERS

In every single case the answer is **d**; in some cases, the development was announced during 1983 and is not yet commercially available, in others, the equipment has been in active commercial use for some years. So if you rated many **a**, **b** or **c**, be warned that the pace of change is faster than you realized.

What are the implications of all this for the business of today? It has often been suggested that computers are as significant in the microelectronic revolution as were railways in the industrial revolution. Certainly many of the social institutions which we now take for granted would have been unthinkable without the rise of the railway network: a common time zone, overnight postal service and national leagues for cricket and football, for example. Although a number of fortunes were made from the railways, there were also a great many bankruptcies, especially in the latter half of the nineteenth century. Entrepreneurs who arrived on the scene too late and in the wrong place tried to cash in on the boom and got it wrong. The microcomputer industry is showing signs of similar stress at present: too many companies seem to imagine that they will make an easy killing with products and services that are all too similar.

Certainly it would be a mistake for businesses to rush into computerization for its own sake, or to jump on the software-selling bandwagon, without doing some market research and careful costing. The high technology route is often also a high-risk one and many firms would do better to stick to their manual systems and traditional products than to rush into new and untried methods and markets.

Nevertheless, the technological imperative rules out a head-in-the-sand posture. If a business operates in such a way that computers can contribute to profitability, then it *must* computerize to stay alive; its competitors certainly will.

Between these two extremes lies moderation. If those who manage businesses will view computers calmly and apply their normal business sense and experience to computer-related decisions, they may find the middle way. If they understand the basic concepts and vocabulary of computing and have the wisdom to know when they need expert advice, as well as the business judgement to apply this knowledge to their own organization, they may face the 21st century with confidence.

Appendix 1
Sources of advice and information

NOTES
1 Most of these bodies are in some sense 'independent', i.e. without commitment to any particular product or manufacturer. However, the two sources of the software used in the preparation of this book (Computer Concepts Ltd and Gemini Marketing Ltd) are also given here for convenience.
2 In the case of networks (like the NCC Microsystems Centres and the ITeCs), there is not enough space to list all the centres, but note that, wherever you live, there may be one nearby. The single contact given below can put you in touch with the others.

Association of Independent Computer Specialists
c/o BEAMA
Leicester House
18 Leicester Street
London WC2H 7BN
Tel: 01-437 0678
An association of (micro)computer consultants and software producers; runs newsletter. Members must disclose financial interests (if any) to their clients.

Association of Professional Computer Consultants
109 Baker Street
London W1M 2BH
Tel: 01-267 5858
A professional organization, all of whose members are independent; in 1984, around 25 specialized in microcomputers.

Appendix 1

British Computer Society
13 Mansfield Street
London W1M 0BP
Tel: 01-637 0471
Major professional organization, with interests in standards and dissemination of good practice; publishes various periodicals, codes of conduct and practice, handbooks and information sheets (list available on request). International links, e.g. with International Federation for Information Processing (IFIP). Various specialist working parties, e.g. Payroll Policy Committee, Schools Committee.

Computer Concepts Ltd
16 Wayside
Chipperfield
Herts WD4 9 JJ
Tel: 09277 69727
Suppliers of software and firmware for the BBC micro, notably Wordwise, the word processing ROM with which this book was prepared.

Computer Referral Service
PO Box 7
London W3 6XJ
Run by Broadcasting Support Services, a registered charity, this is a postal enquiry service that puts members of the public in touch with regional and national clubs and user groups and supplies details of college and self-study courses; publishes a useful series of free factsheets, including ones on microcomputers in small businesses and jobs in computing. Send large stamped addressed envelope for these. Broadcasting Support Services also publishes *Computerfax*, a valuable guide to all the Open University and British Broadcasting Corporation broadcasts, courses and resource materials in computing.

Computing Services Association
5th Floor, Hanover House
73–4 High Holborn
London WC1V 6LE
Tel: 01-405 3161
Around 200 companies belong to this association, which represents over 80 per cent of the organizations involved in computing services in Britain. Offers consultancy, computer bureau and a useful set of twenty free leaflets on topics like contract guidelines. Members' facilities

include seminars and conferences. Free information service about members' services.

Council for Small Industries in Rural Area (CoSIRA)
141 Castle Street
Salisbury, Wilts SP1 3TP
Tel: 0722 336255
Initial discussions free, technical advice at reasonable rates; branches elsewhere.

Department of Industry
Information Technology Division
29 Bressenden Place
London SW1E 5OT
Tel: 01-213 3000
Source of information and funding, mainly geared towards the application of microprocessors in new products. Grants available for certain types of consultancy and feasibility studies. Holds list of authorized consultants.

Gemini Marketing Ltd
18a Littleham Road
Exmouth
Devon
EX8 2QG
Tel: 0395 265165
Suppliers of low-cost serious business software for a wide range of microcomputers, notably payroll and integrated spreadsheet with graphics, as quoted in this book.

William George's Sons Ltd
89 Park Street
Bristol
BS1 5PW
Tel: 0272 276602
Source of *George's Computer Book Catalogue*, a comprehensive listing of thousands of titles, helpfully classified and indexed. The 1983 edition cost £3; an invaluable reference aid. George's will supply any book in the catalogue direct, more than 600 of them from stock.

Information Technology Centres (ITeCs)
Manpower Services Commission
Press Office, 166 High Holborn
London WC1V 6PF
Tel: 01-379 3344
ITeCs are a nationwide network of over 150 centres set up under the Youth Training Scheme, with substantial funding from the Department of Industry and the Manpower Services Commission and sponsorship from industry. Primary purpose is to help young unemployed people to find jobs, but by late 1983, over 55 per cent of ITeCs had some kind of open access. Although non-profit-distributing, all ITeCs have revenue targets to meet and are generally orientated to cooperating with local businesses. Although MSC is based in Sheffield, London press office will direct you to the nearest ITeC.

The Law Society
113 Chancery Lane
London WC2A 1PL
Tel: 01-242 1222
Can put you in touch with consultants with legal and computer expertise.

Microsystems Centre
11 New Fetter Lane
London EC4A 1PU
Tel: 01-353 0013
The London base of the Microsystems Centre network, a division of the NCC (see below). Business people welcome to drop in to browse in bookshop and look at examples from range of microcomputers. Technical advice, courses and consultancy available by appointment; 1984 rates were £65 per hour or £325 per day for consultancy, £125 for training course. Distributes self-study course in *Business Basic* (£19.50, including cassette). There are Microsystems Centres in most major UK cities.

Mine of Information Ltd
1 Francis Avenue
St Albans, Herts
Tel: 5652801
Direct supplier of computer-related books; also maintains data base and distributes annotated bibliographies. Good direct source, failing local bookshops.

National Computing Centre (NCC) Ltd
Oxford Road
Manchester
M1 7ED
Tel: 061-228 6333
A non-profit-distributing agency, backed by government and industry, with branches in London, Birmingham, Bristol, Belfast and Glasgow. Provides a variety of support for businesses including publications in various media, e.g. *Guidelines for the Selection and Purchase of Packaged Software* (booklet, £0.50), *How to Choose your Small Business Computer* (booklet with useful checklist and audio-cassette, £12.50) and *Small Business Computers for First-time Users* (book, £7.95). NCC also publish directories of hardware, software and suppliers. Organizations can participate (apply to NCC for subscription details) and there is a low-cost Guidance Service (package of information and advice). Can put you in touch with network of around twenty Microsystems Centres.

National Extension College
18 Brooklands Avenue
Cambridge
CB2 2HN
Tel: 0223 316644
A non-profit-distributing organization with extensive experience of self-study and distance learning. Involved in the BBC Computer Literacy Project. Have published many books and learning materials, including Clive Prigmore's *30 Hour BASIC*.

Prestel	also	**Micronet 800**
Birmingham Prestel Centre		Bushfield House
Berkley House		Orton Centre
245 Broad Street		Peterborough
Birmingham B1 2HQ		PE2 0UW
Tel: Freefone 2296		*Tel: 0733 237111*

UK public viewdata service, with many specialized services of interest to businesses, including electronic mailbox. Produces helpful information sheets, publishes *Prestel User* magazine. Micronet 800 is a major Information Provider (launched April 1983) and source of home and business telesoftware. Telex facilities interesting to low-volume users (from £0.50 per message).

Small Firms Information Services
Ebury Bridge House
2/18 Ebury Bridge Road
London SW1W 8QD
Tel: 01-730 8451 or Freefone 2444
The London branch of a network of a dozen Department of Industry centres, offering information and advice on the applications of new technology to small businesses. Counsellors offer independent and impartial advice by appointment; first three interviews are free.

Society for Computers and Law
c/o Mrs D Hasting
11 High Street
Milton, nr Abingdon
Oxfordshire OX14 4ER
Tel: 0235 834986
Organizes conferences, publishes booklets and a quarterly journal, *Computers and Law*.

Appendix 2
Further reading

NOTES

1 There is such an enormous recent literature on computing in business that I have had to be very selective. My criterion for including a book has been if I believe that someone who has just read this book might want to refer to it. This ruled out many otherwise excellent books. Where a book has special relevance to specific topics in the book, the relevant chapter numbers are given in brackets at the end of the reference. In case of difficulty in obtaining these books from a library or bookstore, consult the entries under *George's* and *Mine of Information* in Appendix 1.

2 There has been an immense proliferation of computer-related magazines, as a visit to any bookstall will confirm. Buy cautiously: many are thick only because of the number of advertisements, yet they cost as much as a cheap paperback. Some can be read only with a glossary in hand, others are useful only for home users with particular kinds of micro, others again go out of business after a short existence. Nevertheless, if you want regular, up-to-date purchasing information, taking a good magazine is invaluable. The one most likely to appeal to readers of this book is

Micro Decision, published monthly at about £1. (Subscription enquiries to VNU Business Publications, 53–5 Frith Street, London W1A 2HG). It is readable and reliable, includes regular case studies of first-time users, portrays the difficulties as well as the successes and includes a comprehensive listing of specialized software packages. There is a Consumer Line for technical advice and consumer problems (write to Evelyn House, 62 Oxford Street, London W1, or telephone *01-636 6890*).

3 In almost all cases, the comments represent my personal opinions based on reading the book; in three cases, however, the books were not available by the time this one went to press, but the titles sounded promising enough to justify inclusion in this list. These books are identified by asterisks, and the comments that follow were based on the publisher's description.

Aleksander, I. and Burnett, P.
Reinventing Man: the Robot becomes Reality. Kogan Page, London, 1983
A demanding but stimulating book, which reviews recent developments in robotics, especially in robot vision and artificial intelligence. It develops the implications of breaking away from the preprogrammed intelligence typical of computers and, instead, modelling the processes of the human brain. (15)

*Beech, G.
Computer Based Learning. Sigma Technical Press, Wilmslow, Cheshire, 1984
Subtitled 'Practical methods for microcomputers', this book is aimed at those interested in using microcomputers in education and training. It is illustrated by case studies (including primary schools, the Open University, Mobil Chemicals, British Petroleum and British Airways). Apple PILOT is developed as an example of an author language, and Super-PILOT as a sample authoring system. Well-known systems like PLATO, COMBAT and WISE are compared on cost and performance. There is also material on program generators and simple financial models. (14)

Bradbeer, R.
The Personal Computer Book (Second Edition). Gower Publishing, Aldershot, 1982
This might be useful if you are thinking of buying a small microcomputer, but beware the speed at which the product information (which comprises the main part of the book) dates. Make sure you look at the latest edition and double-check everything. Useful appendices, including a list of many UK clubs and specialist groups. (1, 9)

Clarke, A., Eaton, J. M. and Powys-Lybbe, D.
CP/M: The Software Bus. Sigma Technical Press, 1983
This book is subtitled 'A programmer's companion' but neither this nor the offputting title should disguise its potential value to users of any CP/M micro. Although much of the book contains technical material, this is an invaluable reference work for *any* CP/M user. The first few chapters, and the first few paragraphs of *each* chapter, are well within the grasp of non-technical readers. The last chapter consists of vital program modifications to surmount limitations and errors in CP/M which can be typed in even if you don't follow the details. This book is complementary to the CP/M manual, and much easier to follow. (2)

Cluff, E.
Computerisation for the Small Business. Gower Publishing, 1980
Subtitled, 'A layman's guide for directors and senior line-management', this book is by the Secretary-General of the Institute of Data Processing Management. Although somewhat dated, it contains much wisdom and good sense and would make rewarding follow-up reading, especially for those working in larger organizations. (8, 9, 12)

Connell, S. and Galbraith, I. A.
The Electronic Mail Handbook. Kogan Page, 1982
An introduction to the concept and practice of electronic mail, this book gives numerous case studies and includes a policy and market analysis covering Western Europe and North America; it also contains an international directory of suppliers. (15)

Curran, S. and Curnow, R.
The Penguin Computing Book. Penguin Books, 1983
Substantial (458-page) reference work on computing, strong on electronics and programming (in machine code, BASIC and other languages). Good glossary, bibliography and index.

Dean, C. and Whitlock, Q.
A Handbook of Computer Based Training. Kogan Page, 1983
A good starting-point for exploring the issues raised in Chapter 14. Contains details of some authoring systems, useful checklists and glossary. (14)

Deeson, E.
Easy Programming for the BBC Micro. Shiva Publishing, 1982
One of the first and best books on programming in BBC BASIC: attractively written, starts simply, full of original programs and sensible ideas. Sets a standard by which programming books for other BASIC dialects and other languages can be judged. Part of *Shiva's Friendly Micro Series*. (10)

Derrick, J. and Oppenheim, P.
A Handbook of New Office Technology. Kogan Page, 1983
A comprehensive and detailed guide to office equipment of all kinds, including printing, typewriters, word processors, photocopiers, fax, telex, telephones, computers and integrated office systems. The authors (see below) are well aware of the implications of the converging technologies, and this marks the book out from conventional buyers' guides. (1, 9, 15)

Derrick, J. and Oppenheim, P.
Telecommunications: A Businessman's Guide. Kogan Page, 1983
A valuable and timely book by the founder-editors of *What to Buy for Business* magazine. Contains authoritative material on telephones and cost control, fax, telex and teletex, digitization and computer communication and the imminent effects of liberalization on British Telecom (text finalized in Spring 1983). Useful index of suppliers. Much of the text previously appeared in their magazine (in places, the joints are all too obvious), but in such a rapid publication its minor faults are forgivable. (15)

Dobres, M.
Financial Modelling on a Microcomputer. Sigma Technical Press, 1983
This book is most valuable for users of PLANNERCALC and MASTERPLANNER, and is officially approved by Comshare Ltd, the source of these spreadsheet planning systems. Users (or potential users) of other spreadsheets may find it valuable for reference, however, as it gives a clear idea of what is involved in the process of financial modelling, with plentiful illustrations of screens, print-outs, and the instructions which generated them. (4)

Feigenbaum, E. A. and McCorduck, P.
The Fifth Generation. Michael Joseph, 1983
A stimulating and readable account of artificial intelligence, the Japanese plans for fifth-generation computers, the response (or lack of it) from the rest of the world, and the implications of mass production of intelligent machines. (15)

Foy, N.
Computers and Commonsense. Longman, 1972
Not many books from the 1970s stand the test of time, but Foy's commonsense pro-consumer approach is still well worth reading. Her insights on the recent history of the computer industry cannot have pleased its giants, as she systematically challenges sacred cows. The book is superbly readable and practical.

Gibson, D.
Wordprocessing and the Electronic Office. Council for Educational Technology, London, 1983
This is a collection of articles on the technological, social, economic and educational implications of information technology in the office. Although sponsored by the Microelectronics Education Programme and primarily aimed at teachers, this Reader contains a wealth of material of interest to business readers, much of it reproduced directly from magazines such as *Management Services*, *Business Education*, *Which Word Processor?*, *Practical Computing*, *The Office*, *Educational Computing*, *Journal of Information Processing* and *Microelectronics Journal*. Some effort is needed to locate relevant contents (page numbers are only alternate and typeface and layout varies disconcertingly), but the collection still provides a worthwhile short-cut. (6)

Hypher, B. I.
Computer Users' Yearbook. Computing Publications, London, annual
Massive and authoritative guide to the whole world of professional computing, especially minis and mainframes. Valuable reference source, widely available in public libraries. Comes out annually, but often as late as September, so check that you have access to the most up-to-date edition. Useful complement to Longley and Shain's *Handbook* which is confined to microcomputers.

Longley, D. and Shain, M.
The Microcomputer Users' Handbook 1984, Macmillan Reference Paperbacks, 1984
Comprehensive but not always authoritative guide to 200 microcomputers and 278 peripherals, with details of prices, suppliers and available software. Includes details of recent operating systems (CP/M-86, MS-DOS, UNIX and VisiOn), telesoftware and networking, also buyers' guide to insurance, maintenance and performance.

Meadows, A. J., Gordon, M. and Singleton, A.
Dictionary of New Information Technology. Kogan Page, 1982
Over 2500 entries on all aspects of computing, electronic mail, telecommunications, videodiscs. Authoritative, clear explanations, with good illustrations. Valuable reference work when you are ready for more technicalities than this book's glossary.

Megarry, J.
Computer World. Piccolo/Pan, 1983
Cheap, cheerful and colourful paperback for young readers and terrified adults. Fits in a pocket, lots of illustrations and can be read from cover to cover in an hour or two. Might be useful introduction for managers or employees who have not enough time or interest to read this book.

Megarry, J., Walker, D. R. F., Nisbet, S. and Hoyle, E.
World Yearbook of Education 1982–3: Computers and Education. Kogan Page, 1983
Not directly concerned with business, but many contributions (especially Chapter 1) of interest to anyone who wants to follow up on education and training applications. (14, 15)

Naylor, C.
Build Your Own Expert System. Sigma Technical Press, 1983
This book is a curious mixture of rigorous thought and chatty introduction. If you don't find the author's facetiousness too offputting to persevere with the text, it serves as a valuable and practical introduction to the process of constructing an expert system. Program listings are provided for Sinclair Spectrum and Apple II, and there are good descriptions of famous expert systems like MYCIN (medical diagnosis), PUFF (breathing disorders), DENDRAL (chemical structures) and PROSPECTOR (searching for minerals). (15)

*Naylor, C.
Programs that Write Programs. Sigma Technical Press, 1984
An introduction to software generators in three parts: the first is an introduction to programs, file handling and flowcharting. Part two introduces specific programming languages and software generators, like THE LAST ONE, P.I.P.S., CODEWRITER and QUICKCODE. Part three gives a general overview of input/output and ease of manipulation, and gives information about suitable hardware and sources. (2,7)

*Parsloe, E.
Interactive Video. Sigma Technical Press, 1984
The book introduces the necessary hardware and software, explaining the problems of differing formats, interfaces and compatibility. Examples of applications are given in marketing, education/training, entertainment and information storage. There is guidance for those who want to 'do it themselves' and/or adapt material shot for conventional video, including information on costs. There is also a useful glossary of interactive video terms. (14)

Rowan, T.
Managing with Computers. Heinemann and Pan (paperback) 1982
Systematic and sensible, if somewhat traditional, approach to the management of computers, especially in large organizations. Says little about microcomputers but contains valuable appendices, especially the sample statement of hardware requirements and software evaluation checklist.

Samish, F.
Choosing a Microcomputer. Granada, 1983
Good, practical book to read if you are thinking about buying a microcomputer. Contains useful thirty-page guide to business micros available and brief summary of a few of the better known packages. (9)

Sigel, E., *et al*.
The Future of Videotext. Kogan Page, 1983
Contains up-to-date and readable accounts of videotex in most Western countries, especially in the UK and US. Don't be put off by their non-standard spelling: videotext *is* the same thing as videotex (i.e. viewdata and teletext, see glossary). Good, balanced coverage and interesting international comparisons and material on future implications. (15)

Appendix 2

Silver, M. A., Jeacocke, J. and Welland, R.
On-line Computing for Small Businesses – Silver's Wall. Pitman, 1983
A stimulating and well-written short paperback that deserves a wider readership than its title suggests. The source of the Pound Note Game quoted in Chapter 13. Silver's Wall is a metaphor for the great divide between the 'clean side' (people who are overheads to production) and the 'dirty side' (people whose work can be invoiced at the end of the month). Highly recommended, especially if you are interested in manufacturing businesses.

Townsend, K. and K.
Choosing and Using a Word Processor. Gower Publishing, 1981
Worth consulting for its detailed glossaries, specifications and lists of suppliers, but be prepared to hunt for them, as the book is badly organized (poor contents page and terrible index). Reproduction direct from daisy-wheel output has made it bulky in relation to its content. Weak on the microcomputer/software combination, stronger on dedicated equipment. (6)

Varley, H. and Graham, I.
The Personal Computer Handbook, Pan Books, 1983
A well-illustrated and attractively produced handbook with a wealth of practical information about the electronic home and office. Contains a useful buyer's guide, list of sources and other reference material. Good source of illustrations (colour and black-and-white). (1,2,9)

Weston, P. and Roberts, M.
Computers: Applications and Implications. Harrap, 1982
Well-written computer studies text with many suggestions for follow-up activities, examination questions and illustrations. Text prepared in 1980, so inevitably dated on videotex, computer-assisted learning and microcomputers generally.

Glossary

Note: Principal cross-references are indicated in **bold**.

6502 A fast and flexible 8-bit **microprocessor** made by Mostek and used by microcomputer manufacturers like Acorn, Atari, Apple and Commodore. Well-suited for use with a BASIC **interpreter**, but cannot support CP/M operating system.

8080 One of the first **microprocessors**, introduced in 1974 by Intel, now outmoded but still found in early 8-**bit** microcomputers. Can support CP/M.

3-voice music Sound output with three channels that can be controlled independently, e.g. to produce three-note chords.

8-bit processors deal with information in 8-bit 'chunks', i.e. they process one **byte** at a time.

16-bit processors deal with information in 16-bit 'chunks', i.e. they process two **bytes** at a time. In theory, 16-bit processors can work faster and address more internal memory (typically 256 K instead of 64 K of **RAM**). In practice, it greatly depends on the supporting software.

40-track Each complete circular groove on a **disc** is called a **track**. Normally they can only be read by 40-track **disc drives**.

80-track discs (other things being equal) can hold around twice as much as **discs** with 40 **tracks** (see above). 80-track **disc drives** cannot normally read 40-track discs, though special software can make this possible.

A

acoustic coupler A sort of cradle for a telephone hand-set which can also be linked to a computer through a cable. The coupler turns computer information into sound signals and vice versa. This method is not as fast as using a **modem**, and is sometimes unreliable, but couplers are cheaper and more flexible.

alphanumeric Literally, alphabetic or numeric; an alphanumeric **character** can be any letter, number or symbol on a typewriter or computer keyboard.

analogue Anything that varies continuously (e.g. time, temperature) is analogue. **Digital** computers deal with such quantities by assigning numbers to them i.e. digitising them. Analogue computers – still used in some control processes – represent quantities directly by means of varying electrical currents and voltages.

animation Moving pictures. Computer **graphics** are made to appear to move by changing them too fast for the eye to detect.

ANSI American National Standards Institute, an influential body that publishes standard versions of selected programming languages from time to time, setting the seal on their respectability.

applications software Any program that applies the computer to a real-world problem e.g. accounts. This includes all **software** except systems software.

array A list of numbers or words laid out in an orderly way.

artificial intelligence Some computer programs display intelligence in the sense that, if humans were to perform the same task, you would describe them as intelligent. For example, programs can add to their 'knowledge' from previous runs, interpret the meaning of a question from its context, prove mathematical theorems and diagnose diseases or electronic faults. See also **expert systems**.

ASCII American Standard Code for Information Exchange: an internationally accepted system for coding keyboard characters for computers. For example, the letter A is always coded as 65 (base 10) and B as 66.

ASPIC One of several systems for coding instructions for layout and heading so that a disc containing **word processed** text can be inserted directly into a typesetting machine to produce camera-ready pages.

Glossary

assembler Program that translates assembly-language program into machine language.

assembly language A low-level **programming language** that uses shorthand versions of English words to give instructions to the processor. These are automatically translated into **machine language** by the **assembler**. Assembly language is harder for humans to work with than high-level programming languages.

A-to-D converter A device that converts **analogue** information (e.g. time or temperature) into **digital** form (e.g. an on/off control signal) and vice versa. Converters allow digital computers to interact with real-world analogue quantities.

author language A very high-level programming language designed to speed up and simplify the job of writing applications software. Author languages can be especially useful to enable people who are not professional programmers to write their own software, e.g. for training; these are sometimes called **authoring systems**.

B

background A **processor** can divide its attention so as to do several jobs at the same time. The simplest form of this **time-sharing** is where one job (like a spreadsheet) is worked on 'in the foreground' and another job (like printing out) is done whenever there are no other demands on the processor, i.e. in the background.

backing store External memory. Supports and communicates with computer's **internal memory**.

back-up equipment duplicates crucial items in case of break-down. Back-up discs are kept in case of damage to the originals. To back-up a disc is to copy it in its entirety.

bar code Pattern of printed lines common on books and groceries. Contains coded information and can be used for direct input of data to a computer.

BASIC Beginners' All-purpose Symbolic Instruction Code. At present, the most popular programming language for beginners, almost universally available on **microcomputers**. Exists in many **dialects**, with minor incompatibilities. BBC BASIC, a powerful dialect, is introduced in Chapter 10.

304 Glossary

batch infill Process of filling in standard details in a batch of documents in **word processing**.

batch processing Computer processing in which jobs with common features are collected together and run in one batch. The opposite of **interactive** processing.

baud One **bit** per second: a measure of the rate of transmitting information within or between computers; e.g. **telext** operates at 50 baud; programs are often loaded from cassettes at 300 baud; **teletext** operates at 1200 or 2400 baud.

bespoke Custom-designed for a particular application and/or customer. Commissioning bespoke software is the opposite approach to buying a **package** off-the-shelf.

bi-directional Printers that work both left-to-right and right-to-left are called bi-directional. The advantage is that the print head spends less time travelling over blank paper than in uni-directional printing. (The characters are automatically printed out in reverse order on the right-to-left traverses.) See also **logic-seeking**.

bit A bit is a **binary** digit, 1 or 0. Eight bits make a **byte**.

binary system A method of counting which uses only two digits (1 and 0) instead of the usual ten (0 to 9). Deep down, **digital** computers work in binary.

bootstrap (boot) Programs can be made automatically to load other programs so that the system 'pulls itself up by its bootstraps'. This process is known as **booting**.

buffer Temporary memory, e.g. for storing a document until a printer has completed its print-out, thus releasing the processor for other tasks. More generally, any electronic protective device.

bug A mistake, usually in a program. To **debug** is to remove mistakes.

bureau A commercial agency providing computer time, software and consultancy to a number of clients.

burster A machine for separating **fan-fold** paper along its perforations.

byte A group of eight bits that can represent any keyboard character. An 8-bit processor handles information 'by eights' i.e. in bytes.

C

cartridge Software for some microcomputers is sold as a sealed plug-in cartridge. Popular for arcade games and personal computers without **disc drives**.

cassette An ordinary audio cassette can serve as **external memory** for most microcomputers, though short high-quality tapes (sometimes called data cassettes) are preferable. Since the tape travels at its usual speed (less than two inches per second), cassette loading is very slow compared with **discs**; it is still popular for personal computers because cassette recorders are cheap and widespread.

catalogue Place on the disc that lists its contents. Also called directory.

CBT Computer Based Training. Use of computer systems for training purposes.

CCITT International Consultative Committee for Telephones and Telegraphy. A body which issues standards for telecommunications and data transmission.

Centronics interface A standard **parallel interface** widely used by microcomputer manufacturers for connecting printers to processors.

character A number, letter or symbol on the keyboard, screen or printer. The collection of all symbols that can be displayed or printed is called the **character set**.

check digit A digit conveying no information except to confirm whether other digits are likely to be valid.

chip A tiny sliver of silicon that can carry complicated electronic circuits.

clean-edge Fan-fold paper can be obtained with an extra-large number of perforations to the inch, so that when the sheets and **sprocket-holes** are separated, the edges appear 'clean', i.e. almost like a machine-cut sheet. Although clean-edge paper is more expensive than ordinary fan-fold, for low-volume users it may work out cheaper than the capital cost of a paper **feeder**.

clock The basic rhythm of a **processor** is controlled by a clock that keeps its activities in step. Its frequency is measured in millions of cycles per second (MegaHerz or MHz). Microcomputers usually have a clock frequency in the range 1 to 8 MHz.

306 Glossary

Closed User Group (CUG) A group of subscribers to **Prestel** that has access to the public pages but can also communicate with each other privately.

COBOL Common Business Orientated Language. A **high-level programming language** used widely in business computing.

code (1) the process of writing out a computer program is called coding; parts of the program are called bits of code. Thus **code generators** are simply **software generators**. (2) Codes are a way of compressing information so that it takes up less space in the computer.

command mode A style of software in which the user controls the program by typing in commands, as opposed to choosing options from a menu (cf. **menu-driven**).

compatibility The ability of two devices or programs to work together; a rare quality in the world of computers and almost unheard-of among microcomputers. Even when two systems are described as compatible, it may not mean that you can take programs or data from one and feed it straight into the other.

compiler A piece of software inside the computer that translates a program written in a **high-level language** like COBOL into **machine language**. Compilers do this as a once-and-for-all job, unlike **interpreters**.

consumables Discs, paper and ribbons – generally anything that you need a regular supply of for computing.

continuous stationery Paper supplied in continuous form, e.g. **fan-fold** as opposed to cut sheets.

control codes are used to make printers produce a variety of effects, like margins, boldface and underlining.

correspondence-quality A subjective measure of printer quality meaning 'good enough to send out'. Some people consider that only **daisy-wheel** printers qualify, others regard a good **dot-matrix printer** (suitably set up) as perfectly adequate. It also depends on whether you're buying or selling!

CP/M The nearest thing to a standard **operating system** for **8-bit** microcomputers. It's always known by its initials (or sometimes as **CP/M-80** to emphasize the **processors** for which it is designed), though you can think of it as Control Program and Monitor or Control

Program for Microprocessors. The **16-bit** version is called **CP/M-86** (which has not achieved the same monopoly) and the multi-user version **MP/M**. **CP/M Plus** is another name for CP/M Version 3.

cpi Characters per inch; used to measure printer typefaces.

cps Characters per second; used to measure printers speed.

crash When a program stops and cannot be restarted, it is said to crash. If good software design prevents this, it may be described as **crash-proof**, though this sometimes tempts Providence.

cursor Something on the screen that shows you where you are. Cursors may be square blobs or underlines; they usually flash.

D

daisy-wheel printer A printer that stores characters on an interchangeable wheel like a typewriter golf-ball. Usually slower, higher-quality and more expensive than a **dot-matrix printer**.

data Generally, information in the form of letters or numbers. Sometimes restricted to mean information after it has been prepared for computer processing.

data bank A collection – usually a large one – of data held in a computer. The term is sometimes interchangeable with **data base** (see below).

data base A collection of information files organized systematically so as to make processing easy. **Data base management systems** (DBMS) are computer programs for designing, setting up and managing a data base.

data processing Loosely, the handling of information by computer. In practice, usually refers to **batch processing** of large volumes of prepared data, e.g. telephone bills, payroll.

debug To remove mistakes.

dedicated Specially designed for, or limited to, a particular purpose.

default The value or behaviour that a computer system assumes unless it is otherwise instructed: thus **word processing** software might take the default value of page length to be 66 lines, or a **disc operating system** may default to drive 0 (usually on the left or top of a twin **disc drive**) unless told to address the other drive.

dialect A variant of a **programming language**. For example, BASIC exists in hundreds of different dialects, most of them incompatible in various degrees.

dialogue An exchange of questions and answers between a computer program and a user.

digital Anything that can be counted in numbers; the opposite of **analogue**.

DIM Short for dimension: a BASIC instruction that forewarns the processor how much space it needs to reserve for an **array**.

directory Place on a disc that lists its contents. Also called catalogue.

disable To prevent from operating; sometimes it is useful to disable a key (e.g. the BREAK key which may wipe out a program) or a device (e.g. a printer, if print-out is unnecessary). Opposite of **enable**.

disc A flat circular sheet of magnetic material used to store information. Sometimes called **floppy disc** or spelled 'disk'. Can store large amounts of information (usually in the range 100 to 1000K) depending on their sizes, quality and the characteristics of the disc drive.

disc drive A device that reads from and writes to a disc. Disc drives only work with discs of a suitable size, density and number of tracks. They locate information quickly because the disc spins at high speeds and retrieval is random-access.

Disc Operating System (DOS) A program inside the computer that controls the storage and retrieval of programs and data on **discs**.

disc-pack A stack of magnetic discs.

documentation Printed instructions and manuals that are vital if a user is to get the best out of any **software**. An important – but often-neglected – part of a software **package**.

dot-matrix printer A printer that forms characters from a matrix (grid) of dots; the more dots, the better the shape of the character. Generally cheaper and faster than **daisy-wheel printers**, but only the best can produce remotely comparable quality.

downwards-compatible Able to work with simpler, cheaper or less up-to-date hardware or software.

DP Short for **data processing**. Large firms often have separate DP departments with DP Managers at their head.

E

edit To improve, cut or rearrange text or programs.

electronic mail Immediate transmission of messages or data across a distance. May use telephone lines, broadcast waves or satellites.

emulation Making one device behave like another.

enable To make a key or device operate; opposite of **disable**.

enquiry language A high-level language specially designed for interrogating (asking questions of) a **data base**.

enter To put instructions or data into the computer. The ENTER or RETURN key sometimes has to be pressed afterwards.

ephemeral Not permanent. A computer's RAM is usually ephemeral, i.e. its contents are forgotten when you switch off.

EPROM Erasable Programmable Read Only Memory. A **ROM** chip which can be loaded with a program that can subsequently be erased. This is usually done by passing ultra-violet light through a circular window over the circuit. EPROMs are a useful way of distributing **firmware** that is still being developed and refined.

expert systems Software that builds up expertise in making judgements and displays **artificial intelligence**. Some expert systems can coverse with humans in a relatively natural way, and some can explain and justify their line of 'reasoning'. So far, the most successful ones tend to operate in a restricted field of knowledge; they are sometimes called **Knowledge Based Expert Systems** (KBES).

external memory The storage of information outside the computer, usually in magnetic form.

F

fan-fold Paper folded in a long zig-zag consisting of thousands of sheets joined end-to-end by perforations.

fax Facsimile transmission: the entire contents of a sheet of paper (including letterhead, signature, etc.) are scanned, coded and sent to a remote terminal connected by a telecommunications link. The receiving and sending fax terminals must be compatible.

feeder Device for feeding paper to a printer automatically (see **hopper**).

field A single item of information in a **data base**, e.g. a name or address. Each field may need a large number of **bytes** to store its information.

file A collection of instructions, text or data. A text file might be a short letter or a book chapter; a data file could consist of a handful of items or a hundred thousand.

file manager A program to help the user to create, edit and update files of information.

filename The name by which a **file** is known to the computer system; this may be an abbreviation of the name by which the user normally refers to it.

firmware Intermediate between **software** and **hardware**, firmware instructions are fitted to the computer semi-permanently, usually in the form of ROM chips.

flicker A shimmering instability in the image on a computer screen; flicker can be tiring and even unhealthy in prolonged use.

floppy Short for floppy disc (see **disc**).

floppy tape Form of external memory that is a halfway-house between **disc** and **cassette** tape in speed and cost.

flow chart Method of showing logic of a computer program or sequence of operations in a data processing system using boxes and arrows (see Figure 50).

format (1) The format of a piece of text refers to headings, spacing and margins. (2) The arrangement of data in a file, on a disc or on a screen. (3) As a verb, to format a disc means to prepare it to receive information in the format appropriate to the disc drive and computer in use; this process deletes any information which was on the disc before.

footer Standard information printed at the foot of the page in a long document (see **header**).

friction-feed Method of gripping paper used on a typewriter. It is needed if a printer is to deal with single sheets of paper; but if fan-fold paper is acceptable, **tractor-feed** is preferable to friction-feed.

function keys Special keys on a computer keyboard that do certain operations at the touch of a button. Sometimes they can be defined and redefined by the user, so that the same key which justifies text while word processing might also be used to recalculate a spreadsheet, for example.

G

Gateway A system that gives **viewdata** users access to external computers and their **data bases**. The data has to be rearranged into a suitable page format.

Gigabyte (Gb) Unit of mass storage, around a thousand **Megabytes** (actually 2^{30} **bytes**).

GIGO Garbage In, Garbage Out. A long-standing cliché about computers.

GOTO A BASIC instruction to **jump** to a different part of the program.

graphics Pictures that the processor can draw on the screen or print onto paper. The higher the **resolution**, the better the picture.

graphics tablet An input device on which the user traces a shape that is coded in digital form for the computer to process.

H

handshake An agreed convention for control signals so that two electronic devices can communicate with each other.

hands-on Practical experience of using, as in 'getting your hands on' a computer.

hard-copy Printed output; jargon word for print-out.

hard disc A high-speed, high-density form of external memory. Hard discs hold much more information than **floppy discs**, but because they are fixed into the computer, they cannot easily be duplicated for back-up. Removable **hard disc cartridges** may overcome this problem.

hard-sectored Floppy discs that have the boundaries between their sectors marked by the punching of holes (hard-sectored). This method leaves all the disc space available for storage. Contrast **soft-sectored**.

hardware Equipment that makes up a computer system: processor, memory and input/output devices.

312 *Glossary*

header Standard information printed at the head of the page in a long document (see **footer**).

hex or hexadecimal number system based on 16. It uses 15 digits (represented by 0 to 9, A to F). More compact than **binary**, but inconvenient for humans.

hierarchy Generally any arrangement in which there are several levels with higher levels more general than lower ones. Hierarchical **data bases** represent the relationships between different levels in their structure.

high-level (programming) language A language like BASIC, COBOL or ADA in which instructions are written in words resembling English for subsequent translation into **machine language**.

high resolution graphics Computer pictures that can show true curves and crude photographs. Professionals usually mean at least 500 by 500 pixels, but microcomputer salesmen use the term much more freely.

hopper A device holding a stack of paper sheets that feeds them automatically to the printer. Invaluable if you want to do unattended printing onto single sheets. Using **fan-fold** paper is cheaper but has the disadvantage that you have to deal with perforations.

I

icon A picture that represents a particular function: for example, in the Apple LISA system you point to a rubbish bin icon to delete a file.

information manager A program to help the user to create, edit and update files of information.

input Anything you put into the computer. Also used as a verb meaning to feed in. A keyboard is an example of an input device.

INPUT A BASIC instruction to read in.

integrated software Programs which are designed as a collection, so that the output of one can automatically be fed into another.

interactive Two-way communication in which what the user does depends on the response just received just like a telephone conversation. Thus interactive computing is the opposite of **batch processing**, which is more like an exchange of letters.

interface Junction between two things; twilight is the interface between day and night. Computer interfaces often involve specially written software as well as plugs and cables, and can be expensive. To interface two devices is to do whatever is necessary to make them communicate; unless the manufacturers intended them to, this may involve some research and development – not a job for amateurs.

internal memory Inside the computer, information is stored in two ways: **RAM** and **ROM**. Internal memory is more limited and expensive than **external memory**.

interpreter Software that translates a program written in a **high-level language** like BASIC line-by-line into **machine language**. Each line of an interpreted program has to be re-translated every time it is obeyed.

J

jack A prong on the end of a lead. A **jack socket** is the hole it fits into.

jump An instruction to pass control to a different part of the program. Unconditional jumps are always obeyed, conditional ones only sometimes.

justify Normally, typewriters produce text that is unjustified i.e. has a ragged right-hand edge. Word processing software can often rearrange the spaces automatically (justify the text) so that the lines are all the same length, as in the pages of this book. (See also **proportional spacing**.)

K

K See **Kilobyte**

KBES Knowledge Based Expert System. See **expert system**.

keyword (1) Some **data bases** can be searched by keywords that 'unlock' their contents; each item is known to the system by a number of keywords that convey the gist of what they are about. (2) In programming, keywords are words that have a special meaning to the computer. Some personal computers (e.g. the Spectrum and Electron) have such words on individual keys on their keyboards.

Kilobyte or **K** About a thousand **bytes** (actually 2^{10} or 1024). Since 1 byte is needed to store each character, 1 K holds around 150–170 words of text. See also **Megabyte** and **Gigabyte**.

KIPS Knowledge Information Processing Systems. Name given by the Japanese to the imminent fifth-generation computers to emphasize how different their role will be from traditional computation and data processing.

L

laser A narrow, high-energy light beam with important applications in computing and telecommunications. **Laser printers** are very high-speed and high-quality computer printers. Some **videodisc** systems depend on lasers.

light pen A pen-shaped pointing device which can be used to select from choices displayed on the screen, or (sometimes) to draw shapes directly onto the screen.

line printer Fast expensive printer that puts a complete line of text (not just one character) at a time.

list To make the computer display all the instructions of its current **program**. If the program is printed out, this is referred to as a **listing**. LIST is a valid BASIC instruction.

list processing The processing of data arranged in the form of lists; in word processing, sometimes used to describe the insertion of standard information into mail shots.

LOAD BASIC instruction to copy a program or data from disc or tape into the computer's RAM.

logic-seeking When the movement of a printer-head is planned so as to minimize time-wasting travel over blank paper, the printer is described as logic-seeking.

log on To register your presence on a system, perhaps by identifying yourself as an authorized user.

loop A section of program that is repeated over and over again, sometimes using different values or data.

low resolution graphics Crude pictures in which individual pixels are clearly visible. Resolution might be 40 across by 20 down, suitable for bar charts but not for curves.

lpi Lines per inch; a measure of line spacing.

LSI Large Scale Integration. Method of packing a large number (100 to 1000) of electronic components (and their connections) onto a single **chip**. (See also **VLSI** and **ULSI**.)

M

machine language The language of binary numbers in which the processor works. Instructions in machine language are also known as **machine code**.

Magnetic Character Recognition (MCR) Automatic recognition of characters printed with special magnetic ink.

mail merge A word processing facility where details from a customer file are merged into a standard letter.

mainframe A large powerful computer with many users, often spread over a distance, sometimes using a variety of different **programming** languages or software at the same time (see **time sharing**).

Maltron An experimental keyboard with a more ergonomic lay-out than the standard QWERTY arrangement.

master file A file containing standing information which basically does not change although it may be updated from time to time; contrast **transaction file**.

medium resolution graphics Pictures of medium quality, adequate for diagrams but unable to show good curves; technically, around 300 pixels across by 200 down.

Megabyte (Mb) Around one million bytes (actually 2^{20} or 1,048,576). The text of this book could be stored 20 times over in 1 Mb.

Megahertz (MHz) Measure of **clock** frequency in millions of cycles per second.

memory Computers have **internal memory** which contains standing instructions and temporary working space. They also need **external memory** for permanent storage of larger volumes of information.

memory map A diagram of what type of information is stored where inside the computer's memory.

menu-driven A style of software in which the user controls the program by choosing options from a menu, as opposed to typing in commands (cf. **command mode**).

Glossary

microcassette A small audio cassette, common on dictation machines, sometimes used as **external memory** especially for hand-held computers. Compared with standard cassettes, the information can be packed more densely and the motor controlled more precisely.

microcomputer (micro) Any computer you can easily carry. Nowadays, some are quite fast and powerful and may have sizeable memories (see also **minicomputer**).

microfloppy A floppy disc of diameter less than 5 inches, generally between 3 and 4 inches.

microprocessor A computer **processor** on a single tiny **chip** of silicon.

Microwriter A hand-held **word processing** device with its own system of coding characters using only five fingers of one hand. (See Figure 38.)

minicomputer (mini) More compact and cheaper than **mainframes**, but more likely than **microcomputers** to have several simultaneous users. It is becoming increasingly difficult to see a dividing line between the power, speed and memory of top-range micros and bottom-range minis.

minifloppy A 5¼-inch floppy disc.

mips Million Instructions Per Second. A measure of the speed of computer processors.

mnemonics Abbreviations that are easy to remember.

modem MOdulator/DEModulator. A device that allows computers to transmit information through a telecommunications link by turning it into an **analogue** signal. Modems can be built into computers or connected to them separately. They have to be plugged into a jack socket. See also **acoustic coupler**.

monitor (1) A high-quality screen designed to display computer output, giving a steadier display than a television set. (2) Set of basic **systems software** to control and monitor overall operation.

monochrome One colour only: for example, a black-and-white television or an amber (or green) monitor.

mouse Input device around the size of a cigarette pack, which the user rolls around on a desk-top to control the movement of a pointer on the screen. Choices are made by pressing buttons on the mouse.

MP/M A multi-user operating system derived from **CP/M**. MP/M II was the 1982 release.

MS-DOS A 16-bit **operating system** designed by Microsoft Inc. Originally commissioned by IBM for its Personal Computer (on which it is known as PC-DOS) but available on many other machines. Its main rival is CP/M-86.

multi-tasking A system that can deal with more than one program at a time.

multi-user A system that can deal with more than one user at a time.

MUSIC One of several systems of coding instructions for layout and headings so that a disc containing **word processed** text can be inserted directly into a typesetting machine to produce camera-ready pages in the right format.

N

network (1) System for linking one or more computers and **terminals** so that they can communicate with each other and share facilities like disc drives and printers. (2) A network **data base** is one in which network relationships between entries are represented.

O

object code The machine-language instructions and data into which the **source code** must be translated before the processor can obey the program.

OCCAM A programming language developed by Inmos Ltd specifically for **parallel processing**. Although intended for use in systems with multiple processors working in parallel, OCCAM can also be used on some recent single-processor microcomputers.

OEM Original Equipment Manufacturer. Firms who manufacture, and may also service and distribute, their own hardware and software.

on-line Connected to a working computer system, often through a telephone link.

operating environment A comprehensive **operating system** complete with **integrated software** and special hardware – e.g. Apple's LISA system.

operating system (OS) Vital program in overall control of the computer whenever it is operating. Without the OS, the computer could not load programs, process data, retrieve from disc or send output to printers: it would be useless. Personal micros often have **resident** operating systems on ROM chips. **CP/M**-compatible micros load the CP/M operating system from disc. Many 16-bit micros give the user a choice of operating system. The characteristics of the OS determine how the user perceives the computer and how easy it is to use.

Optical Character Recognition (OCR) Method whereby a printed page can be scanned by a machine which 'recognizes' the printed characters by their shape. At present it depends on special typefaces called OCR-A and OCR-B (see Figure 4). These can be produced by **daisy-wheel printers**.

OS See **Operating System**.

output Any result which comes from the computer; usually it is in the form of text and graphics displayed on the screen and/or printed on paper.

overwrite To record on top of. In **word processing**, it is a mode in which the letters typed in replace whatever is there already.

P

package Program or set of programs complete with **documentation**, designed for a particular application.

parallel interface Connection between two devices capable of parallel processing, i.e. that handle information more than one **bit** at a time.

parallel processing Sometimes only refers to the way that data is processed in chunks (e.g. of 8 bits) simultaneously, as in ordinary microcomputers. More generally refers to computers that can perform more than one operation at a time (vital for tasks like pattern recognition and for some kinds of **expert system**); may involve multiple **processors**. Crucial aspect of Japanese fifth generation project.

password Secret word to prevent unauthorized use of a computer or viewdata system. Passwords can give different categories of user access to different levels of privileged information.

PC-DOS IBM Personal Computer's **operating system**. See **MS-DOS**.

Glossary 319

peripherals Any computer equipment other than the processor e.g. input/output devices.

phosphor coating The layer on a monitor screen that produces the display. Different coatings produce displays of varying colours and legibility.

pin-hole Holes at both edges of fan-fold paper; they are used to pull it through the printer; also called **tractor-hole** or **sprocket-hole**.

pixel Picture cell: tiny squares of light that make up pictures on the screen. The more pixels, the higher the **resolution**.

plug-compatible Any two devices that will work properly when plugged into the same socket are said to be plug-compatible.

port A point of access to the processor.

portable (1) Easy to carry, like a small microcomputer. (2) Capable of running on other equipment, like a standard CP/M program.

Prestel A British public **viewdata** system which contains large amounts of information in page format. Subscribers can order goods and catalogues as well as getting up-to-date information. Prestel subscribers with microcomputers only need an **acoustic coupler** and some software to be able to access, save and print Prestel frames.

PRINT BASIC instruction to display something on the screen.

printer A machine like a typewriter without a keyboard that prints computer output. **Dot-matrix** and **daisy-wheel** printers print one character at a time, but more expensive **line printers** print a complete line as one unit.

processor The part of the computer that actually does the arithmetic and makes the decisions. In **mainframes** sometimes called the central processing unit. In micros, often consists of **microprocessors**.

program A list of instructions for the computer to obey, written in a special language (see below).

programming language A special language for giving instructions to computers. There are hundreds of different ones available. All have to be translated into **machine language** before the computer can obey the instructions.

prompt Any sign given by the computer (a symbol on the screen or an audible bleep) to indicate that it is waiting for a response from the user.

proportional spacing Method of printing letters so that the space for each character is proportional to its width when handwritten, e.g. *m* is wider than *i*. Proportional spacing is generally more legible than uniform spacing; although some computer printers can produce proportional spacing, it often cannot be combined with justifying the right-hand margin (as is normal in most printed books).

protocol A set of conventions about the format of messages that allows them to be exchanged in a communication system.

PSS Packet Switched Service. A network dedicated to computer communications that gives higher speeds and lower error rates than the **PSTN** (see below).

PSTN Public Switched Telephone Network. The ordinary telephone system, which can be used to transmit data in addition to conversation using a dial-up connection charged like an ordinary phone call.

Q

query language A high-level language specially designed for interrogating (asking questions of) a **data base**.

QWERTY The standard arrangement of keys on a typewriter or computer keyboard is known by its top row of letters: QWERTYUIOP, or QWERTY for short.

R

RAM See **Random Access Memory**.

random-access Any part of a floppy disc can be found quickly without having to read through all the other parts. Random-access is the opposite of **serial-access**, e.g. the way a cassette recorder has to play the cassette through from beginning to end.

Random Access Memory (RAM) The storage space inside a computer where software is stored while it is worked on. Its contents are forgotten when the computer is switched off.

read (1) A disc drive is said to 'read' information from a disc when it retrieves it, and to 'write' when it records it. (2) The BASIC instruction READ is used to enter data.

read-only Anything that can only be read, not written on, e.g. a protected disc, **ROM** (see below).

Read Only Memory (ROM) Part of the computer's internal memory that stores software in frequent use. Unlike RAM, the contents of ROM cannot be changed by the user and are not forgotten when you switch off. See also **EPROM**.

real-time When a computer obeys each instruction as soon as it is received, e.g. in interactive use or when simulating or controlling a real-world process.

record (1) Each file in a **data base** consists of a number of records, each of which contains a number of **fields** of information. For example, a business's customer file might contain thousands of individuals and firms, with a separate record for each one. (2) To record information on a disc or tape is to **overwrite** whatever is already there with fresh information.

refresh rate The frequency with which the contents of a screen is refreshed (renewed). If this is too low, a visible **flicker** may result.

relational A **data base management system** that represents some of the complicated relationships that exist in the real world between the items of information that it stores is called relational.

REM BASIC instruction for REMark, i.e. a message left for humans to read that the computer ignores.

report Statement of results of computer processing.

resident Permanently fitted to a computer, e.g. held in ROM.

resolution Measure of quality in computer **graphics**. The higher the resolution, the finer the detail. See also **pixel**.

RND BASIC instruction to select a random number.

robot A machine that can be programmed to do a variety of jobs automatically; often controlled by **microprocessors**.

robust Adjective used to describe software that is unlikely to **crash** (fail).

ROM See **Read Only Memory**

Glossary

RS-232 A standard **interface** developed by the Electronics Industry Association for telecommunications equipment. Transmission is serial, at one of a standard range of speeds. The standard has been widely adopted by computer manufacturers, so that many computers have an RS-232 port for connecting processors to peripherals.

RUN BASIC instruction to make a program start running.

S

save BASIC instruction to record a copy of a program, text or data file (usually in magnetic form, e.g. onto a disc).

screen Output device that shows what the computer is doing. The term is often used generally to mean either a monitor or television set used this way.

screen dump The contents of a complete screen (text and/or graphics) printed onto paper.

scroll When a document is larger than the screen, the processor makes the text seem to move up so that the screen can display the next 'page'. Most systems scroll up and down when required; some also scroll from side to side. See **virtual screen**.

sector Smallest unit on a **disc** that can be addressed individually. The boundaries between sectors may be hard (permanently punched holes) or soft (magnetically recorded and erasable).

serial-access When you have to search through something from beginning to end, like a cassette tape, instead of being able to jump to any part of it at random, like a floppy disc.

series (serial) interface Connection between two devices capable of handling information only one **bit** at a time.

shared-logic When a number of terminals share the same processor, the system may be called shared-logic. Now that processor power has become so cheap, **networked** microcomputers are often preferred to shared-logic systems.

shredder Machine that destroys computer print-out after use so that it cannot be read by anyone unauthorized.

soft-sectored Some floppy **discs** have 'soft' boundaries between **sectors**, i.e. recorded onto them by software. Soft-sectored discs can thus have their boundaries changed by re-recording. The price of this flexibility is having slightly less space for data. Contrast **hard-sectored discs**.

software Programs and data. **A software generator** is a program that reduces the labour of routine programming. A **software tool** is any **utility** that helps to make programming faster and easier.

source code The instructions written in a programming language before they have been translated into **object code** for the processor to obey.

spreadsheet A software **package** that displays a set of values (like a firm's accounts) and allows the user to define and redefine the relationships between the rows and columns. The program calculates the consequences automatically.

sprocket feed Method of feeding **fan-fold** paper that depends on two rows of sprocket-holes down the edges of the paper to pull it through the printer.

sprocket-holes See **sprocket feed**.

stand-alone A computer system used on its own, as opposed to being part of a **network** or telecommunications link.

string A set of characters one after the other. The last sentence is an example of a string; note that it includes spaces and a full stop as well as letters. Strings can also consist of numbers or any mixture of **characters**.

structure chart A diagram that displays the structure of a computer program using boxes on a number of different levels; lower-level boxes spell out the details of the higher-level boxes (see Figure 51).

structured programming A method of programming in which each section consists of clearly defined and labelled units, which can be written and revised independently.

synthesizer Device for producing artificial speech or music from electronic impulses.

system facsimile Detailed operational simulation of a computer system used for training users.

systems software Software like the **operating system** and **programming languages** that the computer needs to allow it to do anything useful.

T

telesoftware Software that is sent straight into a computer's memory over a distance, using telephone lines or broadcast waves.

teletex The CCITT system for transmission of text and data between terminals using the public telephone network. It (or something like it) is likely to supersede **telex**.

teletext Information broadcast as part of a television signal e.g. CEE-FAX, ORACLE. Televisions with built-in teletext decoders are known as teletext televisions.

telex A worldwide telegraphic service that allows communication between special printers. By modern standards it is slow and inflexible, but it is well-established and widely available. See also **teletext**.

terminal Equipment that allows the user to communicate with a remote system. It might consist of any combination of a screen, keyboard and printer.

thesaurus Dictionary of **keywords** in a **data base**, showing related meanings and relationships.

time-sharing Whenever a processor works on several jobs at once, it shares its time between them. A simple version (see **background/foreground**) of this is available in some small microcomputers. Mainframe computers tend to have sophisticated **operating systems** to control priorities between time-shared jobs and to ensure that the interruptions are at an appropriate level.

toggle Switch or key which reverses its effect when pressed twice, e.g. light-switch you press once for 'on' and press again for 'off'.

track Complete circular groove on a disc; see **40-track** and **80-track**.

tractor-feed Method of feeding **fan-fold** paper that depends on two rows of **tractor-holes** down the edge of the paper to pull it through the printer.

transportable More accurate name for microcomputers that are too big and heavy to be truly **portable**.

transaction file File containing data to be processed for a particular transaction; it may have to be combined with data from a **master file**. For example, to do a payroll, the transaction file might contain details of hours worked, while the master file might have details of employees and their rates of pay.

turnkey system Computer system supplied in a complete and customized form, so that the user need only 'turn the key' to start it. The term has no connection with security.

U

ULA Uncommitted Logic Array. A type of **chip** which contains circuits not yet connected. The manufacturer can add different final layers containing the interconnections to suit different purchasers' requirements. The result is much cheaper than making a fully customised chip.

ULSI Ultra Large Scale Integration. Method of packing an ultra-large number (more than 1,000,000) of electronic components (and their connections) onto a single **chip**. See also **LSI** and **VLSI**.

Unix A sophisticated **operating system** originally designed for microcomputers at Bell Laboratories, which has been adapted for **16-bit** microcomputers and allows **multi-users** and **multi-tasking**.

upgrade Process of improving or adding to the original hardware or software. A good system will have a well-planned **upgrade path** so that software can be transferred onto expanded hardware without wasted effort.

utilities Programs that allow users to do useful jobs like copying discs or recovering deleted files.

V

variable A 'box' with a name that can take different values at different times. In school algebra, x was a common name for a variable. Computer variables may contain numbers or strings and are called **numeric** or **string** variables.

vdu See **visual display unit**.

verification Process of checking computer input for mistakes. A 'verify' instruction may also be used to check whether the process of saving a file was successful.

vertical markets Software designed for a particular client group (e.g.

326 Glossary

solicitors or estate agents) rather than to perform a particular function (e.g. spreadsheet or word processing).

videodisc Plastic disc 10″ to 12″ in diameter which can store large numbers of moving or still television pictures with sound. Unlike videocassettes, videodiscs can be accessed at random and can store **digital** information. They have great potential as a medium for computer memory because of their enormous capacity. At present, however, videodiscs cannot generally be recorded on by the user.

videotex An electronic method of receiving information at a distance and displaying it on a screen. Videotex may use broadcasting (**teletext**) or telephone lines (**viewdata**). Teletext may be referred to as one-way or broadcast videotex, and viewdata as two-way or interactive videotex. *Videotext* is an alternative spelling, sometimes used in the US.

viewdata Two-way transmission of electronic information, using telephone lines and television sets. Local users not only can retrieve information from large data bases but also can send messages and instructions. **Prestel** was the world's first public viewdata system.

virtual memory A method of making the computer's memory seem larger than it is by swapping information between internal and external memory very fast whenever it is needed, without the user having to intervene or even realize that it is happening.

virtual screen A method of making a small screen act like a larger one by treating it like a moving window that can **scroll** both sideways and up-and-down; popular for hand-held microcomputers.

VisiCalc The first and most famous electronic **spreadsheet**.

visual display unit (vdu) Device that displays computer output on a screen (monitor). Also used loosely to mean screen and keyboard unit.

VLSI Very Large Scale Integration. Method of packing a very large number (1000 to 1,000,000) of electronic components (and their connections) onto a single **chip**. See also **LSI** and **ULSI**.

voice recognition unit Computer input device that can be trained to identify words spoken by humans.

volatile Computer memory that is lost when you switch off is called volatile.

W

Winchester A type of sealed hard disc unit becoming very popular for use with microcomputers. Originally 14" in diameter, Winchesters have become progressively smaller to match the shrinking diameter of floppy discs (8", 5¼" and below).

word Computer processors do not deal with individual bits of information; they group them into 'words' and process them as a single unit. Personal computers generally have a word length of 8-bits, while newer business computers tend to work on 16-bit or even 32-bit words. There is no direct relationship between the processor's word length and how many English words a computer can deal with!

word processor Strictly, a machine **dedicated** to word processing, but loosely used to describe any computer that is running word processing software.

word processing A system for editing, storing and rearranging text so that it can be perfected before it is finally printed out. Word-processed text can be produced easily and without errors to give (for example) 'personalized' letters, containing variations on a standard text. Any computer can run word processing if it has suitable **software** and **peripherals**.

word wrap On a typewriter, the user has to press a carriage return button at the end of each line. Word processing software normally avoids this interruption by taking care of new lines automatically – a process known as word wrap.

wp word processing.

write To record information, e.g. onto a **disc**. See **read**.

write-protected You can make a 5¼-inch disc 'read-only' (i.e. nothing can be recorded onto it) by sticking a bit of paper over its write-protection notch. (In the case of 8-inch floppy discs you take the sticker off.)

X, Y, Z

Z80 A popular 8-bit **microprocessor** developed by Zilog from the 8080, and able to support the CP/M operating system. The Z80A is a high-speed version of the Z80 that runs at 4 MHz.

Index

accounting software 43
account keeping 103–19
accounts
　payable 107
　receivable 103
acoustic coupler (*fig*. 25) 93
acquiring software, options for (*fig*. 44) 181
ACT Sirius processor 197
ADA
　programming language 58
　software cost 50
ADC 66 53
A–D converters 29
advice
　and information, sources of 287–92
　on purchase, independent 189–91
aged debtors 106
ALGOL (algorithmic language) 58
alternative spellings, references for 133
analogue 24–5
animation graphics 40
ANSI (American National Standards Institute) 58
ANSI COBOL programs 57
APL programming language 58
Apple system 168
applications software 43
ASCII code 53
ASPIC code 150
assembly language 52
Association of Optical Practitioners' report on vdus 262
audit trail 106
authoring systems 271
author languages 60–1
　in computer-based training 61
automatic centring 152–3

background in multi-tasking 67
backing store 23
back-up
　copies, necessity for 266
　programmes 32
BACS (Banks Automated Clearing Service) 226
balance forward 105
banking computerization 281
banks' clearing systems and software changes 225
bar codes 28
BASIC (Beginners' All-purpose Symbolic Instruction Code) programming language 22, 51, 53, 55–8, 61, 178, 200, 208
BASIC dialect 205
BASIC-80 compiler and interpreter cost 50
basic input-output section (BIOS) 66
batch
　infill 139
　processing 79, 187
bespoke systems 160–2, 181
binary system of counting 25–6, 27
bits 26
　8-bit words 26
　boot-strapping 66
bought ledger 107
budgetary control 112
buffer 37
bugs, tracing and correcting 51, 155
built-in flexibility 155, 157
bureau processing service (*fig*. 21) 79–80, 187
bursters for fan-fold paper 154
business
　buying computers, points to consider 279
　computerization of 171–223
　　critical period 208
　　market research and careful costing 181, 183
　　timing of installation 248
　features specified 183
　information from microcomputers (*fig*. 20), 76, 77
　software, future trends 280

Index

writing 218
Business of Data Processing
  (Carter) 105, 237
buying software 183
byte(s) 26, 31, 196

cardboard disc jargon generator
  (*fig*. 46), 215
cassette-based word-processing
  software 139
cassette(s) 198
  recorders 32
chairs, high quality, for comfort
  260–1
characters 26
  estimating number of 195
check digits in validation method 221
chip *see* microprocessor 26
clipboard icon 166
clock 26
Closed User Group (CUG) 137
COBOL (Common Business
  Oriented Language) 51, 57–8,
  280
COBOL-80 software cost 50
COBOL F 57
code generators 163
codes and coding information 105,
  106, 184
coin analysis for cash payment 183
college, advice from 190
colour display graphics 39
COMAL programming language 58
command mode 130
communicating microcomputers
  (*fig*. 22), 83, 86
compilers in language
  programming 61–3
computer-based training 269–74
  author languages in 61
computerization
  in barristers' chambers 87
  for chain stores 95–9
  extent of 174–5
  further reading on 293 ff.
  of wine business 90–5

computerized
  data bases, controversial nature
    of 129
  mailing lists, sale of 129–30
  system for warehouse 85
computer(s) 21
  bureau 187
  and business future 279
  comfort and health in using 259–63
  contracts, precautions before
    signing 248–50
  expertise, acquiring 177–8
  familiarization, value of 267
  future of 178–9
  hardware for 21
  helping business 101–70
  hostility towards 255
  impact of 279
  installation, diary for 238–42
  introduction of, effect on
    workforce 237, 257
  as a learning medium 270
  mainframe 21
  managing 237–52
  micro 21
  mini 21
  myths and half-truths 254
  programming 200–17
    in business 177
  software for 21
  sound output 37–9
  system, discipline and flexibility in
    working 257
    handheld (*fig*. 24), 92
  and training 270
computing, attitudes to 253
consultants, advice from 190
contracts, precautions before
  signing 246–50
control codes 151
correspondence quality 36
costs, check list, one-off hidden 247
  counting 246
  recurring hidden 247
CP/M (control program for
  microprocessors) 65, 66, 75, 83,
  164

CP/M-86 68
CP/M libraries 66
  system 198
crash-proof control system 66
creditors' ledger 107
cross-references 134

daisy-wheel printers (*fig.* 7), 33–7, 150, 199, 238
  with dot-matrix printer, information from 76
data base
  business uses for 128–9
  on cards (*figs* 35, 36), 123–7
  computerizing 126
  language 131
  management systems (DBMS) 103, 120–37
    accounting procedure 134
    using 130–1
  software 143
  problems 127
data
  computers 21–2
  processing 134
    in business 177
    flow charts for (*fig.* 47), 223
    commercial 57
    decentralisation of departments 251
    managers dislike of microcomputers 251
    and program flow-charts, standard shapes in (*fig.* 49), 230
    validation 222
Data Protection Bill (1983) and software changes 26
DATA statements 216
DBMS *see* data base management systems
debtors' ledger 103
debugging 62, 218
decentralization and large organizations 251–2
decoders 29
Department of Industry, assistance from 191

Department of Industry's Microprocessor Application Project (MAPCON) 191
developments for business 282
Dewey classification number 124, 125
dialects in BASIC 56
DIALOG for keywords 133
digital computerization 24–5
disc(s) 48
  capacity 179
  drives (*fig.* 6), 32, 48, 72
  filing 266
  floppy (*fig.* 6) 32–3
  handling precautions 266
  hard-sectored 48
  house-keeping 266
  packs 34
  problems 44
  soft-sectored 48
  40-track 48
  80-track 48
  system 198
  twin drive 148
Disc Operating System (DOS) 63, 65, 197
documentation 185
dot-matrix printers (*Fig.* 7), 36, 76, 150, 199, 238
downwards-compatible 56

edge-punched cards (*figs* 35, 36), 123–7
  sorting 124
editing 131, 139
electronic
  mail 137
  spreadsheets (*figs* 31, 32), 112–19
employee(s) and computers 253–63
  attitudes 253
  employment prospects 257
  involving and consulting 258–9
  job satisfaction 256
  money 257
  privacy 256
  and new technology 255
enquiry 131
environmental problems 259

ephemeral memories 23
ERIC
  a relational DBMS 134
  system for library data bases 131, 133, 134
errors 218
  estimating 180
  message 65
  removing (debugging) 140
  reports 221
external memory 32
eyesight, effect of vdu on 262

fan-fold paper 153–4
fax 86
field 121, 122
files 121, 122
  author cataloguing (figs 33, 34), 121
  characters for 195
  managers 126
financial
  forecasting software 43
  planning 112
firmware 49
  bugs in 155
floppy discs (fig. 6), 32–3, 47, (fig. 34), 122
  effect of cigarette smoke on 260
  8-inch 148
  environmental threats to data on (fig. 53), 267
floppy tape 33–4
flow-chart(s) 233
  showing processing of payroll data (fig. 47) 223
format
  commands (figs 39, 40), 151, 152
  stages of 140
FORTRAN (formula translator) 58
four-stage model computer 22
friction feed 153

Gemini payroll (fig. 48), 227–8
GOTO instruction 206, 207, 208
graphic(s) 45
  output 39
  animation 40
  colour 39
  resolution 39
  three dimensions 40
  printing 36
  tablets 29

handwriting, processing 29
hardware 43
  acquiring 186–99
  buy, lease or bureau 186–8
  and applications software, link between (fig. 16), 63
  buying, precautions 249
  for computers 21–4
hard discs 34
hard-disc cartridges 34
high-level languages 55, 58–9
high resolution graphics 39
histogram 166

icons 166, 168
IIS language 61
income and expenditure computerization (fig. 30), 113
industrial relations and profitability 263
information
  four basic stages 22–4
  managers 126
  processing stages 22
Information Providers (IPs) 136
Information Technological Centres (ITeCs) 191
incompatibility, levels of 46
input(s) 23, 72
  automated 220
  devices 27, 194
integrated software 157
integration
  in business, levels of 175–6
  by LISA 166
interactive video, advantages of 274–5
internal memory 30–1
International Standard Book Numbers (ISBN) 222

International Standards Organization
    and letter spacing 262
interpreters in language
    programming 61–3

JARGON program 211–17
    flow-chart (*fig.* 50), 233
    output from (*fig.* 45), 215
    structure chart (*fig.* 51), 233
journal or day book 106

Keep Account (Etor and
    Muspratt) 103, 105
keyboards 27–8, 148
    resistance 141
    typewriter 141
keyword(s) 131, 133
    combinations 133
kilobytes 31
knitting needle for sorting cards 124

languages 131
    future 280
    programming 21, 51, 55, 58
        assembly 52
        different levels of (*fig.* 15), 60
        high-level 51
        machine 51
        special purposes 61
laser
    printers 37
    videodiscs 35
layout 151
LDA 65 52–3
leasing a system 186
letter spacing 262
library information in DBMS 121
line printers 37
LISA (Apple) microcomputer system
    (*fig.* 42), 164
    high-resolution screen 166
    integration by 166
LISP programming language 58
list processing 139
LOGO programming language 58
loop 62
low resolution graphics 39

machine language 25, 51
Magnetic Character Recognition
    (MCR) 28, 226
mail
    merge 139
    order, buying by 198
    mini computer for 237
mainframe(s) 21, 24, 44
    computers and high-level
        language 55
    OS facilities 64
maintenance
    agreement 137
    contract 250
    service 250
Maltron keyboard 141–2
management control 77
Manpower Services Commission 191
manuals
    and training 265
    understanding 183
MAPCON 191
MBASIC, processing 197
MCR typeface for machine
    readability 226
megabyte (mb) 34, 196
memory
    external 32
    internal and external 23, 30–5
        buying 194–5
    internal (RAM and ROM)
        (*fig.* 5) 30
    requirements 194
menu-driven software 130
micro-cassettes 33, 48
microcomputers 26, 178, 189, 251
    buying from dealers 188
    communication by (*fig.* 22) 85
    increase of in business 280
    internal memories 30
    language processing 65
        programs 61
    medium-priced personal 71
    network of 192
    operating systems 67
    programming 228, 267
        pros and cons 268

and software compatibility 44
software for word processing 138
system, where to purchase 188–9
  ground-rules for 194
  networked 148
microprocessor 26
MICROTEXT language program 61
microwriter, hand-held input device (*fig.* 38), 142–3
minifloppy discs 48, 49
mistakes, tracing and correcting 51, 62
mnemonics, use of in assembly language 52–3
modem input process 29, 83
monitors 35
mouse input (*fig.* 42) 166
  disadvantages 168
MP/M II operating system 67
MS-DOS for personal computer system 67
multi-tasking 63, 67
multi-user operating systems 63, 191
MUSIC code 150
music, 3-voice 45

National Computer Centre 191, 195
  formula 196
network
  of computer sharing (*fig.* 23), 88, 89
  of microcomputers 192
networked systems 148
nominal (or general) ledger 106, 109–11
  computerization 106
  inputs and outputs (*fig.* 29), 110
Norwegian Labour Inspectorate and vdu health aspects 261

OCCAM programming language 280
OCR typeface for machine readability 226
office requirements 175
On-line Computing for Small Businesses: Silver's Wall (Silver *et al.*) 258

on-line data base searching 131–4
open items 105
operating
  discipline 266–7
  environments 164
  skills 264–6
  systems (OS) 63
    disc operating (DOS) 63
    future trends 280
    multi-tasking 63
    multi-use 63
    personnel for 176–7
    and users 70–90
Optical Character Recognition (OCR) 28
Original Equipment Manufacture (OEM) 188
outputs (*fig.* 18, 19), 23, 73
  automated 220–1
  computer 25
  devices 194
  graphics 39
  printers 36
  sound 36
overwrite 32

package(s) 43
  choosing 182
page-numbering, automatic 149
paper
  feeders 37
  handling 153–4
  with sprocket holes 239
parallel running 248
PASCAL language 58
payroll
  discs, safeguarding 256
  system 111
PC/DOS (Personal Computer of IBM) 67
personal computer systems (*fig.* 17), 72
PERT (Program Evaluation and Review Technique) charts 167
PILOT language for micro and mini computers 61
pin-holes 153

Index

pixels (picture cells) 39
plan and review 245
PL/M program for microcomputer 58
PL/1 program 58
polytechnic or university, advice from 190
posting the ledger 103
Pound Note Game 258, 259
Prestel, public data base 88, (fig. 37), 135–7
price trends in buying or leasing 186
PRINT command 203, 204
printer(s) 35, 36, 140
   buffer 37
   daisy-wheel 36, 37, (fig. 7), 150
   dot-matrix 36, 150
   laser, 37
   line 37
   quantity of paper used 153–4
   software for 150
privacy and security of computerization 256
processor 23, 26–7, 148
   requirements 194
production planning 112
professional advice 194
program(s) 21–2
   accommodating change within 222, 223
   flow-chart for JARGON (fig. 50), 232
   output 35
   production, joint use of 75
   resident 25
   transferring problems 64
   writing and adapting 163, 267
programmers 185
   professional, working principles 228
   qualifications for 255
programming 268
   languages *see* languages
   process of 228
   professional 181
   self-assessment quiz 200–2
   skills in-house 177
   software 44

PROLOG language 58, 280
public viewdata systems 136
purchase ledger (fig. 28), 107–9
   computerization 107
   inputs and outputs 107
   order 111
purchasing a system, secondhand 186

query 131
QWERTY typewriter keyboard 27, 141, 142, 143

RAM (random access memory) 32
random access 32
random access memory (RAM) (fig. 5), 30–1, 32, 55, 61, 62
   chips 43
read only memory (ROM) (fig. 5), 31
real-time system 270
records 121, 122
reference sell in buying 183
reflections, effect on vdu 260
refresh rate 261
relational DBMSs 134
REM instruction to processor 204
repetitive sorting 52
REPLICATE command 115
resolution graphics 39
   high 39
   low 39
   medium 40
Rico system 199
robots 29
Roget's Thesaurus 133
ROM (read only memory) 55, 62
   chip 74
   software 49
ROM-based word processing 149
rotating 3-dimensional graphics 52
RPG (Report Program Generator) 58
running heads 149

sales
   invoice 111
   ledger system 103–7
      computerization 105

inputs and outputs (*fig.* 27), 104
  main activity 105
screen 35
search-and-replace facility 149
serial access 32
shades (*fig.* 43), 166
shared-logic system 238, 148
shift system for workers 261
shredder for disposal of waste
  paper 154
single file applications 128–30
slides and videotape in training 273
small business microcomputer system
  (*fig.* 8), 37
SMALLTALK language 280
smoking in computerized offices 260
  effect on floppy discs 260
software 43, *see also* systems software
  acquiring 173–85
  backed-up 184
  buying precautions 249
  compatibility problems 44
  for computers 21–4
  current business price list 50
  generators 163–4
  initial training in use of 270
  installing 184
  integrated 157
  language learning 178
  maintenance change 184
  modification 223, 267
  options, business 155–69
  packages 182, 183
    buying 183
    modifications 184, 185
    specialized 158
  plug-in cartridges 49
  production commissions 75
  in ROM chip 48–9
serious 218–33
    stages in designing 229
    special for CBT 270
  spectrum (*fig.* 41), 157
  storage capacity (*fig.* 11), 46–7
  tools 178
  training to use 265
  transference 45, 64

special inputs 45
special purpose languages 61
speech
  input 29
  output 37
spelling
  checker facility 149
  errors in data base 132
spreadsheet 139, 157, 168
  electronic (*figs.* 31, 32), 112–19
sprocket holes 153
STA 67 mnemonic 53
Statutory Sick Pay (SSP) changes in
    software for 225
  calculations 183
stand-alone microcomputer
    systems 191, 192
stock control 111, 248
storage
  devices 34–5
  requirements 196
structure chart (*fig.* 51), 233
super-programs 51, 61, 163
synthesizers for computer sound 37
systems software 43
  designer and workforce 258
  facsimiles 269
  or software houses, buying
    from 188
  requirements, stating 193

tape, floppy 33–4
telesoftware 49, 137
telex (*fig.* 23), 86
terminal equipment 81
thesaurus for data base 133
three-dimensional graphics
    (*fig.* 10), 40
tractor feed printers 153
tractor holes 153
trade unions and introduction of
    computers 257
training
  for computer working 264
  sessions, basic principles 265
turnkey system, high cost of 160, 161
TUTOR language 61

Index

tutors for training 265
typing
  puddle 238
  tutor program 264
typewriting, processing 29

Unix system 67
upgrade path 196
  for systems expansion 192
upgrading 194
USA software 168
Using Statistics in Business 2 (Clark) 119
utilities 68–9

validation 221
variables 205
vertical markets 158–9
videodiscs 35
  laser 35
  as 'live' catalogue 96, 98
  player under computer control (*fig.* 26), 96
  random-access advantage 275
  for staff training 98
  system 275, 277
videotape recorders, serial access 274
viewdata system 136
VisiCalc spreadsheet 112
VisiCorp system 168
visual display unit (vdu) 35
  effect on eyesight 262
  ergonomics and health 260
  technology 66
  work-stations, conditions in 260
    furniture for 260–1
    features of well-designed (*fig.* 52), 261
Vdus on Site report by Association of Optical Practitioners 262
voice recognition 29, 141

voting information from computer 79

wages
  calculations 203
  and computerization 257–8
  flexibility 219
  information, privacy and security 219
  program 203–5, 205–6, 206–8
    automated inputs and outputs 220–1
    minimum human intervention 220–1
  reliability 219
Winchesters, hard disc units 34, 89
word
  insertion 139
  processing (wp) 62, 138–54
    facilities 139
    making it work 138
    microcomputer network 87
    quiz for would-be operators 145–7
    replacing copy typing 141
    software 43, 139
    and telephone interviews 145
    training for 267
  processors 31, 143
words, 8-bit 26
Wordstar 149
workers, education on computers 255, *see also* employees *and* workforce
workforce
  computerization and 257
  consulting and involving 258–9
  and introduction of computers 264
write-protected discs 32
writers, advantage of word processing 144

Xerox system 168